Penelope J. Corfield was born in York and loves Yorkshire; resides in Battersea, south London, and loves metropolitan vitality; is a Briton who enjoys the British sense of humour; and is a citizen of the world who loves Planet Earth.

By profession, she is a historian, lecturing on that subject for many years at Royal Holloway, London University; and she writes on British history, global history, and the history of greetings, including the social spread of the handshake.

Penelope has friends and family around the world. Her recreations include gardening, reading, debating, swimming, listening to Beethoven, stroking cats, and green-travelling. And by temperament, she is an optimist.

This book is dedicated to Henry Ford and to all
who argue that 'History is Bunk',
because they are so gloriously wrong.

Penelope J. Corfield

TIME-SPACE

We Are All in It Together

AUSTIN MACAULEY PUBLISHERS®
LONDON * CAMBRIDGE * NEW YORK * SHARJAH

Copyright © Penelope J. Corfield 2025

The right of Penelope J. Corfield to be identified as author of this work has been asserted by the author in accordance with sections 77 and 78 of the Copyright, Designs and Patents Act 1988.

All rights reserved. No part of this publication may be reproduced, stored in a retrieval system, or transmitted in any form or by any means, electronic, mechanical, photocopying, recording, or otherwise, without the prior permission of the publishers.

Any person who commits any unauthorised act in relation to this publication may be liable to criminal prosecution and civil claims for damages.

The story, experiences, and words are the author's alone.

A CIP catalogue record for this title is available from the British Library.

ISBN 9781035871568 (Paperback)
ISBN 9781035871575 (Hardback)
ISBN 9781035871599 (ePub e-book)
ISBN 9781035871582 (Audiobook)

www.austinmacauley.com

First Published 2025
Austin Macauley Publishers Ltd®
1 Canada Square
Canary Wharf
London
E14 5AA

I have greatly benefitted from encouragement from my family and an international range of friends, lovers, colleagues, correspondents, and students, who have debated Time with me, over many, many years. Special gratitude goes also to my publisher, Austin Macauley Publishers, for grasping the nettle; to Edwina Hannam for admirably apt and witty illustrations; to the sight-savers at Moorfields Eye Centre at St George's Hospital Tooting; and to my stern but friendly critics, physicist, Jack Devlin, historian, Susan Whyman, and my life partner, Tony Belton.

Table of Contents

Preface	16
Part 1: Walking on Earth	19
Chapter 1: Inheriting the Past	21
Living in Time	21
Needing Secure Roots	23
Being Synchronised in Time	24
Knowing About the Past is Not 'Bunk' but Essential	26
Noting the Massive Scope of History	28
Summary First Steps: Getting a Good Grounding	31
Chapter 2: Growing and Learning	33
Living on a Learning Curve	33
Experiencing the Present	35
Inhabiting the Sexual Body	38
Thinking Ahead	40
Learning from Experience	42
Summary Next Step: Looking Backwards and Thinking Onwards	45
Chapter 3: Remembering and Forgetting	47
Gaining Anchorage in Time	47
Walking Together 'Down Memory Lane'	49
Forgetting	52

Offsetting Memory's Weaknesses	54
Cross-Checking	57
Summary Next Step: Keeping Track of Time	59
Chapter 4: Generalising and Questioning	*61*
Thinking Big and Small	61
Detecting Big Patterns	63
Detecting Past Stages	66
Spotting Complications	68
But Rejecting Total Doubt	70
Summary Next Step: Building and Testing Knowledge	72
Chapter 5: Coming from Deep Time 'We are Stardust'	*74*
Looking at the Stars	74
Counting Nights and Days	75
Probing Deep Space	77
Probing Deep Time	79
Dreaming (Vainly) of Time-Travel	83
Summary Way Station to End the Journey's First Stage: Being Earth-Bound While Thinking Free	86
Time-Out: I—Meditating	88
Part 2: Scanning the Stars	**91**
Chapter 6: Dwelling in Time-Space	*93*
Understanding Time	93
Representing Time	95
Understanding Space	96
Yoking Time with Space	98
Looking within the Sub-Atomic World	103
Summary Next Step: Grasping the Dynamic Unity of Time-Space	104

Chapter 7: Identifying Continuity   *107*

   Assessing Deep Continuity   107

   Naming Deep Continuity   109

   Praising Constancy or Blaming Inertia?   111

   Detecting Through-Time Constants   113

   Finding Routines in Daily Life   115

   Summary Next Step: Appreciating the Role of Continuity within Time-Space   119

Chapter 8: Spotting Slow Change   *121*

   Assessing Gradual Change   121

   Naming Slow Change   122

   Praising Gradualism or Castigating Timidity?   124

   Detecting Evolution in the Natural World   126

   Recognising Gradualism in Human Affairs   129

   Summary Next Step: Recognising Slow Momentum within Time-Space   133

Chapter 9: Bracing for Turbulence   *136*

   Assessing Explosive Change   136

   Naming Explosive Change   138

   Praising or Fearing the 'Terrible Beauty' of Revolution?   139

   Detecting Upheavals in the Natural World   141

   Coping with Turbulence in Human Affairs   144

   Summary Next Step: Bracing for Turbulence within Time-Space   148

Chapter 10: Experiencing Time-Space in all Its Dimensions   *150*

   Co-ordinating in Time-Space   150

   Making Music/Marking Time   151

   Living Unique Lives Together   152

Rejecting Time Denial	156
Embracing Temporal Complexity	160
Summary Way Station to End the Journey's Second Stage: Experiencing Time-Space in all its Dimensions	161
Time-Out: 2—Laughing	163

Part 3: Mapping the Journey — 165

Chapter 11: Coping with Deceptions — *167*

Taking Nothing for Granted	167
Being Aware of 'Sweet Nothings' and 'Polite Lies'	169
Spotting Historical Fakes and Forgeries	171
Uncovering Factoids/False 'Facts'	174
Noting also Practical Limits to Deception	176
Summary Next Step: Becoming Ever More Vigilant!	178

Chapter 12: Generating Shared Memory-Markers — *181*

Relying on Shared Information	181
Noting Stability in (Most) Personal Names	182
Acknowledging Longevity in (Many) Place Names	185
Sharing Significant Milestone Dates	186
Raising Special Monuments to Memory	189
Summary Next Step: Generating Shared Knowledge	192

Chapter 13: Encountering and Judging Conflicts — *195*

Being Combative	195
Experiencing the Spectrum of Hatred	197
Making War	199
Memorialising Past Conflicts	202
Assessing Criminality in Warfare	205
Summary Next Step: Judging Conflicts at the Bar of History	207

Chapter 14: Boosting Cooperation   *210*

   Being Resilient   210

   Intermarrying and Sexual Partnering Amongst the Human Family   212

   Generating Conventions of Daily Behaviour   214

   Enjoying Concord and Cooperation   217

   Seeking Reconciliation After Discord   220

   Summary: Building a Global Civics   222

Chapter 15: Putting the Pieces Together   *225*

   Understanding the Knowledge Spectrum   225

   Enjoying Historical Fiction as Fiction   226

   Testing Factual Evidence   228

   Exposing Biases   230

   Seeking Impartiality   232

   Summary End Station: Travelling Together from Past to Future, Fortified by Reliable Knowledge   233

Time Summary Next Steps Together…in Time   *237*

   Step One: Being in Time   237

   Step Two: Appreciating Time's Three Dimensions   238

   Step Three: Living Together on Planet Earth   238

Index   **241**

This book fuses biology, physics and history to reveal how humans can best live in Time and its co-partner, Space.

Preface

'Time, Time, Time is on my side!' sings Mick Jagger, to a chorus of *Yes it is!* from his companions in the Rolling Stones rock group. And quite right too: without time, there would be no humans. Yet, wait a minute. 'Time is the Enemy', states a musical track by Quantic (2001). Can it be both friend and foe?

This book, which is aimed at thinking readers worldwide, reveals how humans can best cope with the mighty power of Time and its cosmic co-partner, Space. These great phenomena do not have room for sentiment. Time coolly brings triumphs and disasters; life and death; wars and peace; laughter and grief; and everything in between. So it can be either friend or foe, and sometimes, both at once.

Time-Space, what's more, has its own unstoppable momentum. It is not subject to human control. So proverbially speaking, Time, like the tides, 'waits for no one'. And it affects everyone. No one stands outside the grasp of Time and its physical location, which is Space: 'We are all in it together'.

Taking a fresh approach to the collective human journey calls upon evidence from biology, physics, astronomy, geography, and history. And there is no lack of material to debate. From their earliest existence, humans have explored the globe and worked at 'telling the time'. They have invented clocks and calendars. Astronomers nightly scan the skies, while scientists send space probes to study distant galaxies or to gather cosmic debris. Human expertise thus stretches from ancient days of dodging dinosaurs while scanning the stars, to contemporary days of dodging crowds while consulting mobile phones.

Three sections within this book cover three key elements of the collective journey. The first shows how human life unfolds within the grasp of Time-Space. It includes strategies for coping with both over-retentive memories (traumatic flashbacks) and under-performing memory (forgetfulness); all this is part of the notable human capacity for 'thinking long'.

The second stage then explores the fundamentals of Time and Space. They set the parameters of all existence. Unsurprisingly, the picture is not simple.

There is no simple formula that states T = … Moreover, the great cosmos is restless, 'unsleeping'. Yet humans strive, undaunted, to understand its dynamics. While we cannot travel (to date) beyond Planet Earth and its close vicinity, our thoughts and research probes are not so confined. We can investigate the cosmos. Plus we share and debate our research results.

Thirdly, then, the last section shows how humans map the collective journey. There are obvious impediments. Gaining reliable knowledge may be hampered by misinformation, lies and deceit. Let alone by the warping effects of enmity, hatred and warfare. Nonetheless, people strive to study the past, whether in history or science, as accurately as possible. It's a group endeavour.

Thinking globally is a good challenge. People sometimes ask if I am offering a purely 'Western' view. Well…we all come from 'somewhere' in Time and Space. Nothing can change that. Nevertheless, humans can and do share and debate global perspectives. (By the way, a notional moon-resident might have an outsider's clear view of Planet Earth. But then Earthlings would rightly object that such a moon-being lacked practical experience of terrestrial living.) So humans have to study from our shared planetary home-base, while trying to eliminate undue biases (as further discussed in later chapters).

Thanks are finally, and paradoxically, due to all the doubters and nay-sayers. Those who deny that there's any value to understanding the past. Who find history irrelevant and 'dead'. Who dismiss science as abstruse and 'boring'. And especially the minority of philosophers and physicists, who claim that Time is nothing but an illusion.

These naysayers are annoyingly but gloriously wrong. Between them, they have given me a massive kickstart to write this book. The human journey, past and present, provides vital information, not least for coping with the current global climate crisis. Yet it's not enough for just one person to say these things. Readers, please join the journey and see what you think. *Time to hit the road…*

P. J. C: London, Winter 2023

Part 1
Walking on Earth

Chapter 1
Inheriting the Past

Chapter 1 starts the journey with the obvious point that all lives are rooted in Time and Space, and then explores why people need a secure sense of their origins within the big picture.

Living in Time

Time is the pulse-beat of the cosmos... Its grasp includes the entire animate and inanimate world. The obvious point then follows that all humans are rooted in Time (and therefore in Space, the intimate connection of Time-Space is further explained in Chapter 6). All people are born and die in Time. Moreover, Time exists within them as well as all around them.

Moreover, mighty Time is itself unidirectional. It unfolds implacably from nano-second to nano-second. Today, the modish term for the immediate moment of 'Now' is 'real-time'. The wording is suitably brisk. And each moment of 'real-time' is followed by another such, in an unending line of Time that stretches steadily from the deep past to the present and onto the future. Within the lifespan of this cosmos, it doesn't stop suddenly. Or jump about randomly, from one era into another different one. And Time does not suddenly reverse itself and *run backwards*. (That last trick would require not only all words to be reversed and *backwards run* but all component letters also to *sdrawkcab nur*.)

The same propositions apply to humans. While they can direct their thoughts and imaginations into both the past and future, their minds and bodies always remain in the ever-updating present moment. Real people live in 'real-time'. Hence, as Time steadily unfolds, nano-second by nano-second, so all people grow steadily older, not younger.

Collectively and individually, that means that all humans are living histories. They come from the ever-expanding past. They live in the present, gaining experience which, moment by moment, becomes part of their past life stories. And they face a future, which steadily turns into the present. As a great English story-teller C. S. Lewis once dryly remarked: these epic changes happen for everyone at the same pace, which unfolds at a steady sixty minutes per hour.

Hard as it is sometimes to believe, all today's old people were once loose-limbed youngsters, capable of dancing the night away. And, before that, they were tiny newborn babies. And, before birth, each was a growing foetus, created by a long-ago act of conception. And, before their parents became active lovers, they too were tiny babies… And so on back in time, until the human species began.

That collective human saga has generated a massive legacy, which is inherited anew by each successive generation. Here are a few daily examples. Communities today speak languages that are inherited from the past. They dwell in houses, which, in almost all cases, were not built yesterday. They share in societies with rich cultures, traditions, laws, and religions which have not been created on the spur of the moment. Every day, people use (or fumble at) technologies that they have not themselves invented. They sing songs with words and tunes that have survived through Time. They play organised sports with rules that are already established, even if those are not always upheld with complete fidelity.

And each individual is born with a personal variant of an inherited genetic blueprint, known as the human genome. It has evolved throughout the lifespan of the human species, and it belongs equally to all. As a result, all people, whose lives are inextricably rooted in Time, gain a massive inheritance from their collective past—a legacy that is not only vital but also unavoidable.

Needing Secure Roots

Given that context, individual well-being is greatly enhanced when people have a solid grip on the links between past and present. They need basic information about the unfolding of their own lives, and those of their fellow humans who are close to them. And they need to know equally confidently where they are located in Space. Those individuals, who lack a sound sense of their own location in Time and place, are left feeling disorientated and 'unrooted'.

But why should *that* matter? The answer is that people, who feel basically rootless, live rootless lives. More than that, they often harm themselves and others in the process.

Reported experiences of people, who are suddenly rendered homeless, give clues to the adverse effects of rootlessness. Being taken abruptly away from known surroundings can cause sharp psychological pressures, even for those who were expecting a move. And for those who were unprepared, an abrupt switch, forced amidst a crisis atmosphere of conflict, can cause major disturbance. Involuntary refugees are all too familiar with these problems, and they understand the vital need to recreate a semblance of normality as soon as possible. That requirement is especially urgent for unaccompanied child refugees who are cast adrift during key years of personal development.

Feeling lost in Time and Space is utterly disconcerting. And those individuals who, distressingly, suffer total memory loss cannot manage for themselves at all (This point is further explored in Ch. 3).

By the way, the importance of rootedness does not mean that people have to stay only in one place. On the contrary, humans belong to a hugely successful migratory species. Yet even those undertaking a desired relocation may be temporarily shaken by arriving, friendless, in unfamiliar terrain. That's the moment for experiencing the dull yearning (and, sometimes, serious misery) that is known as 'homesickness'. It's a feeling that can initially take people by surprise, even though it usually wanes once new local contacts are established.

Having a secure sense of location in Time and Space acts as an essential human sheet anchor. Being well grounded then permits people to move around freely and to encounter the multiple branches of the human family.

In other words, historical and spatial roots successfully mesh individuals into Earth-bound existence, rather as the invisible force of gravity effortlessly holds them physically onto the terrestrial globe. The analogy, of course, is not exact. Gravity is a force of nature, whose properties can be precisely measured. Human legacies from the past are far too varied for easy calibration, but they still provide vital personal and communal ballast.

Indeed, talking of the importance of Earthly rootedness, space travellers living for any period of time in zero gravity have to be highly trained to cope with an experience which is both mentally testing and physically shaking. This latter challenge is not discussed much in public as it detracts from the 'romance' of space travel. Yet it's taken very seriously by all who plan and direct such voyages. Humans are by nature gravity-bound Earthlings.

Manifestly, none of these 'rooting' factors have prevented humans from migrating around Planet Erath—and, with the aid of rocket boosters, from exploring nearby space. On the contrary. The fact that humans share a total global dependency encourages them to explore Earth's length and breadth, to climb its heights, to investigate its depths, to chart its astronomical location, to probe its spatial vicinity, and, very wisely, to study its bio-climate.

For these reasons, all people need to know about a host of related subjects, including biology for their origins and evolution; astrophysics, ecology and geography for the advent and ever-changing state of their terrestrial home; and human history and sociology for their shared past, which is growing daily through the collective actions and inactions of all people living in the present.

All such knowledge helps mightily towards survival. Therefore, every scrap of reliable information should be stored in humanity's shared memory banks.

Being Synchronised in Time

Humans, being a large-brained species, have a notable capacity to reflect upon their collective experiences. They use this signal ability to keep their footing within the roller-coaster of survival on the beautiful and dynamic Planet Earth.

Two special qualities make the process possible. In the first place, like all living creatures, humans are instinctively geared into their own immediate moment. At times, individuals may feel subjective that 'the times are out of joint'. But that emotion is felt chiefly by people who are seriously ill or hungover, or really frightened or disturbed. And feeling discontented or disorientated does not mean in practice that anything has really changed 'out there'. Time continues to unfold steadily. And that is experienced by all, whether they are contented or discontented with the current state of the world.

Instinctively, therefore, all are *synchro-meshed* (to borrow a term from motoring) into the present moment. It's the norm and there are no exceptions. Time keeps everything within a common temporal framework, so that people don't get out of synchronisation with one another, or with the cosmos.

This vocabulary uses the Greek term 'Chronos' as a name for the great power of nature, sometimes domesticated as 'Old Father Time'. And variations then pinpoint differing temporal states. For example, the immediate instant is sometimes known as the 'synchronic'. It is not a very elegant usage. But it makes a point. All alive at this instant NOW are sharing a synchronic moment. They are experiencing 'real-time'.

A second term, also with Greek derivation, is comparatively rarely used. It does, however, point to an instructive contrast. The *diachronic* refers literally to 'through-time' or the very long term. It acknowledges the dynamic unfolding of temporality throughout the cosmic lifespan.

Therefore, it can be said that 'the synchronic is always in the diachronic': that is, each passing moment is part of a longer process. And conversely, 'the diachronic is always in the synchronic': the long term infuses each passing moment, which is part of an unfolding process.

Sounds heavy? Not really. These are ways of pinpointing the 'mystery' of Time, when each moment seems unique but is then instantly absorbed into a bigger picture. The immediacy of 'real-time' is thus a component of what may be termed 'real-long-term-time'.

Thinking then about human responses, it can be said that people not only have a natural sense of '*synchro-mesh*' but also share a capacity for *diachro-mesh* (to coin a term). They take the experience of temporal unfolding in their stride. Humans do not just think in terms of micro-moments. They regularly think long. They write histories. They recount tales of olden times. They have invented calendars and clocks. They measure not just the fleeting nano-second but also calculate the span of millennia. They use astronomical evidence from former times to predict future movements of far-distant comets.

Their capacity to 'think long' as well as 'immediate' makes humans truly exceptional animals. All living creatures respond instinctively to the changing of the seasons. A number also have strong powers of memory.

But the mental as well as instinctive calculations made by humans have no parallel. They use their brains and memories to turn their sense of *diachro-mesh* into a grand intellectual system of calendrical dating that is shared around the globe. Impressive.

What's more, young human children can be taught successfully to *tell the time* long before they have the capacity to ask searching adult questions about the nature of temporality. Humans are thus habituated into Time, which is the cosmic dynamo within which all life is lived.

Knowing About the Past is Not 'Bunk' but Essential

Unfolding temporality includes the past that was—the present that is—and the future that will be. Humans can certainly anticipate and predict elements of events to come (as shown in the next chapter). Yet the huge mass of evidence, available to help humanity decipher its ever-changing environment, comes from the ever-growing past. Much effort is devoted to its study, within a great range of subject specialisms.

Yet grumpy individuals sometimes assert that: *We don't learn from the past.* An extraordinary dictum! People certainly don't learn from the future, which has yet to unfold. And while people do learn from the present moment, each nano-second of real-time is constantly morphing into the past. There is no permanent boundary between 'Now' and 'Then', but a permanent blending.

Critics of studying the past probably mean that humans don't necessarily use such knowledge very intelligently. But that is quite a different point. Gaining understanding from the past is certainly not always a precise or easy process. Evidence is often disputed—and people may well disagree about its implications—and decide to discard warnings in favour of rival views.

Well! All the more important, then, to give everyone a good basic training in collecting and assessing evidence, and learning to spot and reject fake versions. Such skills can only strengthen the innate human powers of *diachro-mesh*. The more that can be learned about the effects of unfolding Time—and how to live within its grasp—the better.

Studying the past, whether in biology, astrophysics, ecology, climatology, zoology, sociology, economics, literature, linguistics, and human history (as well as many other subjects), is thus fundamental, not optional. Everyone should be made familiar with basic information about the history of the cosmos, and of human history within that.

There has not always been agreement on that latter point. 'History' is the name given to the past, particularly the human past. (And, just to double down, 'history' is also the name given to the study of the human past.) Either way, the subject has its critics. Legacies from many millennia ago are said to be 'dead and buried'. By implication, irrelevant to 'modern times'.

Most famously, too, knowledge of the human past is said to be 'useless', and unproductive. Or, in the pithy 1916 dictum from Henry Ford, America's pioneer of the Model-T Ford automobile, 'History is bunk'. This succinct phrase (which was quite possibly polished by a journalist) has been much repeated. The term '*bunk*' has a catchy resonance, like a four-letter Anglo-Saxon swear word. And its meaning is sweeping enough: *Rubbish!*

However, as already noted, there is no clear dividing line between past and present. Historical studies stretch seamlessly from 'Then' to 'Now'. Their remit is both distant and impersonal; *and* up close and highly personal.

History covers every aspect of past times. Many historical factors from long ago—such as the power of human sexuality; human inventiveness; the need for basic resources; the risks of warfare; the capacity of humans to work cooperatively—apply equally well today. Thus humans can learn from (say) the past rise and fall of different civilisations. And, equally, past experiences of ecological and climatic crises can provide both apt warnings and guidance for human life today.

Henry Ford himself, when making his dismissive remark, was in full flush of enthusiasm for his new invention, the Model-T Ford motor car (1908). That was a significant moment in the history of mass transportation. And he was entitled to revel in the 'shock of the new'.

New motorcars, however, do not appear out of the blue. Ford and his team had already spent fifteen years experimenting with designs and honing their engineering skills. They also needed a developing steel industry to supply the light steel alloy for the motorcar's frame. Plus they relied upon the savvy of historic oil prospectors and of the refiners who turned the crude oil into usable petroleum. Moreover, Ford's novel design for electrical ignition drew upon scientific research, starting in the 1770s, into the storage and use of electricity.

Above all, too, the steady motion of an automobile depends upon humanity's oldest technical invention, dating back some five thousand years: the rotating wheel.

Innovations thus have a history, just like everything else. Inventors look to the past to find building blocks for change, while simultaneously looking ahead to spot opportunities for novelty. If they were to dismiss literally everything from the past as 'rubbish', they could find that they had invented a motorcar one day but, the next day, lost the knowledge of how to start it, let alone how to repair it if and when things go wrong. Not for nothing is the inventor's true mantra: *trial and error*. Which inescapably means learning from the past.

Incidentally, Henry Ford later repented of his sassy dictum. He became a noted collector of classic automobiles as well as of early American antique furniture and artefacts. And to house his collections, he sponsored in Dearborn (Michigan) a Museum of American Innovation as well as the open-air Greenfield Village Museum complex. In that way, others could look, learn and share lessons from history.

It may be said, then, that studying the past has had a modest last laugh. Today more than a few leading scientists urge that an exclusive training in science and technology, without any knowledge of the Humanities (including history), is excessively narrow. It is harmful to innovation and to society at large. Some specialisation is of course required, as learners study to advanced levels. There is much data to process, many skills to polish. But excess specialisation leaves individuals, and societies, with lop-sided minds.

Inventions and experiments draw upon many sources, including the buzz of conflicting ideas: *outside the box*. Attempts at cutting down or removing entirely the Humanities from educational programmes are seriously harmful. The great, complex, human heritage of both the arts *and* sciences belongs to all.

Without knowledge from and about the past, people are left in a state of mental childhood. In sum, the dismissive assertion that 'history is bunk' is…well…(words fail me!) *bunk*.

Noting the Massive Scope of History

Nothing in the past is exempt from study. And no discipline has a monopoly. Human history is a broad-based subject, shared with many adjacent specialisms.

Archaeologists study physical remains from earlier times. Anthropologists compare and contrast the diverse forms of human communities that have appeared over millennia. And historians share fruitful overlaps and mutual borrowing with sociologists, economists, political scientists, literary scholars…and many, many others.

No types of sources are excluded from scrutiny. Once, historians focused chiefly on the written record and often upon the doings of governments. But today, all aspects of life are examined, using all kinds of evidence. Anything can convey a message when studied closely. Historians accordingly study: past housing, past buildings of all kinds, surviving clothing, the great array of material objects (some surviving only in fragments), ground plans of towns, the layout of fields, the contents of rubbish tips, bones, *bric-à-brac*…and so forth. Intangible evidence in the form of old jokes, sayings, and songs can also be consulted, albeit without being taken literally (Only very few people who sing 'I am a Lincolnshire poacher O' are actually Lincolnshire poachers).

None are excluded from the remit of history. It is true that, until recent times, there was much emphasis on studying powerful countries with abundant written records. And massive research attention has been—unplanned but understandably—focused upon the troubled global twentieth century.

Nevertheless, the full remit of history is democratic and universalist. As long as historians can find relevant evidence (or reconstruct it from other sources), they investigate all communities around the globe throughout Time.

Nor is any aspect of life on Planet Earth immune from retrospective attention. There are studies of global climate and of the world's ecology, viewed over the long term. All aspects of human behaviour also have a past, including topics which are hard but not impossible to study.

Notably tricky, for example, is the history of human sexuality. First-hand accounts are notoriously unreliable (People often exaggerate their sexual prowess and quite a number lie, when denying that they have cheated on partners). But the inventive variety of human sexual practices can certainly be studied, and without being 'boring'. But nothing should be omitted. So there is a history of sexual frustration. And one of sexual sadism, violence, and aggression too.

Needless to say, too, all other permutations of human behaviour, whether attractive or unattractive, are also put under the historical microscope. So there is much to be understood by studying the origins, development, and outcomes of warfare; genocides; and all other cases of what Scotland's global bard, Robert Burns, described, bleakly, as *man's inhumanity to man*.

Note, too, that no rules specify how long a period of Time has to be covered in any specific study. Some are intricate micro-histories, focusing upon short stretches of Time in great detail. But others review the entire span of cosmic evolution. This approach, running from the Big Bang to Now, is known as Big History, where cosmologists and historians work amiably together.

Normally, students combine getting to grips with in-depth micro-studies and with long-term macro-trends. Putting different timespans together can help to answer questions, such as: Why did things develop in this or that way? How far do core factors change? Are there deep forces of continuity? When and why does conflict escalate into warfare? Why did some past civilisations disappear when others flourish? Does history (or indeed Time) convey one or many messages? Studying the past has sufficient breadth, depth, length, and variety to cater for all interests. The subject is inexhaustible…and daily growing.

Numerous signs confirm the great public thirst for perspectives on the past. Factual and fictional accounts find ready markets. TV, theatre, films and radio constantly address historical themes. People pay good money to get printouts of their genetic ancestry. The heritage industry—and the associated heritage institutions—flourish. Umpteen children's toys and games have historical themes. The past contains rich matter for laughter and entertainment as well as for instruction and cogitation. There is something for everyone.

National and international policy-makers have, of course, to grapple with both current issues and past legacies (the two being often intertwined). At times, there have been intellectual fashions which throw doubt upon the reality of Time (a point later discussed in Ch. 10). And some (but far from all) politicians have tried to reduce the amount of history studied in schools.

Nonetheless, these passing elements of Henry Ford-type hostility to studying the past are today waning fast. Indeed, unfolding history has a way of cruelly tweaking the tails of those who claim to live wholly in the current moment.

Nowadays, commentators are detecting instead a newly powerful 'temporal turn': that is, a return to understanding developments in their full historical context. Scientists are also taking a renewed interest in Time. As for 'ordinary' people, their interest in yesterday as well as tomorrow has never waned.

Summary First Steps: Getting a Good Grounding

Knowledge of the cosmic and human past is basic for present living and future survival. Therefore, crucially, the true question is not: *What is the use or relevance of studying history?* The subject is inescapable. *All of cosmic life is there*, including the lives of all readers of this book. The true question is:

Given that people are living histories, how can they best learn about their collective roots in Time, as part of an unfolding cosmic story?

Of course, no one knows every detail. At advanced levels of study, selectivity is necessary. Yet everyone should have some grounding in the basics. How did the cosmos come into existence; how is it expanding; how did the planets, including Planet Earth, come into existence; and what are the probabilities for the cosmic future?

Then, closer to home, individuals need to have an account of the origins and history of their own local community, and of the peoples living in their quarter of the globe. Furthermore, it is essential also to have some awareness of the lives of different societies, in different times and places. A comparative approach does wonders for the gaining of a truly global perspective.

Plus, very close to home, all people need to have some outline knowledge about the origins and backgrounds of their own families. That provides the most fundamental of all good grounding. Adoptees, meanwhile, should always be given information about their birth families, while also learning about the families of their prime carers. (For more on this point, see the discussion in the next chapter.)

Often, when reviewing themes from the past—whether personal or cosmic—the issues are complicated. There is not always just one 'right' answer. Explaining such intricacies has to be adjusted for the age and abilities of young learners. Yet, it's good for all to realise from the start that there are complexities as well as simplicities in this world. Learning about alternative views—and how to assess their relative truth or otherwise—is a critical survival skill. So humans, who are all Time-bound and Earth-bound (or very close-to-Earth-bound), need good solid grounding from the cosmic and human past to step confidently onwards through Time.

Introductions to Time

Hawking, S. W. (1988) *A Brief History of Time: From the Big Bang to the Black Hole.*
Lockwood, M. (2005) *The Labyrinth of Time: Introducing the Universe.*
Rovelli, C. (2018) *The Order of Time.*

Philosophy of History

Day, M. (2008) *The Philosophy of History: An Introduction.*
Tucker, A. (2004) *Our Knowledge of the Past: A Philosophy of Historiography.*

Studying History

Black, J., MacRaild, D. M. (2007) *Studying History.*
Corfield, P. J., Hitchcock, T. (2022) *Becoming a Historian: An Informal Guide.*
Tosh, J., Lang, S. (2006) *The Pursuit of History: Aims, Methods and New Directions in the Study of Modern History.*

Ways of Teaching History

Gradwell, J. M., Leacock, K. H. (eds) (2020) *Finding History Where You Least Expect It: Site-Based Strategies for Teaching about the Past.*
Guyver, R. (ed) (2016) *Teaching History and the Changing Nation State: Transnational and International Perspectives.*

And [indicating no hard feelings]
Appreciating the Inventive Life of Henry Ford

Brinkley, D. G. (2003) *Wheels for the World: Henry Ford, his Company and a Century of Progress.*

Chapter 2
Growing and Learning

Chapter 2 looks next at how individuals grow and learn in Time, which is inside minds and bodies as well as 'outside'.

Living on a Learning Curve

Time is a non-stop teacher. Old secrets may come to light. Others become buried beyond recall. Accurate predictions are verified. False prophecies are frequently refuted. Time heals. Yet it also avenges. Time remembers. Time forgets. *Cormorant, devouring time*, as Shakespeare once aptly termed it, is a tough but impartial power. It gets to everyone from the start and in the end.

Sheer existence is instructive. Life is a prolonged learning curve. At all stages, from birth to old age, there are new lessons to confront, both pleasant and otherwise. There's no need to go looking. Life's lessons knock at the door. So human existence not only means surviving *through* time but it also entails living and learning *with* this mighty, all-embracing power—which dwells inside minds and bodies as well as all around.

From their earliest days, young babies are not only growing their bodies and (as importantly) their brains, but they are laying down core experiences. Initially, newborn infants have limited attention spans and their visual perceptions of the world are hazy. Yet they immediately know their own needs and very quickly recognise their prime carers.

Within three months of healthy growth, babies' visual sense of colour and shape is already sharpened, followed soon by a sensitivity to directional motion. It's highly exciting: a new world opening before them. Yet it's simultaneously challenging and exhausting. It takes several years of healthy growth to gain fully mature powers of perception and thought. For that reason, babies sleep a lot as they stock their working memories and replenish their forces.

Care from others remains an essential ingredient for many years. Much is learned, however informally, from families, close friends, and surrounding communities. Knowledge and skills are then supplemented and systematised through formal education. Schools in childhood and youth are followed later by college life or training in young adulthood. Virtually, all countries today make it compulsory for everyone to get at least some formal education. And, ideally, communities should impart both book-learning and craft-lore (widely defined) to transmit and update the collective stock of knowledge and skills.

Young adulthood is a seminal time for most individuals. They leave home and set up their own households. They decide upon careers, lifestyles, and partnerships, whether long-lasting or with a high turnover. It is usually (but not always) very exciting. And the young adult body is usually (though again not inevitably) at peak performance. However, the expected joys of life in one's prime make it hard for those who are having a tough time.

Mid-life then brings further options and challenges. Past decisions may have led to happy and fulfilling lives. But there are also mistakes, wrong turns, and regrets. Physiques change. A few people may remain sylph-like into old age. Yet many bodies spread and sag while people are not paying attention. Joints become stiff. Eyesight may dim. Hearing fade. Suddenly, it's not so easy to run joyously through a meadow. Or to spring up readily from a deep chair.

Life's rewards and penalties sometimes seem justified, but other outcomes remain capricious. The cards are not dealt evenly to all. Indeed, individuals with physical or mental disabilities often face special difficulties, through no wrong-doing of their own. And an unknown number of tolerably healthy people may still feel depressed that they have not fulfilled their youthful hopes and dreams. Indeed, the American social philosopher Henry David Thoreau once remarked (in 1854) that: 'The mass of men [humanity] lead lives of quiet desperation'. Such a proposition is impossible to prove or disprove; but it's a reminder that many who don't outwardly complain may be inwardly bitter, if stoical.

Nonetheless, throughout life, there is always scope for further change, enjoyment and/or learning, in both major and minor ways. The obvious moral is to make the most of Time while experiencing all phases of its handiwork. *It's not over until it's over...*

Experiencing the Present

Songs have a lot to say about everyday experiences because much of their appeal comes from striking a chord of recognition. They distil pleasures and pains, especially those intensely felt in young adulthood. Songs can be both immediate and timeless. In that way, they mimic the experience of learning. Each single moment of real-time can contain a unique and vivid insight. But, like a song, learning is often repeated and layered into people's consciousness, since that is how so much knowledge is gained.

One model of learning does embrace the sudden, blinding flash of illumination. The Christian Bible provides one famous example. St Paul, initially named Saul, was travelling to Damascus to harry the rebel Christians. Then, 'Suddenly, there shone round about him a light from heaven. And he fell to the Earth, and heard a voice saying unto him: "Saul, Saul, why persecutest thou me?" His eyes were temporarily blinded. Yet spiritually, he was enlightened. He switched sides and joined the faith which he had been persecuting.

Perhaps a psychologist might speculate that Saul's earlier hostility hid an unacknowledged fascination with Christianity. At any rate, he reinvented himself as St Paul. And a *Damascene conversion* remains a classic term for an instant change of heart, though Paul still had to learn slowly how to undertake successfully his new role as a Christian apostle.

Another example comes from an English literary classic. In Jane Austen's *Emma* (1815), the socially confident protagonist is a matchmaker, who is ignorant of her own heart. She likes to play at intrigues. So Emma encourages her young protégée to fancy herself in love. But then something unexpected is disclosed. The result is wonderfully described. Emma sits in silence for several moments, 'in a fixed attitude'. Her protégée loves not a handsome young lad but the respected squire, Mr Knightley. And, worse still, her protégée believes that her love is reciprocated. Emma's consternation is total: 'It darted through her, with the speed of an arrow, that Mr Knightley must marry no one but herself!'

She had been blinkered. Yet she 'wises up' in a single moment. Emma then undertakes some mortifying retrospection as she gauges her past errors and blindness. However, Austen's comedy of trial and error kindly allows both women to gain better self-knowledge and, eventually, a suitable life partner.

These cases show how a significant insight can be achieved in a single moment (especially in the case of strong emotions). But then, the breakthrough has to be consolidated in the subsequent minutes, hours, and years. The flash of illumination needs to be mentally consolidated and 'owned'. Otherwise, it is just one of those 'bright ideas' which can come and, as quickly, go.

Effective learning can gain mightily from inspiration, but it also entails repetition, cogitation, debating, and practice. Such through-time application applies whether people are gaining physical or intellectual skills or both. The role of perspiration, as well as inspiration, is the stuff of many mottoes: 'If at first you don't succeed, try and try again'; 'Stick at it'; 'Trudge another mile'; and, especially, the succinct formula: 'Practice makes perfect'.

Some aspects of learning may come easily and 'naturally'. Overall, however, the journey requires sustained effort over Time. Just as physical routines are practised again and again until they become 'muscle memory', so repeated mental efforts are needed to inscribe knowledge into 'mind memory'. Going over things is a necessary chore for effective learning. Inventive educators do their best to make the processes as interesting as possible. Reiterating things in different ways. Getting students to discuss or to re-enact, if appropriate. It takes much effort in many present moments to learn effectively. And it's generally helpful to share with others in the process.

Getting to grips with the stock of human knowledge and experience is far too massive and complex a task to master in an instant. Indeed, there's so much to know that no one today can become truly omniscient. There has to be some specialisation and cross-sharing between specialists. Societies need an ever-growing range, from astronomers and archivists to zinc miners and zoologists.

Choices of subjects to study are key decisions, made in the present, by individuals—while pressures from families, schools and friends, as well as available options and sheer necessity, all play a part. Moments of choice can be hard for those who don't like being put on the spot. Others meanwhile sail through, unconcerned. In all cases, educational systems should give people chances for pathway switches and later-life learning, so that single decisions, made in youth, do not close down all future options.

So intense can be today's bombardment of images, ideas, information, news and messages by social media in multiple outlets that many twenty-first century citizens feel shocked and dizzied. 'Tired, wired on my back on the floor/Overthinking thoughts like never before', as the American singer R.LUM. R. wryly records. In this era of information overload, all sane advice on how to decide about lifestyles, careers, and partners, is at a premium.

At times, indeed, some people escape into simplified group-think, with a separate or parallel view of reality. It's been tried in the past—and is still tried today—by intense religious cults and by some obsessive secular groups as well. People in these groups communicate solely with each other in an enclosed loop. There are parallels here with the view proposed in 1981 by the French cultural theorist, Jean Baudrillard. He thought that the fast-paced, multi-stimulated, increasingly techno-reliant lifestyles of twentieth-century societies were pushing their citizens into an acute state of 'hyper-reality', indistinguishable from the real thing. People were allegedly living in a fake but plausible 'virtual' world.

In practice, Baudrillard's claims were overdone. Worldly matters, like hunger, cold, conflict, emotions, human companionship, laughter, sex, birth, and death, continually override the hype and restore a sense of mundane reality. The outside world intrudes even into closed cults, sometimes with drastic consequences.

Today, the most common experience is for individuals to be pummelled by a blitz of news, views and information, including serious misinformation. The sheer amount and diversity of inputs arriving in real-time are genuinely overwhelming. As a result, it's a good social rule that everyone should have a daily allowance of 'time off', away from all forms of social media. Families and schools should enforce this practice especially firmly to protect the growing young.

People need Time to take stock; cultivate their 'personal space'; to find their true selves. A sense of individual identity is needed to live well in Time—and to learn, whether through slow repetition or instant insight—or both.

Inhabiting the Sexual Body

Intimately personal knowledge also comes from individual bodily sensations. No matter how much (or little) forewarning has come from family, friends, and teachers, nothing in sexual matters can match direct personal experience. After all, it's very bodily intimate. For that reason, it's well attested that many people, especially in their youth, think a lot about sex. That's partly in anticipation (biology calling!) and also in retrospection (Mmmmn).

Young women at puberty in their teens not only discover that their breasts are growing (larger or smaller as the case may be) but they also have to cope monthly with the messy business of menstruation. Moreover, a sizeable minority face the unfairness that their menstrual downflow produces debilitating period pains, while others feel little more than vague discomfort. The message that biology is priming females for reproduction is clear, even though far from all adult women will actually bear children.

No doubt because of this biological readying, many women find the first sensation of an erect phallus penetrating the vagina as thrilling, shocking, but somehow also 'familiar'.

What's more, societies take a collective interest in these intimate matters. Over time, a variety of mechanisms have been invented to assist conceptions in a bid to aid 'Mother Nature'. But there are also some who want to terminate unwanted pregnancies. So there are also options (whether legal or illegal) to seek an abortion. However, all interventions either to stop or to assist births have to cope with obstinate individual bodies. Those have their own rhythms and physicality and do not always respond as expected.

Young men similarly confront in their teens the onset of physical maturity. Voices deepen, testicles grow and dangle, while (variably) facial and body hair sprouts. Shoulders also tend to grow broader and muscles to develop greater power. Such changes occur incrementally, over months and years. Specifically, too, young men feel the stirrings of bodily arousal, wonder at their first erection, and experience the shock/ecstasy of the first ejaculation. While the onset of physical maturity is generally welcomed, a few mourn the passing of boyhood. Again, Time is asserting its irresistible power over very fundamental matters.

Added to physical changes, people begin also to understand the specifics of their own sexual desires. Such realisations may come as a slow awakening or a rapid, breathless discovery. And desires may be controversial if people's sense of gender and/or sexual identity runs counter to the expected norms (and legal rules) of their communities. Discovering how to navigate such challenges takes much psychic effort. And even for those whose desires are conventional, there is still the practical shock of turning inchoate yearnings into direct action.

For that reason, many (though not all) remember their first full sexual encounters. It's best when such experiences come lovingly. And good to have thereafter healthy, happy, non-coercive sex lives, based on affection and trust.

Within that framework, there's then scope for enjoyable hands-on practice to discover personal preferences: what sort of partner; what sort of sexual plays; how best to please and be pleased. Do women prefer vaginal or clitoral orgasms or both? Sexual happiness has many variants. Some women like sex but, especially at first, find it hard to climax. (With sympathy for the unknown numbers of men and women whose plight is sung by Mick Jagger: 'I can't get no satisfaction, 'Cause I try, and I try and I try and I try…')

Notably, amongst these options, a determined minority of people remain celibates. It's a valid way of life, which can be very tranquil. Involuntary celibates, however, are well advised to reach for congenial company, not self-referential anger, as an exit from unwanted sexual isolation. Arousing desire entails building and cherishing mutuality, not raging alone at its absence.

Unsought sexual initiations, especially if violent and abusive, can meanwhile bring bewilderment and heartbreak. 'What doesn't kill you makes you stronger', runs one defiant claim. Possibly but not always. Bad sexual encounters, especially if experienced when young, can, alas, have long-lasting negative effects.

True, it's good for victims to respond with a defiantly positive outlook. Yet much better for societies to stop abusers and for abusers to learn to desist too. Not an easy task. It often transpires that abusers have themselves been abused when young. Learning to 're-set' sexual expectations means breaking one individual's spell cast by past times (as discussed also in the next chapter), while it simultaneously means halting repetitive cycles of harm that continue from generation to generation.

The passing years then bring further implacable messages. Many women experience the upheavals of giving birth. Or the distress of trying to get pregnant and not succeeding. Or, worst of all, delivering a still-born child. A surprising number also face the lonely and often miserable turmoil of abortions and/or miscarriages (sometimes more than once). Then, in mid-life, all women face the menopause, when menstruation stops. A sizeable minority (again unfairly) have unpleasant symptoms, while others hardly notice the change.

All, however, are aware that their 'natural' capacity for reproduction has gone, though not their capacity to enjoy sex. Some women at the menopause experience a loss of libido. Others experience exactly the reverse (The rest—no change). But in all cases, the menopause reaffirms the basics of embodied being: female bodies have a limited window of opportunity for reproduction.

Men in mid-life do not have anything as drastic as an end to fertility. They may continue to father children into old age. However, more than a few older males experience a waning in their capacity to sustain an erection and to ejaculate. Such changes may follow upon illness, or upon alcoholic excess, or may simply accompany the frailties of ageing.

Sexual arousal when younger can be triggered by erotic passion or by a desire to dominate (or a mix of both) as well as by sexual variety and sheer physical delight in being alive. But those triggers don't work automatically throughout a lifetime. Discovering that cold truth can come as an unwelcome shock to individual men—and to their partners—who are used to the ever-ready erections of libidinous young men.

Of course, there are stimulus pills and a range of sexual pleasures other than penetrative sex. Bodies, however, 'tell the Time', even to those who don't want to listen. And sexual bodies in particular quietly convey an intimate in-person lesson: that temporality has an insidious power to give, and to take away. And this often involuntary education in body-learning and sexual learning continues side by side with what is known as 'book-learning'.

Thinking Ahead

Meanwhile, the future holds out the hope of alternatives, at least in aspiration. As young humans grow and learn, they become increasingly aware of the potential of things to come. They have hopes and dreams. As is confirmed by the great repertoire of songs and sayings about future options: 'One day, all this will change…'; 'Somewhere, over the rainbow…'; 'I have a dream…!'.

At the same time, many future high probabilities are known. Routine experience confirms that days habitually follow nights, which precede further days. True, the point is basic. But it can be reassuring, notably in times of trouble. Cue for yet more song: 'There is always another day'.

Additionally, humans undertake careful calculations, based upon past data, which allow for future predictions. For instance, actuarial tables, showing age-related life expectancy, indicate group probabilities. Those are not certainties but are more than random guesses. Based on such calculations, life insurance businesses raise money from clients with a guarantee to pay post-death benefits to nominated recipients. All parties are taking a calculated risk. And insurance companies do go bust, sometimes spectacularly so. Yet the business broadly survives while continually seeking to refine its calculations.

Future predictions in some fields are, furthermore, much more precise. It is known, from astronomical observations, allied to calculation, that Halley's Comet (officially 1P/Halley) becomes visible to the naked eye from Planet Earth every seventy-five to seventy-six years. The calculations allow for small orbital variations from fluctuating pressures in outer space. But the next return of Halley's Comet, into view from Planet Earth, is forecast for mid-2061. Many alive today will be able to check. But they are unlikely to make bets against the outcome since the evidence is well attested.

True, knowing the date of a future cometary visit is not immediately helpful. (Some may ask, Henry-Ford like: *what use are astronomers?*) Yet such calculations show that humans can calculate forces far beyond the immediate vicinity of Planet Earth. Such knowledge offers a foothold in a turbulent cosmos. A basis for coping—or attempting to cope—with predictable and unpredictable future happenings, not all of which will be pleasant.

Advance calendars are also available. Forecasts, both adventurous and precise, abound. Humans regularly plan for future events, months, years, and even decades ahead. People enter into long-term contracts. At weddings, couples solemnly promise to sustain their mutual commitment for a lifetime. In practice, of course, plans are regularly modified as Time unfolds. Promises aren't invariably kept. Yet, the interplay between hopes/plans for the future and actual outcomes is highly educational. Sometimes joyously so, sometimes painfully.

Soothingly, a well-known ditty declares that: 'Que sera, sera/Whatever will be, will be/The future's not ours to see…' Having at least some tolerably secure basic information about what is to come does, however, help to diminish the terror of the unknown. The future is not a complete void. Instead, it is full of options, possibilities, and high probabilities, verging on certainties. The betting industry flourishes by encouraging people to wager money on their predictions. And there is a huge semi-covert world of seers, soothsayers, astrologers, clairvoyants, crystal-gazers, and self-styled prophets who offer to foretell the future. They also seek to dispel the clouds of future uncertainty.

It goes without saying, meanwhile, that no one can halt or change the unfolding course of Time. Nonetheless, humans can make informed predictions, and if those are unfavourable to human life, can take steps to avert or to minimise the severity of expected trends.

To be sure, it is not easy to get agreement about remedial actions. For instance, many eloquent songs warn about the hideous perils of warfare. But their message doesn't halt conflict. The anti-war ballad, *Where Have All the Flowers Gone?* thus ends with a poignant lament: 'When will they ever learn?'. Good question. Nonetheless, humans have the capacity to cast their thoughts backwards and onwards, along the line of Time. So they can learn, if they want, from the anticipated/predicted future, and take steps accordingly.

Learning from Experience

But, undoubtedly, the great repository of human experience—both for individuals and for society at large—is knowledge gained in and from the past (as already noted in the previous chapter). Such know-how shapes behaviour in the present and plans for the future. Yet messages from former times can be read in diverse ways. On emotive issues, there are often strong rival views. Historians also may disagree, as do the public, which is why informed debate is crucial.

Learning from the past is, after all, not just a matter of being told. People have to want to understand as well. And, having understood, then to take heed. Desperate or careless individuals are capable of drinking bottles marked *Poison!* Reckless humans wander beyond points marked *Danger!* And, less dramatically, lots of good advice (for example, from doctors) is daily ignored. Much information goes, proverbially: 'in one ear and out the other'.

Thus older people often remark about the rising generation: 'Young people have to learn from their own mistakes'. Indeed, it is frustrating to give advice, based upon hard-won experience, which is then ignored. Even the bittersweet pleasure of later saying, after a disaster: 'I told you so', does not compensate.

Past experience, while a valuable resource, cannot, furthermore, be relied upon blindly. Not all old ways are right. And they certainly don't define the limits of the available options. Many things, once thought impossible, can be done after all. Again, however, not every innovation works. There are new blind alleys as well as old ones. Learning from the past requires a continuous critical assessment.

Memories from earlier times are, meanwhile, readily shared with others, without the need for argument or debate. The past provides a deep psychological and mental homeland. Talking with others about earlier shared experiences is one of life's habitual pleasures, whether chatting at the marketplace or by the fireside or on today's social media. The past cannot be brought back as it was. Yet its reverberations can be shared, pondered and enjoyed.

Collectively, there's so much accumulated information and experience that the load can seem overwhelming. That's why educational pathways are needed. And why learners need to be enthused. Much is gleaned unconsciously and subconsciously. But conscious study requires learners to be primed to offer full attention not just at one instant but with a sustained 'fix'.

Finding out about the world is an awesome task, undertaken from the moment of birth onwards. Patterns of learning are laid down very early. As a result, young babies need a special concentration of favourable circumstances (which remain helpful throughout life). That is, they need ample nutrition, personal security, regular physical exercise, sustained and non-capricious human love that is clearly and safely demonstrated, and lively mental stimulus. The role of primary carers is crucial, while adult friends and family members contribute too.

But children also learn, both emotionally and mentally, from other children. Shared fun and games give great scope for creativity and for the through-Time repetition that embeds knowledge and skills.

Given the obvious nature of those propositions about love and nurture, it is dispiriting to realise that there was once a period, from the 1950s to 1970s, when scientists experimented to test the power of animal attachment and stimulus. Young monkeys were locked in total isolation for many months (being fed automatically) at the bottom of a dark, featureless steel tube, horribly named the *Pit of Despair*. They emerged as pitiful, huddled wretches. When later returned to the ordinary simian company, they behaved in aberrant and destructive ways.

Such unethical experiments (which were controversial at the time) did at least provide unequivocal answers. Successful mammalian growth and well-being depend upon very much more than regular food supplies alone.

Observations of human orphans in 1990s Romania confirmed the point. Sadly, some children were reared in underfunded orphanages without adequate nutrition or focused adult attention. Many of these youngsters developed behavioural disorders. What's more, scans showed that a number had restricted brain sizes and limited mental activity. The need for reciprocated affection, comforting touch, mental stimulation, lively company, regular physical activity, and lack of confinement are universal basics.

Growing well and learning manifestly go together. The young are being inducted into the collective experience of their species, while simultaneously laying down their individual mental trackways for future development. Hence serious harm to growing children can cause deep long-term damage, which then takes many years to reverse or alleviate.

All societies thus provide formal education systems for their young citizens (details vary globally). Pupils are progressively guided through a range of knowledge. Large sums are spent on schooling because an effective intergenerational exchange is essential for human survival. Historically, the trend everywhere is for populations to become more highly educated, with greater numbers moving from school into tertiary institutions for advanced training. Educated brainpower is a valued resource whose stock is always rising.

Adults, moreover, continue to learn, long after their formal schooldays. Many receive in-work training. Others follow hobbies, attend courses, or take up new skills. The precise degree of involvement varies with needs, aptitudes, and interests. All also learn to cope, happily or otherwise, with their changing corporeal and mental powers. Such long-term lessons can be tough. But the best response, as is well known, is to keep as physically and mentally fit as possible.

Hence it is a fair prediction that demand for lifelong education will continue to grow. In particular, with the forecast expansion of automated work, people will seek more and more non-workplace activities to keep their brains and bodies alert.

Expanding the prediction, it may be guessed that one day new mind clubs will open (*with a better name!*), alongside today's gymnasia (*body clubs*). And all will expand in numbers and geographical spread.

A crucial proviso should also insist that both mind and body clubs must cater for all interests, from chess to crochet, from dance to drama, from walking to word games…and as many forms of applied knowledge as possible. 'All in good Time', to adapt an old saying, 'can be shared in good Time'.

Summary Next Step: Looking Backwards and Thinking Onwards

Once an eighteenth-century American lawyer, when confronted with a new constitutional problem, gave a splendid response: 'I have but one lamp by which my feet are guided, and that is the lamp of experience. I know of no way of judging the future but by the past'. It was a graphic image. A lantern throws light. It does not insist dogmatically but provides sufficient illumination for good judgment. 'Experience' is also a key component. It implies not just bare 'facts' but a capacity to think about past events and to learn from them.

Historical studies—for example, of past pandemics—provide suggestive evidence of what was done, what was not done, and what could have been done better. Imaginative literature also offers reflections upon the range of human reactions when daily life is disrupted by unexpected plagues. Medical reports meanwhile strive to explain the source of contagion and available antidotes. In such diverse ways, people respond to present dangers and also undertake mental rehearsals for future crises. Experience helps to confront the unexpected.

By the way, the remark about the 'Lamp of Experience' is often attributed in web-listings to Edward Gibbon (1737–94), Britain's pioneering historian of ancient Rome. He seems a plausible person to make such a point. Yet, the wording does not match Gibbon's impersonal writing style. So who was the true author? In fact, it was a near-contemporary Virginia-planter-turned-lawyer named Patrick Henry (1736–99), as some web-listings do correctly report. His appeal to precedent was characteristic of the legal mind, then as much as today.

If cited in casual conversation, the statement does not lose any of its force by being misattributed. Yet, credit should go where credit is due. Accuracy matters (both Edward Gibbon and Patrick Henry would emphatically agree).

Reliance upon knowledge from the past is much more effective if the evidence is trustworthy. In fact, Patrick Henry's observation, while poetically put, is not bold enough. Past experience provides much more than a single beam of light. Time not only teaches intimate bodily lessons but also gives scope for conscious learning. Humans have collectively amassed a huge knowledge stock, which illuminates all aspects of temporal living. That key point was made long ago by Confucius, the sage of classical China. He advised looking backwards while thinking onwards: 'Study the past, if you would define the future'. That is: combine both perspectives to live well in the long trajectory of Time.

Childhood Learning

Gerhardt, S. (2004; 2015) *Why Love Matters: How Affection Shapes a Baby's Brain.*
Hassett, B. (2022) *Growing Up Human: The Evolution of Childhood.*
Yawley, T. D., Pellegrini, A. D. (eds) (2018) *Child's Play: Developmental and Applied.*

Deprivation Studies

Blum, D. (1994) *The Monkey Wars.*
Nelson, C. A., Fox, N. A., Zeanah, C. H. (2014) *Romania's Abandoned Children: Deprivation, Brain Development and the Struggle for Recovery.*

Human Sexuality

Bolin, A. (et. al) (2021) *Human Sexuality: Biological, Psychological and Cultural Perspectives.*
Rathus, S. (et. al) (1997), *Human Sexuality in a World of Diversity.*
Zeldin, T. (1994) *An Intimate History of Humanity.*

Futurology

Andrews, S. (2005) *Lemuria and Atlantis: Studying the Past to Survive the Future.*
Weigend, A. S., Gershenfeld, N. A. (eds) (2018) *Time Series Prediction: Forecasting the Future and Understanding the Past.*

Adult and Lifelong Learning

Brown, L. J. (1995) *Learning, Liberty and Social Purpose: A Reminder of Our Radical Liberal Inheritance in Adult Education.*
Hadjar, A., Gross, C. (eds) (2016) *Education Systems and Inequalities:International Comparisons.*

Chapter 3
Remembering and Forgetting

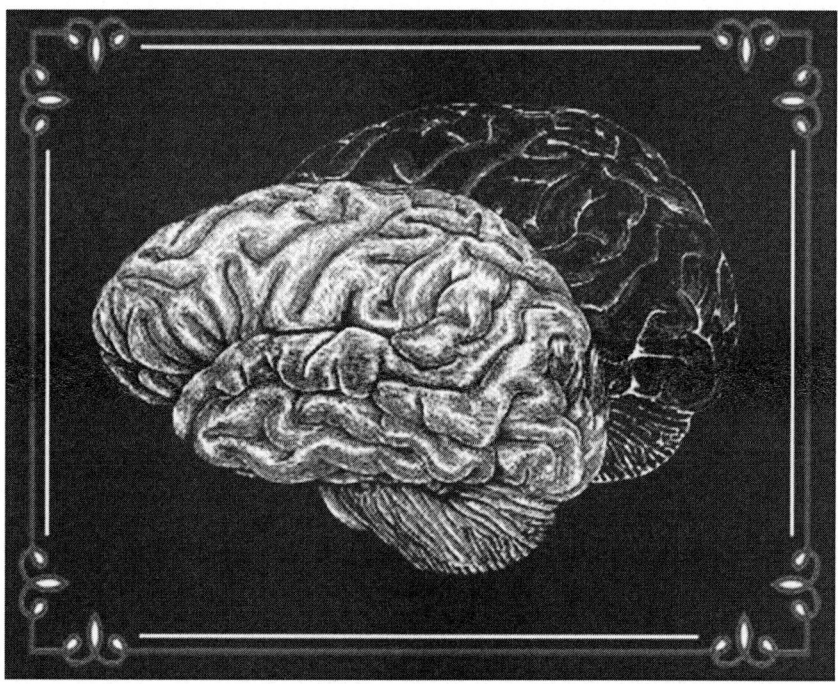

Line drawing of a human brain, looking rather like a barrister's wig—
and, behind, a shadow-brain.

Chapter 3 explores the powers of human memory and strategies for offsetting its weaknesses

Gaining Anchorage in Time

Time is the parent of memory. True, not all parenting works perfectly, Nonetheless, proverbially, *All today's moments are tomorrow's memories.* In healthy humans, the recall power functions doggedly—non-stop, from birth to death. So it can work, tenaciously, for decades—and, in a small but growing number of cases, for over a century.

Moreover, personal memories automatically supply individuals (short of mental decay or accident) with a lifetime's worth of information about themselves. Memories are human footholds in Time. *The remembrance of times past* (in Shakespeare's resonant phrase, famously borrowed by Marcel Proust) provides a spontaneous and natural form of *diachro-mesh*.

Notably, too, this sense of personal anchorage in Time does not depend upon remembering precise dates. It is an intrinsic human capacity that precedes the advent of calendars (with important implications that are discussed later).

The ability to remember is not identical to human consciousness. In some distressing cases, otherwise healthy people remain conscious without any memory or with fragmented recollections. These clinical cases of amnesia are generally associated with traumatic brain damage (on which more below).

Yet, the normal expectation is that, in healthy people, consciousness co-exists with memory-making. Even very young babies quickly recognise their prime carers, aided by sounds, smells and touch. And with further growth, healthy children and adults develop an active memory which sustains their sense of identity and an outline backstory (without recalling every detail). Even after a riotous night on the tiles, it's much more common for people to wake, groaning: 'Oh my poor head!' than asking seriously: 'Who am I?'.

A functioning memory thus provides the basis for living coherently through Time. With absolutely no powers of sequential recall, people could not complete a sentence, or string sentences together to make a speech. It's true that trains of thought can be broken. People stop mid-sentence and ask, distractedly: 'Where was I?'. But then they either recover the thread, or they laugh and say: 'Oh well, I'll tell you when it comes back to me…' And often, it does.

Generally, such hiccups in recollections are the equivalent of minor stumbles from a regular walker, quickly corrected. They may occasion a passing comment but nothing more. At times, moreover, people may have unpleasant episodes that they struggle to erase from their memory banks. 'How can I remember to forget?' asks one plaintive song. Hearts and minds can hold unwelcome as well as welcome memories, and suppressing such unwanted recollections can be surprisingly difficult.

Nonetheless, tenacious as it is, human memory can, simultaneously, be fallible. That reality is no secret. Memory is selective. It can fail, and it can be outright wrong—even if the memory seems totally vivid and true to life.

Accordingly, humans have, in response to such known weaknesses, developed an impressive range of strategies for coping. Memory works to anchor people in Time. It is one of the greatest of all human mental powers. It is, therefore, vital for everyone that it be assisted to operate at its best.

Walking Together 'Down Memory Lane'

Many framework recollections—such as knowing one's native language—are accumulated unwittingly and almost effortlessly from early childhood onwards. Deep memory provides a long-term storage system. Thus even if people in later life become mentally confused, they generally continue to speak grammatically long into their illness.

Specific memories may also be prompted by well-known sights (such as photos of family or pets), by familiar touch, and by distinctive smells and tastes. Marcel Proust made famous his sudden recollections of childhood, which were unexpectedly triggered by consuming a small cake, known as a *madeleine*, which had been dipped into a cup of lime-flower tea.

Strikingly, too, sounds and music often manage to evoke deeply buried memories. In particular, songs, which often combine pleasing tunes with insistent rhythms and repeated phrases, can open pathways into the brain's deepest echo chambers. After all, long before the advent of codified languages, it was customary for early humans to communicate by sounds (and gestures). As a result, even people with serious mental impairment can at times be jolted into unusual feats of remembrance when hearing again a long-forgotten song from their youth. That reality is supported today by much practical evidence from the successful use of music as therapy (even if not a total cure) for dementia patients.

Remembering greatly multiplies the brain's power. Thoughts are not just one-off flashes of illumination (though some are). They can be retained, developed and shared. Moreover, memory operates both consciously and unconsciously. As already noted, performers striving for supreme bodily self-control (as in sports, dance, and music-making) repeat their actions again and again. Movements are thus embedded into muscle memory. Then performers in action can hit the heights without fussing about remembering the basics.

Emotions are also entwined with both thoughts *and* memory. In that way, remembrance is often boosted by feelings of (say) love, hate, regret and/or remorse. As a result, people are often offended and angry if one of their cherished memories is later revealed to be inaccurate. Have they been nurturing false illusions all along? It is not a happy thing to discover. (Cue song: *Don't Shoot the Messenger!*)

Pleasant and positive feelings are good to recall. Long-lasting loves are bolstered by happy memories which reinforce emotion. It's good to walk metaphorically *down memory lane*, in the company of others who are sharing the experience. People sometimes add extra details. Or correct minor uncertainties. And laugh together in shared retrospective delight.

Happy sensual memories also add to the pleasures of sex. Recollections may be warmly blurred and fuzzy. Or sometimes highly specific and erotically stimulating. Thus couples sometimes have a joint repertoire of intimate gestures or words which are used as 'starter signals' for the next round of dalliance.

On the other hand, memories of both sex and love can also be bittersweet, or purely bitter. Love betrayed or lost often leaves galling, agitating, and even tragic memories. The contrast between former happiness and later misery induces both melancholia and romantic yearning. 'Now I long for yesterday'; '*Mais où sont les neiges d'antan?*'; 'Ain't no sunshine when she's gone'; 'Where have all the flowers gone?'; 'Missing you'; 'Baby come back'.

Unpleasant feelings, unsurprisingly, are rarely savoured. Instead, people frequently try to corral negative emotions into a mental box marked *Do not open*. Yet, there's no absolute rule. People with persistent mentalities, who have been treated badly or faced serious losses, may hold onto anger and other grievances. They replay them mentally to sharpen their sting. And they may share them with others, generating a mass cauldron of hatred.

Confronted with such circumstances, religious teachers, moral counsellors, and therapists usually give unequivocal advice. They urge that hatreds, whether ancient or recent, be shed, and enemies forgiven. People who cultivate emotional negativity for long periods harm themselves as much (or more) than they harm others. But not all strong haters see things that way. 'Forgive and forget' is a hard lesson to accept. And some, who do manage to forgive, will still confess that they have not forgotten. Some memories are scorched into the mind.

It has already been noted how past adversity often has long-term negative effects. Even when people seem outwardly to have recovered from earlier damage, their tenacious bad and/or sad memories may later impact subliminally upon their behaviour. The replication of parenting styles provides one example. Adults, who when young were treated coldly, cruelly or capriciously, often announce that they will behave differently with their own offspring. Some manage to do so. But others find it hard to break ingrained patterns.

Changing the dynamics of family life requires more than just good resolutions. Different behaviour is needed—not once, but daily. It's challenging. People accustomed to being physically remote with their close family can be helped, with the right sort of encouragement, to become more 'touchy-feely'. But individuals, who have lived from early youth with capricious and inconstant adults, can struggle to learn for themselves the exercise of self-discipline.

One particularly difficult syndrome occurs when some victims, who have had horrific experiences in their youth, feel a need to pass on the pain to others. As already noted, numerous adult sexual abusers of children were themselves abused when young. Their later behaviour seems to constitute a form of retrospective revenge upon an uncaring world which failed to protect them. Indeed, it may be speculated that dominating forcibly over a weaker victim offers a form of self-exorcism: 'Look, now it is I who have power and I am using it to override my bad memories by passing them to you'. (Morally and legally wrong in every way but psychologically understandable).

To outsiders, it may seem paradoxical that adult abusers should inflict the same damage that they themselves bitterly resent. Yet, evidence confirms that those who have suffered childhood abuse tend to have impaired empathy and fellow feeling with others. Victims are left in a moral void, with nowhere to 'park' their negative feelings. To repair such damage, counsellors advocate a super-effort of memory. Adult abusers need to reconnect to their young selves as they were pre-abuse. To remember what life was like before suspicion, pain, bewilderment, self-disgust and anger became ingrained—even if later masked in adult displays of power, dominance and control. The challenge is great indeed.

Above all, it's clear that emotions, like thoughts, have a great capacity for long-term survival in human memory banks. All individuals have deep subconscious recollections, which may resurface at specific moments. And traumatic experiences can endlessly 'flashback' unless conscious efforts are made to come to terms with the negative experience and to 'park' it safely.

Emotional memories, meanwhile, embrace a rich spectrum. They feed into creativity, for example in the arts, music, dance and literature. Furthermore, human brains are simultaneously channelling the products of rational memory. Much recollection is undertaken consciously, especially during formal education. Some bits of basic information, such as multiplication tables, are commonly *committed to memory*.

In sum, human minds can remember countless ideas, impressions, experiences, emotions, values, and snippets of information, as well as consciously learned formal knowledge and rational calculations. There's a lot in play. Memories do not control destiny but they certainly feed into it.

Forgetting

Fortunately, no doubt, the normal human mind copes with a super-abundance of information by not remembering everything. Much in daily life is lightly noticed at the time but then forgotten. It's helpful for people to reserve both the frontal working memory and their deeper memory banks for items which really matter to them. A constant sifting and winnowing process takes place. It's managed partly by rational calculus (*Make a mental note of that!*) and partly during the routine housekeeping undertaken by the brain during sleep.

Scientific research throws instructive light upon the physiology as well as the psychology of remembering and/or forgetting. People who sleep well are liable to generate clear and well-retained memories. Humans are social beings. They like to be out and about, meeting others. At the same time, they have evolved with a countervailing need to shut down their systems for a good stretch of time in every twenty-four-hour cycle. If their hours of sleep are peaceful, their minds and bodies take stock effortlessly. Some memories are ingrained. Others shed.

Conversely, daytime stress and disturbed nights are always unhelpful. Tired and distracted people have tired and distracted minds. Their instincts may remain alert, as in 'the burnt child fears the fire'. Yet, their capacity for learning is in disarray. So those who regularly lack quiet, dark, and safe places for repose will have 'jangled' memories, with only blurred recall of uncertain details.

Forgetfulness that is over and above the average is particularly damaging to students in formal education. Those with poor memories become frustrated and can lose motivation.

Teachers are aware of these difficulties. Studies show that some proportion of all freshly learned information is regularly forgotten within a relatively short period. However, there is no standard rate of loss. Figures sometimes cited, showing that x percentage is forgotten within y days, are no more than estimates, concealing dramatic variations.

Key factors that minimise student forgetfulness are well known. They include (no surprise) the learners' desire to learn; the learners' sharing with fellow learners; the teachers' capacity to inspire, and the effectiveness of the chosen teaching method for each subject and age group. In addition, too, forgetfulness is reduced when the learners are physically well and have regular access to a good night's sleep.

Muddled memories are, of course, experienced by everyone at some stage during a lifetime. It can be infuriating when something well-known is *on the tip of one's tongue* but cannot be retrieved at the required moment. In response, people either just laugh gaily, or look up the missing item.

All the same, it is a worrying sign when moments of forgetfulness begin to multiply unduly. It's an experience that may well signal the onset of serious illness, or simply the 'scattiness' stereotypically (but not invariably) associated with advancing age.

Rarely, forgetful people with emptied memory banks may be suffering from full or partial amnesia. That syndrome is often caused by traumatic head injuries. Or, exceptionally, by drastic alcohol abuse, leading to severe psychosis. Amnesiacs typically lose not only past memories but also the capacity to lay down new ones. Sufferers are in this world but out of it. The condition is dangerous and distressing, though it can right itself with time—fortunately since there's (to date) no reliable cure.

Interestingly, cases of amnesia appear in literature and films more frequently than they do in real life. But whether factual or fictional, they convincingly demonstrate the centrality of a sound working brain, with accessible memories, for independent human living.

Far less immediately dramatic than cases of total amnesia, but often far more distressing—both for sufferers and for their friends and family—are cases of progressive dementia (Sadly, this condition of brain-scrambling can be caused by hundreds of different diseases, often but not invariably associated with old age). Sufferers forget even routine things. They become self-neglectful. Their personalities may change, not always for the better.

Commonly, dementia sufferers appear vague and listless. A few become aggressive. Some behave in sexually inappropriate ways as normal self-control erodes. Furthermore, as the illness worsens, sufferers can become dangerous to themselves and others, for example by accidentally starting fires.

Witnessing the spreading forgetfulness of dementia is a desolating affair for friends and family. They see a loved personality 'die' in stages, while the body continues to live, thus rendering any official mourning premature. There is no clearer indication of the vital role of a working memory. It's needed not just for independent living but for retaining individual identity.

Many dementia sufferers will eventually need institutional care. And as greater numbers of people are surviving into advanced ages, so the potential need for special nursing assistance is rising, as are the financial costs.

Hence, memory loss poses a great challenge not only for individuals and families but for society as a whole. It's a hard one to resolve. But all cases of dementia do underline once more the crucial need for people to keep their minds and memories in good working trim, and to sleep well.

Offsetting Memory's Weaknesses

Memory's fallibilities are well known. To recapitulate: It is often imperfect. It fades. Unkindly, it also plays tricks. Details that people recall with immense clarity can prove to be false. Wishful thinking may have secretly prevailed. Discovering the truth can be disconcerting, even shocking, as already noted.

None of these points are surprising. Most people's memories are selective. If absolutely everything seen, read, heard and/or experienced was recalled in complete detail, the overload would be intolerable. Some selectivity is needed for survival. Yet, the scope for errors and omissions is also apparent.

As a result, much human attention has been devoted to finding strategies for storing and transmitting knowledge that do not depend upon one fallible memory alone. Group sharing is indeed a wise project for group survival.

Communal storytelling is one social practice of great antiquity. Long before literacy allowed tales to be put in writing, those with good memories would recite stylised accounts, later known as 'sagas'. Listeners could also chime in, at favourite points, or prompt speakers should they falter. Sharing familiar stories helped to shore up communal memories. And the process of oral transmission conveyed them to the next generation.

Another mechanism for remembering was (and is) to use significant places or objects as memory-markers. This habit still continues today (as explored in a later chapter). The many monumental standing stones, surviving from very ancient times, are testaments of this practice.

Historically, one example of using special places as memory-markers was sadly misunderstood. When the first European settlers arrived in Australia, they viewed the distinctive 'walkabouts' of its indigenous peoples as aimless wanderings. Whereas, in fact, they functioned as communal memory tours in which specific locations and objects (rivers, trees, rocks) had specific collective associations. All individuals, who today choose special places where they go for personal acts of remembrance, can empathise with this historic practice.

Over the course of history, furthermore, humans have found many ways of systematising knowledge. Personal memory, as already noted, is pre-calendrical. People don't habitually remember by reference to precise dates, excepting only special occasions or consciously learned information. So there is often a great mismatch between detailed recall of a specific event and utter vagueness about its exact date. (*Several years ago…but how many? Hard to say…*)

Normal human memory thus provides a broad sense of Time but not a precise calibration. This 'unreliability' factor was offset by developing systematic Time measurement. Calendars, mechanical clocks and all forms of timekeeping devices provide the missing accuracy. They were made by humans applying their minds and memories to calculate and mark the passing of Time. And, in turn, such devices, once invented, are used to prompt memory. Need to remember when to do something? Cue song: *Listen to the clock upon the wall* (Or these days: *set the timer on the mobile phone*).

With the advent of literacy, people could further refresh their memories by consulting the written word. The stock of recorded knowledge began inexorably to expand. And, with the later advent of printing and the spread of literacy skills, the relevant records not only multiplied dramatically but so did their availability. Summary guides of all sorts began to appear: dictionaries, encyclopaedias, atlases, bibliographies, and a multitude of handbooks. And today, the support systems for human memory are enshrined not only in texts but also in electronic format. The resources are truly formidable.

Individuals, meanwhile, still need to cultivate good working memories. Those are as much needed as they ever were. Hence, there are plenty of handbooks which offer advice on improving powers of recollection. There are also a host of mnemonic systems (as they are termed) or traditional techniques for laying down memories. One common tip is to concentrate very deliberately on the process of remembering. It's called 'fixing' an item of information in the memory. Remembering to remember. That method reinforces long-term remembrance and assists rapid retrieval from the brain's storage system.

People with disturbed memories can also seek help from therapeutic experts. They try to free troubled minds from endless loops of recycled negativity. In particular, victims who experience horrific flashback recollections of traumatic events can be advised on how to come to terms with 'bad' memories, and then to 'store' them safely away. (Simply refusing to think about past disasters can initially seem to work but the tactic often leaves too much scope for later relapses, signalling the all-too-vivid 'return of the repressed'.)

Meanwhile, in different and much less emotional cases, people have to undertake their own sessions of mental housekeeping. That process is needed if individuals fail to forget too many minor details. The result is chronic memory overload. Some with this problem have the rare (and disputed) syndrome of total photographic recall. And others have consciously trained themselves in feats of memorisation. They can scan multiple pages, even of gibberish, and then recite every word with total accuracy. But such mountains of recollected information still have to be consciously shed. Otherwise, remembering a mountain of trivia seriously clogs a good working memory.

Given these intricacies, it is entirely normal for people to have a mix of recollections. Some memories will be strong and clear. A good proportion will be hazy and semi-remembered. And some may be mythic, arising out of hearsay and suggestions from others. Thus, witnesses on oath in a court of law can at times be wrong-footed. They may testify in good faith. Yet, other unassailable evidence shows that their memories are mistaken.

When and if that happens, lawyers pounce to discredit the witness entirely. They quote the Latin legal tag: '*Falsus in uno, falsus in omnibus*/Wrong on one point, wrong in all'. Yet such an assumption is far too sweeping. Inadvertent (or even deliberate) errors on some points may be counter-balanced by truths elsewhere. It's for the courts to decide. Still, it's best for witnesses to be both accurate and consistent. It's wise, therefore, mentally to double-check evidence before making statements on oath. And then stick to the original story, without deviations that may later be used to discredit a muddled witness.

Lawyers, like detectives and historians, still cultivate an attitude of due scepticism. They don't like to rely upon one uncorroborated source. They know the potential flaws of memory, even if reported in good faith. Hence, the art of gaining reliable knowledge relies on extensive challenging and cross-checking.

Why, it may be asked, has human memory evolved with this hit-and-miss quality? One obvious answer is that furnishing legal precision is not its prime function. Instead, memory serves well enough, in a healthy person, to sustain a lifelong sense of personal identity, alongside much useful information both in storage and in daily use. Some areas of haziness do not normally matter much.

Working memories have thus evolved to provide sufficient coherence and operational capacity for human survival. (As noted above, those without such key mental resources need additional help from families and/or institutions, depending upon the severity of their dementia.) But, at the same time, people have simultaneously developed an impressive array of mechanisms for providing greater levels of precision when such precision is required.

Cross-Checking

Sharing is a very common feature of everyday social and cultural life among humans. And that applies very notably to the making and testing of memories. All societies have known meeting places—at churches, shrines, parks, sporting venues, resorts and transport interchanges as well as in shops, markets, drinking dens, inns, restaurants, coffee bars, schools, community centres, and workplaces—let alone at wells and oases in even the most sparsely populated desert. People exchange news and views daily. Cue song: '*I heard it through the grapevine…*'

Casual conversations are not, of course, designed to test the accuracy of memory, unlike appearing in a law court. Gossip and general chatter move lightly from topic to topic without a care. Yet, while memories are being shared and compared, there is scope too for a degree of chaffing and scepticism.

Retrospective accounts ('She said…; then he said…; and then she hit him'. 'Well I never, did she really?') may seem rambling and inconsequential. Yet, they provide ways of rehearsing and underlining memories. Indeed, some accounts turn into polished anecdotes that recur regularly in people's conversational repertoire. Stories that contain the spice of scandal spark closer attention. And spicy stories frequently grow more 'interesting' in the retelling.

Listeners, with their own memories to contribute, are, however, not necessarily bound to accept everything that they hear. ('So, after she hit him, what he did do next?' 'Oh, he sat down and cried like a baby'. 'No, I can't believe that! You've got to be kidding me!') People can and do allow for the possibility of exaggerations and outright lies (further explored in Chapter 11).

Furthermore, the entire story may anyway be a joke, reflecting the notable human sense of humour. A number of mammals laugh and like to be tickled. But verbal humour is uniquely human. Cue another song: '*I was only joking, my dear…*'

What people are doing, informally, is sifting through proffered memories, and taking the opportunity to adopt, adapt or shred the mental record. Moreover, groups, as well as individuals, maintain their coherence by the same mechanisms, equally informally.

Shared memories have immense potency. Thus gatherings of friends, families, lovers, local communities, religious faiths and entire nations have their own repertoires of remembrance. Walking together *down memory lane* is a pleasure that can be shared by both small and large groups, as already noted. People also boost their shared stories with other memorabilia, including letters, photos and all sorts of meaningful souvenirs.

Collectively, therefore, humans can tap into memory banks that stretch well beyond their own immediate worlds. In particular, the cohesion of large groups is often welded by the acceptance of one big 'framing' narrative. Of course, communal memories can be also biased and inaccurate. They are often debated and contested, both within the group and by rival groups.

Crucially, however, communal remembrance does not depend upon just one fallible individual. And the sharing of a common 'through-Time' story is a powerful resource. It can be formally feted in public places of commemoration (see Ch. 12) as well as recorded in history books and casually celebrated in songs and sayings. The literate become well-versed in the narrative, and the illiterate (now dwindling in numbers worldwide) can glean much from oral recitations.

Informal and instinctual ways of cross-checking ideas and information are thus very ancient indeed. They help humans to share and test memories. And these informal mechanisms have been incomparably expanded and rendered much more sophisticated and systematic as the huge superstructure of human skills and knowledge is constantly being updated.

Now, the sum of collective 'learning' has expanded far beyond the capacity of any one individual, no matter how gifted, to recollect. Human knowledge is a continual work-in-progress. Over time, many fundamentals become settled. Yet errors may always remain, awaiting detection. Or the intellectual framework may be fundamentally revised (as when Einstein updated Newtonian physics). Memory banks are thus constantly open for checking and revision. Today, too, ever-improving technological aids are applied to knowledge generation, testing, communication, recalculation, storage, and retrieval. And it also follows that new technologies must equally remain open to critical scrutiny as well. Sharing and cross-checking are alike key strategies for generating secure knowledge.

Summary Next Step: Keeping Track of Time

Good temporal bearings are needed by all living creatures. Many species adapt instinctively to the seasons. Hibernators in late summer seek places to sleep safely; and hoarders, like squirrels, deposit supplies for the winter. In other cases, birds and fish undertake long migrations, sometimes around huge areas of the globe. They seek supplies and/or places to over-winter and/or to breed. Often, they return to the same locations, year after year. Such actions rely upon effective geo-locators, which provide spatial memory.

Mechanisms for coping with changing circumstances are very varied. Some species, like dogs, habitually use their formidable powers of smell to convey key messages to the brain. Possibly they and some other 'bright' species, like rats, have a sense of episodic recall and can fit events into a remembered Time-sequence (Research on this point is not yet conclusive).

Their animal inheritance provides humans too with strong instincts about temporal living. Yet, among all living creatures, they are the most remarkable for their highly developed memory-systems. They recall both the long- and short-term. They blend intellectual and emotional memories. And as earlier stressed, they share memories and try to understand their 'through-Time' story.

Immediately, in that context, medical advisors convey a significant warning to today's humans. People should remove from their bedrooms all fluorescent lights on the latest techno-gadgets. Those are harmful to the memory-making and memory-retaining capacities of the human brain. Outdoors, too, all excess light pollution at night should be eliminated.

Such prudential moves will uphold the historic circadian and seasonal rhythms of life—not just for humans but for all other species as well. Good planetary housekeeping requires nothing less.

Fortified by their mental resources and collective memories, meanwhile, humans live successfully in all quarters of the globe. They have adapted to many varied ecosystems. Their temporal bearings are generally well-adjusted.

Communities, as well as individuals, build upon shared memories and the historic record to generate long-run backstories. They make collective histories that stretch back through 'Time Immemorial'.

Despite their potentially fallible memories, then, humans collectively are not lost in the great cosmos. They build Time-reckoners. They create knowledge which they share and debate with others. Together, they keep critical track of the cosmic journey. And as already noted, information about Time-markers is imparted to very young humans, while they are developing their own memories and their own grasp upon the temporal cycle. Thus, all children in all global cultures are taught successfully, not to speculate about the metaphysical meanings of temporality but simply to *tell the Time*.

Human Memory

Danziger, K. (2008) *Marking the Mind: A History of Memory.*
Fivush, R., Neisser, U. (eds) (1994) *The Remembering Self: Construction and Accuracy in the Self-Narrative.*

Techniques for Memory Training

Yates, F. A. (1966) *The Art of Memory.*
Goldberg, P. (2019) *Memory Improvement Guidebook: Step-by-Step Guide to Improve your Memory, Rewire your Brain and Stop Overthinking…*

Forgetting

MacPherson, S. E., Della Sala, S. (2019) *Cases of Amnesia: Contributions to Understanding Memory and the Brain.*
Schachter, D. L. (2002) *The Seven Sins of Memory: How the Mind Forgets and Remembers.*

Music Therapy for Scrambled Minds

Mahoney, F. (2011) *Music and Memories: Creative Caring for People with Dementia.*

Chapter 4
Generalising and Questioning

Animal proverbially representing different casts of mind, as allegedly hedgehogs always think big while instead foxes always ask questions and spot complications

Chapter 4 assesses how humans view their collective past, noting tensions between those who make big generalisations and others who invariably spot complications.

Thinking Big and Small

Time itself will tell... runs a grand old adage. And indeed Time writes its messages majestically across the skies, throughout the globe, and in the faces, bodies and minds of all living humans. Nonetheless, the evidence, vivid as it is, needs interpretation. To that end, humans think big. They listen to myths and tales about olden times; they recount personal and family stories about the past;

and a proportion of them read serious historical and scientific studies. These activities are all forms of *diachro-mesh*, helping to locate people in Time.

Needless to say, daily lives unfold in the immediacy of the tremendous present. Many self-help manuals and yogic philosophies offer pertinent advice on savouring each moment. No point in dreaming only of the past, or waiting endlessly (hopefully? fearfully?) for a distant future. De-stress. Be alive in the present: 'Quick, now, here, now, always…', to quote T. S. Eliot's wonderfully orgasmic formulation from his *Four Quartets* (1944). However, each single moment morphs constantly into the next. It's a brute truth that becomes apparent to all humans once past very early youth.

Thinking, moreover, is a constant through-Time activity. And it's undertaken with the aid of accumulated knowledge, which is ballasted by memories and documented by stored information in encyclopaedias, guidebooks, history books, libraries of textbooks on every subject under the sun, and the multifarious resources of the web.

So how can people make sense out of so much—often contradictory—information? No one can decide everything from scratch. Much has to be taken for granted. But people also probe and ask questions. One big picture may be opposed by an alternative big picture. Or one big generalisation challenged by sceptical questions. *Yes, it's this! No, it's that!* Or, alternatively: *No to both!*

Polarities in human thought patterns have long been detected. In the mid-nineteenth century, for example, the great biologist Charles Darwin (who was not himself afraid of the big picture) divided thinkers into 'lumpers' and 'splitters'. Those terms are graphic, if hardly elegant. 'Lumpers' assemble fragments of knowledge into one big picture. 'Splitters', by contrast, like splitting hairs. They see complications everywhere. And they certainly don't want to be fooled into thinking that things are really so easily understood.

Rival terms were later popularised by the Latvian-born philosopher Isaiah Berlin. In *The Hedgehog and the Fox* (1953), he contrasted the wily fox, who allegedly knows many things, and the single-minded hedgehog, who, equally allegedly, knows only one big thing. Those animal exemplars were based upon a proverbial dictum from the classical Greek poet Archilochus.

To provide a human example, Isaiah Berlin pointed to the Russian novelist Leo Tolstoy. After a spiritual crisis, he devised his own personal philosophy. Tolstoy thus began to live simply, peasant-style. He gave up meat-eating and became a vegetarian. And he embraced pacifism and non-violent civil disobedience. In all, Tolstoy's vision of peaceful simplicity marked him, for Isaiah Berlin, as a classic 'lumper' or 'hedgehog'. But really? Does the small, shy and prickly hedgehog seem right for a sweeping thinker like Tolstoy, author of *War and Peace* (1869), which is a mighty classic of world literature?

That objection to Berlin's analogy is, incidentally, a good example of critical 'splitting'. No generalisation is immune from challenge. Indeed, a brooding character in a P. W. Anderson sci-fi novella declares that: 'I have yet to see any problem, which, when you looked at it in the right way, did not become still more complicated'. It's a great maxim for splitters.

Big debates, as a result, often spawn multiplying disagreements, rather than one sole answer. It's hard to reduce tangled complexities into just one key proposition. 'Simple isn't easy', as one thoughtful catchphrase announces. To which rival responses quickly state: 'Oh yes, it is'. 'Oh no, it isn't'. Thought characteristically builds upon both 'lumping' and 'splitting'. And there are big and pertinent questions to debate. After all, how exactly did the ever-generalising, ever-argumentative humans manage to get to this point in Time?

Detecting Big Patterns

Making any general argument requires a bit of summarising. It's very hard to extract meaning from an unadorned list of single fact after fact, *ad infinitum*. (Once a learned lecturer, invited to explain the growth of a key trend in the eighteenth century, began with the year 1701, moved on to 1702, 1703, and so forth. After an hour, the talk had got to 1724. The audience was in despair. But their agony turned into general relief when the chair intervened to thank the speaker and stopped the century at 1725.)

Chronology provides an essential framework (hence it's vital to get dates right). Yet, one-thing-after-another does not provide an explanation. So humans often look for big patterns and recount evolving storylines. Various influential examples are examined here, but these don't exhaust all the possibilities. All cultures have their approaches to the collective human story, sometimes with a range of variants. (Readers may well find that they themselves have a number of core beliefs about history, which they have picked up from friends, family or teachers, often without even realising.)

Grand historical trends, meanwhile, rely upon big sources of motor power to effect change. So what are those forces? What about the impact of sex? One example of *lumping* and *counter-splitting* occurred in a disagreement between two early twentieth-century novelists. The apostle of sexual frankness, D. H. Lawrence, stressed the universal power of the sex instinct. He was not a casual libertine but a mystic. 'Sex is our deepest form of consciousness', he wrote in 1922: 'It is utterly non-ideal, non-mental. It is pure blood consciousness. …It is the consciousness of the night when the soul is *almost* asleep'.

Lawrence's claim was wonderfully portentous… indeed, positively 'Lawrentian'. Sexuality does indeed combine physicality and emotions. And there has been a lot of sexual action over Time, to produce the almost eight billion humans in the world today. Yet, Lawrence was criticised as too prone to see sex everywhere. There are other forces in life. Thus fellow author Katherine Mansfield countered him with the wry remark that: 'I shall never see sex in trees, sex in the running brooks, sex in stones, and sex in everything'.

Well, it's a good question to debate. How much importance in human history should be attached to the sex drive? And what other big factors need to be included too? What about (say) the desire of men to establish dominance over women? Or vice versa? Or looking beyond gender roles, what about the lure of money? Or competition for scarce resources? Or the human instinct for aggression? The class struggle? Technological innovations? Or the power of ideas, and faiths? All those have been cited. But equally disputed.

Nowadays, most big pictures of human history tend to avoid relying upon one single factor. For example, the sex drive operates inexorably to renew and grow the species, generation after generation. Yet, lust and procreation cannot explain the many long-term changes that have accompanied the emergence of humans from obscurity, as a minor branch of the Great Apes, into the world's most dominant (even dangerously predominant) animal.

Instead, big stories are likely to involve multiple factors, working together. But stress upon complexity does not mean that things are so entangled that they are beyond explanation.

One early model of change described the human story in terms of the successive rise and fall of great civilisations. From (say) the ancient Egyptians— via the Sumerians—the Greeks—the Romans, and so forth. The pattern of change is seen as cyclical. The parallel is with the human lifecycle: the familiar sequence from birth to maturity to old age and on to death. One key theorist of cyclical change was Giambattista Vico, writing in early eighteenth-century Naples. And a famous case history was penned in Britain by Edward Gibbon in the form of his magisterial *Decline and Fall of the Roman Empire* (1776).

Cyclical accounts can also convey stark threats or warnings. In 1918, Germany's Oswald Spengler darkly warned of *The Decline of the West* (1918; reprinted 1922). His big message was not hard to spot. Lurking behind 'decline' was the prospect of 'fall'. Spengler was pessimistic. But things did not happen as he foresaw. The West, while facing many challenges, has not (yet) collapsed.

Another celebrated big picture came from the historian Arnold Toynbee. He saw history as propelled by a non-stop process of 'challenge' and 'response' between rival powers. 'Winners' rise and 'losers' fall. A later variant followed from the American political scientist Samuel P. Huntington. For him, there was an endless 'clash of cultures'. Conflicts between nations, religions, or ideologies, led some groups to success and others to failure. Interestingly, a board game (2012), entitled *Clash of Cultures*, invites players to *lead your civilisation from a single settlement to a mighty empire* (But it makes no mention of losers, who, presumably, take their cause into oblivion or servitude).

Approaches such as these highlight the role of conflict. On the other hand, 'splitters' are ready with objections. Do cultures always have to compete? Can they not cooperate together for some purposes? Furthermore, do powers always rise and fall so readily? What about those that remain in steady-state for long periods? Or even those that rise and fall more than once? What's more, are the fates of entire nations or entire religions in practice so monolithic? After all, there are plenty of internal conflicts *within* groups as well as *between* groups.

Accounts of history in terms of cycles of 'rise and decline' have not disappeared. But they now compete with a very different picture. Especially in the West in the nineteenth and early twentieth centuries, a bold alternative was adopted by many (though not by all). The reverse of Gibbon's *Decline and Fall* was a linear *Rise and Progress*. It saw the human story as one of progressive betterment. As though walking up a hill together, to the 'sunlit uplands' ahead.

Linear change might face temporary setbacks along the line, but its destination was expected to be glorious. In the West, the concept was linked with confidence associated with imperial expansion, economic innovation, and geopolitical dominance. But optimistic hopes could embrace any topic. Thus, in 1745, an author explained *The Rise, Progress and Improvement of Geometry*.

Such studies boosted confidence in big impersonal trends. A work like William Lecky's *History of the Rise and Influence of the Spirit of Rationalism in Europe* (1869) conveyed its optimism in its title. 'Splitters', unsurprisingly, counter-attacked. How widespread are these alleged trends? Is not historical 'progress' for affluent people in some parts of the world often based upon exploitation and impoverishment for others elsewhere? And how do stories of benevolent change incorporate the endemic role of conflict?

In fact, confidence in universal 'progress' faded—especially after the mid-twentieth-century experiences of global warfare, the atomic bomb, and organised genocide in Nazi Germany, in the heart of allegedly 'civilised' Europe. Optimistic scenarios are still written. Songs with cheery titles continue. But lyrics may express caution, as in Ayumi Hamasaki's *Progress* (2011):'*We can't live in this time with just an innocent smile/But we move ahead*'.

Moreover, today, eco-anxiety rightly poses an urgent counter-narrative to unalloyed progress. Some long-term trends may be benevolent (*say*, improvements in dentistry and medical science). But others simultaneously are disastrous (*say*, environmental degradation, species loss, and climate change).

Ultimately, historical pathways may be pluralistic. More than one big trend may be unfolding in the same era. Furthermore, some major changes may develop in parallel with others. At other times, however, trends may be contradictory. History contains patterns but also options.

Detecting Past Stages

A very different approach is equally bold. But it avoids depicting history in continuous lines, whether running in circles or progressing uphill (or sliding downhill). Instead, it sees things as broadly stable for long periods, but then switching suddenly, from one big stage to the next.

Stage theories have been proposed in many cultures. In the 1830s, the French social theorist Auguste Comte provided an influential three-stage model. He sought a scientific account of the growth of human knowledge. So he announced his 'Law of Three Stages'. The first era was relatively primitive. Knowledge was then dominated by religion. The second was more advanced. Then people believed in abstract principles (like 'rights' or 'freedom'). And the third was his contemporary 'Age of Science', with knowledge based upon evidence-based general laws. Each era had its intrinsic mindset.

All these stages could be readily tested, Comte further explained, by careful processes of 'observation, experiment and comparison'. It was super confident 'lumping' in neatly numbered stages.

'Splitters' might well ask why human mindsets should suddenly switch from one perspective to another. After all, if everyone in one era thought in one specific way, then who could possibly generate new ideas? But Comte was more interested in the outcomes of systemic change than its causation.

However, for sheer intellectual panache, plus subsequent global impact, there has been nothing to match the stage model offered by Karl Marx. He wrote *The Communist Manifesto* (1848) with his political ally Friedrich Engels. In nine brief pages, they summarised all past stages of human history. And that gave them grounds for a bold prophecy. They transformed their outrage at inequalities past and present into a confident belief in a better, fairer future.

For them, the motor force for drastic change was class conflict. A first economic stage of 'Feudalism' (serf labour) had already been replaced after a revolutionary upheaval, by 'Capitalism' (based upon free waged labour). And further conflict was inevitable. Thus, 'Capitalism' would yield to the 'highest' era of 'Communism' (with communal ownership of the means of production).

Marx's heady blend of history, prophecy, and moral outrage combined to make Marxism in the twentieth century much the most globally influential of all stages theories of change. Not that all those living under communist rule were necessarily true believers. Yet, their rulers could and did claim confidently that the dynamic inevitability of historical stages was on their side.

Of course, multiple questions followed. Do entire eras change at a stroke from one economic system to another? What about the underlying powers of deep continuity? Let alone the complicating impact of gradual change? And even if stages are accepted, how many will there be? Do they all follow everywhere in the same sequence? Or is it possible to jump a stage?

And the debates continued. Do people always bond most closely with others from their own class? Or do other issues—(say) religious or nationalist loyalties—cut across economic alignments? In orthodox Marxist circles, people who are motivated by non-economic factors are said to suffer from *false consciousness*: they fail to understand their 'objective' circumstances. Yet that excuse might be considered, in slang terms, *a cop-out*.

Doubters then raise further objections: are there many classes or only a few? Are the boundaries between them always clear? Are economic interest groups always at loggerheads? Or can classes cooperate?

Issues such as these were much debated within the Marxist movement, as well as by critics. For example, the ideas of the French theorist Louis Althusser generated much angst. He had argued for a scientific or 'structural' version of Marxism, deducing the nature of political power from the underlying economic system. (*Had Althusser been channelling his inner Auguste Comte?*) But, leading the critics in 1978, the English peace campaigner and Marxist historian E. P. Thompson denounced Althusser's model as an *abomination* (strong language). It seemed far too abstract, too lacking in historical evidence.

Political systems in 'advanced' capitalist states are not everywhere the same. Relationships between economic 'base' and political, cultural, and religious 'superstructures' don't fit into rigid formulas (*Think of the differences between (say) twentieth-century Brazil, Germany, Japan, and the USA—all 'capitalist' economies but with very diverse societies and political systems*).

Collectively, the Marxist tradition long remained intellectually fertile but became increasingly disunited. There were splits between rival regimes claiming to represent 'true' communism, well before the collapse of Soviet Russia in 1991. And, after that seismic date, belief in communism (however defined) as the inevitable outcome of history was seriously shaken. Some true believers hold onto hope. They view the cause as not lost but betrayed (for example, by Stalin's Russia). Yet, if history can be side-tracked by 'bad' politicians, then clearly its trajectory is not one of cast-iron inevitability.

When considering all these debates, people sometimes ask how much big views of history really matter. They may not have much obvious impact from day to day. Yet, people's underlying sense of history can certainly affect their behaviour and attitudes. Certainly, leaders become bold if they believe that they represent an inevitable force. And fierce conflicts can ensue if they are opposed by rival leaders, believing just as firmly in the inevitability of a rival cause.

Strong beliefs about the march of history can build people's confidence about facing the future. Songs and poems in many cultures attest to that. *Onwards, Christian Soldiers; Onwards and Upwards; Walk on through the Storm; Onward we Rock/Hungry and Hunting...; Climb Every Mountain; Excelsior! [Ever Upwards]; Don't Stop Me Now; Win Any Way* with its punchy chorus: '*They don't want us to win, but we're gonna do it anyway!*'.

Spotting Complications

Against the case for big generalisations, however, 'splitters' note that if there is one big broad-brush account of the human story that is reliably apparent, then it would have been discovered and universally agreed long ago. However, there is no consensus. (By the way, it's worth stressing that the best 'splitting' entails making intelligent objections, not simply giving a blanket denial of *Nooooo*.)

Knowledge grows via a mix of aggregation and disaggregation. ('Look, it all fits together into one big picture'. 'But, hang on, what about this or that big exception?') Debates may reverberate across generations. The classical Greek philosopher Aristotle was a great classifier. He divided the animal world by 'genus' (*category*) and then by species within each category. But his approach was rebuked in the early fourteenth century by the English friar William of Ockham. He dismissed all loose generalisations as *flatus vocis* (meaning: a sound without a matching object in reality, or popularly, *hot air*).

Systems of classification almost invariably gloss over some marginal cases which don't neatly fit into the precise sub-sets. Ockham deplored all abstract 'universalisms'. His solution was to favour simplicity and fidelity to the details.

Among historians, some consciously avoid seeking big 'macro' pictures. Instead, they concentrate on micro-studies. Their accounts are rich in details and diversities. They seek local meanings rather than universal propositions. And often, too, they stress the role of accident and contingency (meaning the unpredictable) over irresistible grand trends or inevitable stages.

Studies of this sort make a great contribution to the warp and weft of historical research. They don't replace big pictures. But they form an excellent counterpoint.

Everyone prone to big 'grand visions' needs to debate regularly with sharp-witted 'splitters'. Not necessarily to halt generalisations but certainly to improve their quality. It never hurts to scrutinise every big over-arching explanation, asking whether its basic premise is: *wholly true?—partially true?—*or not *true at all?*

Incidentally, much depends upon the media of communication. When experts are invited to speak on the radio or to appear on television, the producers (and audience) do not just want to hear: 'Oh, it's all so complicated'. For that reason, public presenters of history tend to make bold pronouncements. (Sometimes thinking to themselves: 'Goodness, what would my students say if they could hear me now?')

Conversely, meanwhile, round tables, panels and critical forums thrive upon disagreement and upon challenges to easy generalisations. There 'splitters' can come into their own.

Yet, interestingly, it is often hard to criticise without falling into some alternative generalisations along the way. Once, many years ago, a venerable and much admired female historian announced to a gathering of younger female colleagues (in my hearing) that: 'We women are no good at generalising'. She was voicing a view that is not uncommon. Women are supposed to be great at details but weak at overview. In other words, they are (allegedly) classic adjutants, not leaders. Her audience was too surprised—and probably in those distant days too deferential—to disagree publicly. But there was irony within the basic proposition. Her negative statement was in itself a massively 'lumping' generalisation, and it was made by a woman.

Furthermore, a (mistaken) put-down of female brainpower can have malign effects. In fact, all social groups, whose abilities are repeatedly and publicly disparaged, can end up under-performing. Their members tend to lose self-esteem and believe in their own inadequacies. It's helpful, therefore, when downbeat generalisations prompt the response: *But is that actually true?*

Critics and doubters force generalisers to check and refine their big interpretations. Paradoxically, however, it's always worth checking to see if would-be 'splitting' remarks do not contain their own covert generalisations, which need to be challenged in turn.

But Rejecting Total Doubt

Total doubt about all developments over time, in both past and present, is, meanwhile, a step too far. In some (but not all) leftish-leaning circles in the West during the 1980s and 1990s, there was a fashionable phase of intellectual rejection of big generalisations about the past.

Simple models of a linear 'March of Progress' had been subjected to major doubts since the mid-century. And confident faith in the Marxist revolutionary stage theory was, by the end of the twentieth century, fast fading too.

Sceptics increasingly dismissed as 'old hat' all the old-style 'Grand Narratives', as these big historical overviews were collectively termed. They seemed to their critics to be part-and-parcel of a failed—and departing—'modern times'. Hence, the new sceptical views were termed *postmodernist*. Opinions remained divided, it is worth repeating. Not all left-wingers and certainly not all students of the past endorsed a postmodernist viewpoint. But its emergence triggered spirited public debates about history as a subject of study.

Postmodernist critics stressed the problems of discovering reliable information about the past. Sources are scrappy and fallible, they warned, and historians are biased and subjective. Therefore, postmodernist critics considered history books to be best understood as a sub-branch of literature. They can be thus classified as either tragedies or comedies (*But, perhaps regrettably, virtually no historical tomes rise to the heights of being successfully comic*).

Dramatically, too, some postmodern theorists, like the American expert in cultural studies, Elizabeth Deeds Ermarth, saw the passage of Time itself as 'broken'. The steady temporal flow is illusory, she argued. Time instead is seen as moving in discrete, rhythmic bursts. Hence, no need to write long-swing accounts. Enough to produce micro-stories which are subjective and contingent, rather than pre-determined (Some total sceptics went further still, to deny the entire 'reality' of Time—an argument which is further discussed in Ch. 10).

Together, the postmodernist theorists adopted a stance of super-'splitting'. They rejected the value of studying history. Instead, they stressed the role of play, humour and accidental outcomes. And the human story does indeed contain unexpected as well as expected outcomes. Meanwhile, in the world of architecture in the 1980s and 1990s, the term 'postmodernist' was attached to a design shift, as imaginative and sometimes humorous buildings began to be built—in lieu of yet more high-rise glass-concrete-and-steel 'modernist' edifices.

But what happened next? 'Big' historical studies have not been halted. Researchers view tricky sources as a bracing challenge, not an insuperable obstacle. Much can be learned about the past, even if not everything can. For example, if all history is open to perennial doubt, then the minority stance of Holocaust Denial cannot be refuted. Yet reliable scholarship does so, effectively. There are still debates over details; but the broad scale of the mid-twentieth-century mass killings of Jews and others deemed 'undesirables', on the authority of the German state under the Nazis, is established beyond doubt.

Readers may have spotted one further paradox, too. Postmodernist doubters actually embrace their own stage theory of history. The advent of whimsical new architecture—like mock Tudor gate-houses in out-of-town shopping malls—was taken to signal that a playful new era of Postmodernity had replaced an outmoded era of rationalist 'Modernity'. And the *Zeitgeist* (spirit) of the new age was simultaneously taken as validating their philosophy of intellectual doubt. Well! Here was macro-lumping on a grand scale.

Renaming an entire era—and associating it with a specific way of thinking (and building)—was a bold manoeuvre. It showed the appeal of claiming the mantle of history to uphold a cultural philosophy.

By the early twenty-first century, however, the mood of the times, even among left-leaning circles in the West, let alone everywhere else, was changing. The mild boom in postmodernist manifestoes peaked at the turn of the millennium. After that, however, their appeal faded. In 2001, one author remarked that the concept of Postmodernity is 'slipping into the strange history of those futures that did not materialise'. In 2019, another tract asks: *Are We Postmodern Yet? Or Were We Ever?*

Commentators these days often refer instead to 'late Modernity' or (in a few cases) to 'post-Postmodernity'. And, coincidentally, architects have not by any means abandoned buildings in steel and concrete after all.

Periods of cultural doubt need to be taken seriously. Lessons can always be learned. Yet, it's not necessary to elevate every phase in cultural fashions into a (notional) new stage in human development.

Nor should intellectual doubts and questioning become exaggerated into total negativism. For in that case, there is a twist in the tale. Paradoxically, to assert that: 'We know nothing' is itself a positive claim to certainty (The true position for perennial sceptics is to murmur that 'We don't know').

Summary Next Step: Building and Testing Knowledge

Human thoughts in practice weave together both complications and generalisations. 'Splitters' press 'lumpers' to refine, improve, qualify, and, at times, reject big broad views. Sometimes such critical debates do prompt the emergence of better generalisations. Yet, sometimes the valid verdict is: 'We still don't know yet'. Or even, on some points: 'We may never know'.

Possibilities and probabilities at times apply, as well as certainties: relative propositions as well as absolutes. By the way, big-thinking Auguste Comte once remarked in 1852 that *Everything is Relative.* It was a dictum later admired by postmodernist thinkers.

Guess what, however? Comte's remark is already a massive generalisation. Moreover, it is an amusingly self-refuting one. 'Universal relativity' is itself an absolute concept. Comte himself noted that point but allowed himself a way out by stating that his dictum constituted the 'only absolute thing'. But, wait a minute! That means that there is at least one global absolute after all.

Building knowledge requires more than choosing between two starkly opposed binary alternatives. 'Lumping' hedgehogs and 'splitting' foxes do not exhaust all the options. Humans, when thinking about their collective past, are well advised to avoid over-simplification on the one hand, and overcomplication, on the other.

Beware, therefore, those who say: 'It's all really: cycles of rise and decline/unstoppable Progress/the class struggle/postmodernist doubt/or any other single factor, even sex' (Here D. H. Lawrence protests but is overruled!). Equally, however, the message is also to beware of those who counter with: 'we know nothing'. The collective story of human life within the restless, unfolding cosmos is intricate but not inexplicable. And it's one to which all people need access. So humans together generate knowledge by a constant mixture of big generalisations and critical questioning—acknowledging probabilities and possibilities along with certainties—and testing everything in Time.

Patterns of Thinking

Berlin, I. (1953) *The Hedgehog and the Fox: An Essay on Tolstoy's View of History.*
Panaccio, C. (2017) *Ockham on Concepts.*
Simon, H. (1989) *Models of Thought*, 2 vols.

Big Pictures/Stages in History

Christian, D. (2004) *Maps of Time: An Introduction to Big History.*
Huntington, S. P. (1996) *The Clash of Civilisations and the Remaking of World Order.*
Lasch, C. (1991) *The True and Only Heaven: Progress and its Critics.*

Postmodernist Doubt

Ermarth, E. D. (1992) *Sequel to History: Postmodernism and the Crisis of Representational Time.*
Jameson, F. (1991) *Postmodernism: Or, the Cultural Logic of Late Capitalism.*

Doubters Doubted in Turn

Evans, R. (1997; 2000) *In Defence of History.*
Sokal, A. D., Bricmont, J. (1998) *Fashionable Nonsense: Postmodern Intellectuals' Abuse of Science.*

Chapter 5
Coming from Deep Time 'We are Stardust'

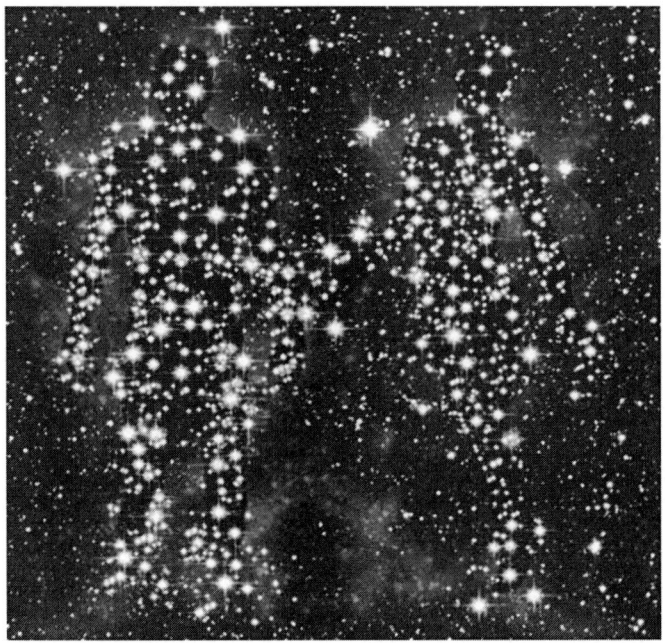

Chapter 5 further explores how humans 'think long'—and dream (vainly) of time-travel—while learning of their deep cosmic origins.

Looking at the Stars

Time has long, long sight-lines. These stretch (both metaphorically and literally) throughout Time and Space. Physical manifestations can be detected by humans, such as when they view the streaming light from a far, far distant star. Thus, while people's synchro-mesh keeps them focused on immediate matters in real-time, they also pick up signals that encourage them to 'think long'.

Much human effort is devoted to probing both deep Time (long ago) and deep Space (far away, and also long ago). Such explorations confirm that the cosmos is not static. It has elements that change profoundly as well as those that remain stable.

Grasping such complexities gives humans a potential evolutionary advantage. As already noted, they both think back and think ahead. And they can plan to cope with transformations (though implementing such plans is always trickier). Humanity's applied brainpower, together with their capacity for cooperation, has given them (currently) global predominance.

Rats provide an instructive comparison. They are a 'bright' species, with a strong sense of smell. They can readily scent their predators and hide successfully. Rats are also wily scavengers who are not fussy eaters. As a result, they are a huge biological success story, being widely distributed across Planet Earth. Indeed, they are globally the second most numerous free-range mammals (that is, excluding domesticated animals).

However, the aggregate size of the rat population, while running into billions, still falls short of the global total of 7.9 billion humans (as estimated in November 2021). Moreover, humans walk forth confidently. They leave their physical imprint everywhere. Rats instead run and hide—a perfect strategy for survival, which may one day (who knows?) give them the last laugh.

To date, however, rats are very far from having global predominance. It is the human population which has plans to exterminate rats (or at least to control their numbers) rather than *vice versa*.

Thinking about both the long- and the short-term together makes humans successful navigators through cosmic and local turbulence. They combine framework knowledge with improvisation. Long-term aims with temporary deviations. They are not stuck in never-changing thought systems. They explore; they debate; and they adapt—even if they sometimes leave necessary changes until late in the day.

Counting Nights and Days

Looking up at the sun and stars has always provided crucial locational information for terrestrial living. People in all known cultures throughout history have made astronomical observations. These have been used from earliest times not only for secular purposes, like navigation, but also for religious purposes, such as establishing ritual dates for worship.

Today, astronomers the world over share the results of their star-gazing. To ensure a perfect global collaboration, they have established an agreed calendar.

It's based upon a continuous day-by-day count (sidestepping any confusion over numbers of years or millennia), with each twenty-four-hour period beginning at noon. Their enumeration starts from a chosen date in the classical Roman calendar under Emperor Julian (The system was invented in 1573 and accepted internationally in 1925). Thus each observation period is known as a Julian Day (abbreviated JD)—though it might, more accurately, be called a Julian Night.

But no matter. The point is that astronomers worldwide share a common timetable for the accurate logging and study of astronomical data. And observations are derived not only from large telescopes on Earth but also from space probes and satellites.

Star-gazing today is a serious business. It's also a basic part of the universal human heritage as supporters of the international Dark Skies movement (opposing excessive light pollution) rightly emphasise.

In a similar effort of global cooperation, astronomical information is today pooled into one agreed system for Time measurement. Definitions of seconds, minutes and hours are universally agreed. And those are aggregated within an internationally accepted calendar.

Meanwhile, it is right to recall that a number of significant world religions maintain separate year counts for their own theological and cultural identification. There are thus many varied motives for 'thinking long'. Yet, all these religious calendars are simultaneously translatable into the international calendar, which is used to coordinate global trade, travel and communications.

Moreover, today's timekeeping is continually updated by communal agreement. Various scientific agencies keep ultra-precise atomic clocks whose results are adjusted to allow for oscillations in the Earth's rotation. When their readings are synchronised, the outcome is taken as the global standard.

That agreed Time-reckoning is called Coordinated Universal Time (UTC). As its name suggests, it is accepted as an impartial system, shared globally by friends and foes alike. Thus, while human societies and languages are very diverse, people worldwide share one temporal measurement system. It is the fruit of observations, calculations, debates and pooled thought over literally countless generations.

Long-term Time is not 'tamed' but it is logged. (As for songs about timepieces—well, infants can start with *Hickory Dickory Dock!* while adults *Rock around the Clock!* or today share short videos on *TikTok*).

Probing Deep Space

Space explorations from Planet Earth are undertaken for many motives. But one significant outcome has been that it today allows scientists to identify the origins of the physical materials of which humans are organically composed. From some viewpoints, the story is prosaic. All human bodies contain mixtures of six core elements: calcium, carbon, hydrogen, nitrogen, oxygen, and phosphorus; plus five trace elements: chlorine, magnesium, potassium, sodium, and sulphur (It's not outwardly the stuff of magic, or of epic passion).

Yet, the story is more dramatic than it seems. Those materials are the products of far-distant galactic explosions. Huge upheavals in outer space leave an accumulating legacy of interstellar dust, which swirls through the cosmos. And that stardust continually replenishes Earth. This theory (with many rival variants) is known as Panspermia, and its details remain disputed.

Nonetheless, it puts each individual life on one tiny planet into a much, much wider cosmic context. Continuing studies further show that individual humans are themselves lifelong dynamic works-in-progress. They absorb star-sourced organic nutrients from plants and then use them constantly to renew body cells throughout each lifetime. It's *mega*, in slang terms.

Poets and songwriters certainly appreciate the romance of extraterrestrial origins. 'We are stardust', sang Joni Mitchell at Woodstock in 1970; 'We are golden'. Another verse is more explicit: 'We are stardust/Billion year old carbon'. Mitchell further concludes with an appeal for a return to eco-simplicity. Chorus: 'And we've got to get ourselves back to the garden'.

Ahead of the scientific curve, the Shropshire poet A. E. Housman had already in 1896 mused on the random factors which create an individual life:

> *From far, from eve and morning*
> *And yon twelve-winded sky,*
> *The stuff of life to knit me*
> *Blew hither—here am I.*

Yet, the apparently accidental nature of being alive did not mean that the experience should be trivialised. On the contrary, Housman's message was stoic but insistent. All life should be lived truly and fully before the winds blow again and eternally dissipate each individual's being.

For many, of course, traditional religious teachings continue to explain both the origins of life and the meanings of death. Impressive bodies of thought grapple intellectually, emotionally, and spiritually, to provide meanings. The world's great religions are classic vehicles for thinking both long and deep.

Meanwhile, secularists are equally challenged to understand the role of humans in the context of a huge and indifferent universe of deep Space and random stardust. There are elements of overlap in their explanations, although secularists do not invoke one divine first cause.

Some astrophysicists are positively exhilarated by their work. 'The cosmos is within us. We are made of star-stuff', wrote the sparky American cosmologist Carl Sagan. He supported the search for Extraterrestrial Intelligence (SETI); and pending the discovery of other scientifically-minded species, Sagan claimed strikingly that: 'We [humans] are a way for the universe to know itself'.

Whether that formulation will prove to be accurate remains to be seen. Nonetheless, the human capacity to explore Space and Time is undoubtedly a source both of confidence and responsibility. Sagan rightly urged that all should learn the basic sciences upon which humans rely. And all should use that knowledge for the vital task of protecting the homestead planet (He might have noted too the urgent necessity to clear the literally millions of pieces of space debris which have been scattered in close orbit around Planet Earth by past space explorations. Good housekeeping in near Space is urgently required).

Sagan further added, somewhat mystically, that: 'Our obligation to survive and flourish is owed, not just to ourselves, but to that Cosmos, ancient and vast, from which we spring'. 'Splitters' might reply sceptically: *Oh, really?* The cosmos shows no interest in human survival. And the quest to find intelligent life forms in deep Space, to swap experiences, has so far drawn a blank.

Improved understanding of the turbulent cosmos is, nonetheless, still invaluable, even if shared only with fellow humans. Investigations by astronomers and astrophysicists continue to probe, literally, the frontiers of knowledge. In response, 'splitters' might ask: *Does it really matter that terrestrial scientists have now obtained, from light-years away, photographs of the super-massive Black Holes that mysteriously stud the cosmos*? To which humans, who live within a notably turbulent universe, can reasonably reply that all information about the death and life of stars is relevant information.

Furthermore, researchers constantly explain, more or less patiently, that new knowledge would not be new if the answers were already known in advance.

There's no knowing what may be found, and therefore, what significance it may turn out to have.

Certainly, human imaginations respond to the speculative allure of Space. 'Fly me to the Moon/Let me play among the stars…'; 'Ground Control to Major Tom…'; 'Walking on the Moon'; 'Space Cowboy'. In addition, there are expressions of dissent, to keep 'splitters' happy, 'Space Travel is Boring': 'I'm shot to the moon/Been there half an hour, I want to come home soon…' But many people find 'Reach for the Stars' a highly appealing aspiration for a migratory species, even if chiefly undertaken metaphorically.

Probing Deep Time

Attention is also directed to understanding the long past of life on Earth. Palaeontologists, who study the fossil record, share their research with biologists, geneticists, archaeologists, and historians. Key for humans is what has happened within one large sub-group among the warm-blooded mammals. 'Primates' are agile, dextrous, sociable creatures, with relatively big brains, as well as with clear bodily distinctions between males and females. All of them rely upon a characteristic visual acuity rather than upon the sense of smell alone. And primates are globally well established, with a fossil record reaching back at least sixty million years.

Amongst their ranks, the Great Apes (known as *Hominidae*) are further noted for their larger brains, their lack of tails, and their prehensile hands, which give an excellent grip. And it is from the Great Apes that one species has emerged as supreme global settlers. Numerous hominid branches existed on a small scale for millennia. No doubt, there was much interbreeding. Eventually, however, humans, noted for their upright stance and preference for walking on two feet, came to predominate. They were classified in 1758 by the Swedish biologist Carl Linnaeus. He took the noun *Homo*, the Latin word for 'Man' (now taken as embracing 'Humanity') and added the kindly adjective *Sapiens*. Humans are thus 'thinking' or 'wise' apes, even if at times there are grounds for doubt.

The precise date of their global 'advent' is uncertain. Evolutionary changes happen slowly, and the fossil record is patchy. Yet, humans had probably become established by a date some two hundred thousand to three hundred thousand years ago. Important among their early locational strongholds was sub-Saharan Africa. But there may too have been some groups in central Europe. (Patchy fossil finds mean that the picture is always liable to be adapted.) And the humans collectively were, from the start, notably restless and given to migration.

Contrasting with their ultimate evolutionary success was the fate of a rival group of closely related hominids, who emerged at roughly the same time. The cave-dwelling genus of *Homo Neanderthalensis* lived in Europe and western Asia. Its people were robust and stocky, with prominent brows and jaws. Yet, they were effectively eclipsed as a separate species some forty thousand years ago (although perhaps some isolated groups persisted for longer). It is worth noting, meanwhile, that the Neanderthal genes did not entirely disappear. Some can be detected within today's humans as a result of ancestral interbreeding.

Reasons for the Neanderthals' eclipse as a separate species are still debated. Overall, they did not cope successfully with harsh climate conditions, with changing patterns of disease, and with competition for finite resources from humans. No global species, indeed, has an automatic guarantee of separate survival as today's loss of biodiversity worldwide is making all too apparent.

Conversely, the runaway success (defined in numerical terms) of *Homo sapiens* indicates that humans proved to be, over the long term, exceptionally adaptive and versatile. Their brainpower, which permits systematic thinking, conferred great evolutionary advantages. Even so, it took millennia for the early settlements of primeval humans to become established in anything other than small numbers. From the start, there was much group migration as well as individual wandering. Yet, there were also failed settlements and lonely deaths.

Patterns of population movements were intricate. There were large mass migrations, followed by periods when some world-regional communities (such as the indigenous peoples of Australia) became isolated from other groups—only to re-encounter them, as a result of explorations, at a much later date. In biological terms, the result was the global diffusion of numerous groups of people, all carrying the human genome. That genetic template constitutes the communal inheritance of all branches of the human family.

Various regional divergences have also become more marked. In specific parts of the world, inherited medical conditions have developed in those human communities which remained relatively isolated and self-contained over long periods. One example is the continuing high incidence of beta-thalassemia (a blood disorder leading to iron deficiency) among the population of Sardinia. Yet, the island was never entirely closed to outsiders. Genetic research can also trace the advent of newcomers at specific times. Their input helped to dilute the gene pool, so that the blood disorder, while widespread, is not universal there.

Convergence and divergence in human history were—and are—common motifs. Innovations, which appeared in some communities, were copied by some. But not necessarily in others. Significant macro-changes occurred. But not in an ordered sequence and not at the same rate everywhere.

Repeated major changes introduced by the ancestral hominids, and then by their successors in the form of the resourceful humans, were truly epic. Think of the implications of the following: the first invention and subsequent refinement of tools, among them weapons (a long process, dating back for over two million years); the first taming and use of fire by hominid ancestors (from four hundred thousand to three hundred thousand years ago, or possibly earlier); and the adoption of sewn and fitted clothing, updated from the earlier cloaks of animal hides. And much more.

Humans impressively gained the capacity to speak and they have evolved many structured languages, which go far beyond the instinctual calls, cries and gestures of their fellow apes (The date of this breakthrough is still disputed. It may date back over two million years, evolving alongside tool-making. Or it may be as relatively recent as fifty thousand years ago). Humans also instituted communal burial rituals. And they developed decorative arts.

With such skills and collaborative support systems, the ingenious humans survived the most recent Ice Age (peaking some eighteenth thousand years ago, before abating some eleven thousand seven hundred years ago) in sufficient numbers to flourish when more benign climate conditions followed. Indeed, it's instructive to consider the sheer tenacity of the first hunter-gatherers. They knew how to evade mammoth predators and to live simply with nature, bequeathing traces of those skills to their descendants.

Eventually, too, inventive humans began to build and to reside in permanent settlements, updating the earlier shelters that had long been used. Again, these developments are hard to date with precision. But especially once the Ice Age retreated, the number of settlements multiplied (though human migrations did not stop). Animals were domesticated and organised farming, with surpluses to trade, was instituted. Standing stones were used as Time-markers and complex annual calendars were formulated. The wheel was invented—at more than one place and moment in history. And human life, with its well-known tensions between conflicts and harmony, blossomed.

By contrast, the Neanderthals were less systematically inventive. Archaeological evidence indicates that they had some clothing (cloaks); they used fire for heating and cooking; they made simple tools; they were able to treat wounds and to apply herbal medicines; some crossed seas in reed boats; and they enjoyed visual decorations (cave art) and music (flute-playing). Moreover, the Neanderthals may have evolved language capabilities, helping them to share information and ideas. Nonetheless, these skills could not save their separate communities from eclipse, even before the most recent Ice Age.

While humanity's long-term emergence to global predominance is a clear enough outcome, it is equally evident that there were many twists and turns in the story of the early hominids. Many factors came into play. A case could be made for explaining human history (say) via stages in communication: from speech to first writing, on to printing and, recently, to electronic media. Or the emphasis could fall (say) upon innovations in tool use: from the flint hand-axe all the way through to the mechanised robot. Such 'lumping' categories offer one approach to history, though they still call for explanations as to why specific inventions were tried, tested and successfully adopted at specific times.

Spotting one big formwork factor in history has its attractions. As noted in the previous chapter, it seeks to provide one definitive trackway through complexity. But (to repeat) there are many big forces in human life. Can one factor alone explain everything? The enthusiasm of the human sex drive can hardly be denied (D. H. Lawrence agrees!). It has produced all the billions of people alive today and all their ancestors. (Equally, the rat sex drive has done as much for the global rat population.)

Single-factor accounts often highlight a genuine historical force—but then exaggerate its universal potency. Take the class struggle (in a simple version of Marx and Engels): classes may often compete but they can sometimes cooperate. And, as already noted, divisions may emerge within socio-economic classes, over (say) religion or ethnic affiliations.

Or—to take another theory that had some influence in the later twentieth century—what about the subliminal influence of power structures? The French cultural guru Michel Foucault argued that power was subtly, and sometimes not-so-subtly, sustained through language. His insight was illuminating. Successful wielding of power relies upon much more than brute force. If rulers were always addressed with respect and awe, and if their subjects were designated as 'inferiors', then it could be very difficult to try to overthrow the social hierarchy.

On the other hand, even the most totalitarian power structures, buttressed by clever propaganda (both visual and literary), can and, at times, do fall. Opposition to power has a history and language, too.

And then there are the claims of the theory known as Evolutionary Biology. Males are supposed to be tough, virile, single-minded beings, motivated by the desire to spread their sperm successfully. Females, meanwhile, are supposed to be gentle, nurturing, empathetic multi-taskers. They favour monogamy, each one seeking to mate and settle down with an alpha male, who will provide good genes and make a protective father. Propelled by such instinctive 'Stone Age' characteristics, human societies thereupon breed and grow. Well! It is possible to identify some men and some women who conform to those stereotypes (Think of some examples). But there are many who do not (Think of some counter-examples).

Stirring claims, based upon recognisable features within human societies, make for suitably stirring debates. Other framework factors that might be named range from: the impact of wars, population migrations, the ever-mutating patterns of disease, climate variations; through to economic, cultural, political, religious and ethnic solidarities and/or clashes—both within and between different human groups across the world.

What a fine brew! Ample material for debates between 'lumpers', 'splitters', and everyone in between. Later chapters revert to all these themes, including sex, power, economics, and warfare. At this stage, it is enough to note that the ingenious humans, who survived the last Ice Age when many species perished, now confront an urgent new challenge. Their historically recent transformation of economic life and transport technology, based upon the intensive burning of fossil fuels, is contributing to global climate change. Today's task is to mitigate and to survive a new Age of Fires and Floods.

Dreaming (Vainly) of Time-Travel

Meditating about the weight of history can meanwhile induce a secret desire to escape. Can Time's steady march be eluded? Is there a temporal bridge, arching over the centuries, which allows people from one era to visit those in another?

Individuals in some folk tales fall deeply asleep…and awaken, with surprise, in another epoch. Sleeping Beauty, cursed by an evil fairy, lies dormant for one hundred years (In some versions, her handmaids sleep alongside her too). When she awakes, the Beauty is as young and bonny as ever. Moreover, she is being kissed by a handsome prince (approximately one hundred years her junior), with whom she falls in love. The story is charming, with an erotic undertow. Yet it's not hard for 'splitters' to see objections.

Perhaps Beauty won't enjoy the uninvited kiss? Or what if her sleeping body awakens, only to catch up rapidly with her real age? In fact, it's such a delayed-action death which happens to the imperious African princess in Rider Haggard's evocative novel *She* (1886). Secret powers of fire have enabled the great lady to wait timelessly for an ideal young lover. All but she have obeyed the laws of temporality. Yet, when the hero arrives and is awed by her beauty, she overdoes the magic. She steps back into the fire of eternal life.

For a moment, she glows with unearthly radiance. But then, to his horror, she ages with extreme rapidity and expires. All that remains is a shrivelled pile of bones, dust and rags—alongside locks of her glossy hair. Time has the last laugh.

Too much alcohol, by contrast, is the elixir that famously causes Rip Van Winkle to fall heavily asleep for twenty years (Hangovers sometimes feel like that). The hero of this American tale, dating from 1819, is totally disorientated when he awakes. No one is kissing him welcome. Instead, Rip Van Winkle finds that his beard is matted, his rifle rusty, his friends altered, and his faithful dog vanished. The only 'bonus' is that his 'nagging' wife is dead. *Ho ho ho* (sarcastically): the benefits of Time-travel.

Wishful thinking plays a role in such stories, as well as mental ingenuity. But there is a limit to the number of variables that change. Within the Time-travel genre, greatly boosted by H. G. Wells' ingenious *Time Machine* (1895), it's axiomatic that the epoch-jumping is done by one person (or, more rarely, a group), while the ambient Time for everyone else continues to unfold normally.

Generally, Time travellers arrive unharmed in a new epoch (whether in the future or distant past). At most, they are bemused, or naked, as in the case of the compulsive Time-nomad who partners *The Time-Traveller's Wife* (2003).

Encounters between people from different eras then lead to an impressive range of imagined outcomes: comedy, romance, adventures, satire, science-fiction, prophetic visions, and endless other excitements. The clash of epochs can wonderfully goad the imagination. And prompt fertile dreams of alternative worlds. However, once each Time-machine or Time-traveller has imaginatively jumped, the surrounding Time in the new location still behaves as normal.

Take another case of changing perspectives. Films can be run backwards, often to amusing effect. Viewers, however, are still watching in a normal 'onwards' Time-frame. They have not stepped outside their own temporal bounds. They are not getting younger, thinking in reverse, or talking backwards.

If, however, one component within all-encompassing Time was actually being rolled backwards, then everything else would have to do so too. Rivers should flow in reverse. Effects precede causes. That happens (imaginatively) at one stage in Lewis Carroll's enchanting fantasia, *Alice Through the Looking Glass* (1872): the White Queen cries first and then pricks her finger afterwards. But nothing else in the story has followed suit. The White Queen's speech does not run backwards. She cries when hurt, 'Oh, oh, oh!', but not with reversed letters, 'Ho, Ho, Ho!'. Her life is not actually running in reverse.

Logical limitations within Time-travel stories indicate the brute truth that people are located inescapably within their own eras because Time encompasses everything and everyone. Humans can't stop the temporal flow, alter its pace, or step outside it. They can't make themselves younger—or older—than they are. They can try to look and act differently. They can use any medical, sporting, cosmetic or psychological means to modify their age-related physical condition. They can doctor their birth certificates. Yet they still remain situated within the unfolding set of years into which they have been born—along with all their peer-group contemporaries.

Only if the temporal flow itself did something astonishing, would things become transformed, oddly and unexpectedly. If the entire Time-bound cosmos fell into a Black Hole (being a focal point of collapsed gravity) and switched into a parallel universe—emphatically not something that scientists predict—only then could people escape their current Time-frame. But all contemporaries would perforce join the journey. Sardonically: *No escaping the wife, husband, kids, or neighbours by disappearing into a Black Hole then.*

And there's a conundrum. If a Black Hole ingested the entire cosmos, then it would also have swallowed Time, within which the Black Hole itself features. It would mark the messy end of everything. (Don't try it!)

Best to stick to investigating the steadily unfolding past with the combined powers of reason, memory, and effective research. There is no practical option to travel to another era to check in person. But no need to fret. There's no limit to mental Time-travel and the charm of imaginative fiction.

When British writer Douglas Adams offers the 'definitive' *Hitchhiker's Guide to the Galaxy* (1979), he advises quizzically that: 'Reality is frequently inaccurate'. Yet, the truth about temporality is that it unfolds very accurately and steadily within an all-encompassing system that never allows people to step outside their own era, except imaginatively. It must be Time to laugh (or cry?).

Summary Way Station to End the Journey's First Stage: Being Earth-Bound While Thinking Free

Being Earth-bound (or in the case of astronauts, bound in near-Space) has some obvious limitations. Yet major compensations too. Planet Earth is an admirable homeland. It provides suitable habitat, food supply, roots, and familiarity. It's the one speck in the cosmos to which humans are perfectly attuned, and the one about which humans have unrivalled first-hand knowledge.

Living there, throughout the successively unfolding years, also provides basic information about temporality. As already noted, Time does not actually fragment, shatter, jump around erratically, change its pace from day to day, or run backwards. So much the better for everyday terrestrial living.

There does seem to be some temporal binding power which operates throughout the cosmos. It ensures that framework Time unfolds steadily (even while relative Time measurements may vary in certain circumstances, as explained in the next chapter). This basic reality prompted the British astrophysicist Stephen Hawking to conclude that there is a Chronology Protection Agency. It sounds like an obscure international quango. Yet, Hawking means that the functioning of the cosmic system requires that there be no disruption to the steady temporal sequencing and to the normal workings of the physical laws of causality. Time is protected by its foundational role.

Alternatively, the point can be made the other way around. 'The only reason for Time is so that everything doesn't happen at once'. It was a wry joke but an apt one, coined by the American sci-fi writer Ray Cummings. (There is no infallible Quotation Protection Agency, which is why that remark is often—but wrongly—attributed to the world-renowned physicist Albert Einstein.)

Different eras in history simply don't overlap. Humans are stuck in the specific epoch in which they live. From that, it follows that they should cherish every moment. As Benjamin Franklin dryly observed in 1747: 'Lost Time is never found again'.

Simultaneously, however, there is no limit to mental exploration. People can set their minds free, to roam throughout the cosmos and all history. Being Earth-based and Time-bound provides a stable foothold for mental roaming.

As cosmic beings, forged from stardust, humans rightly gaze back at the stars that surround them nightly. Little wonder too that people ponder their origins, enjoying both facts and fiction of human and cosmic history. Here ends the first stage of this book's exploration of Time-Space. It shows that all humans who walk on Earth are, inescapably, temporal beings. But that fact gives them the great asset of familiarity when (after a brief break) attention turns to defining the core qualities of that all-embracing all-powerful Time.

Keeping Time

Richards, E. G. (1998) *Mapping Time: The Calendar and Its History.*
Waugh, A. (1999) *Time: From Micro-Seconds to Millennia: A Search for the Right Time.*

Probing Deep Space

Glikson, A. Y. (2019) *From Stars to Brains: Milestones in the Planetary Evolution of Life and Intelligence.*
Schrijver, K., Schrijver, I. (2015) *Living with the Stars: How the Human Body is Connected to the Life Cycles of the Earth, the Planets and the Stars.*

Human Evolution

Harari, Y. M. (2011) *Sapiens: A Brief History of Humankind*, in Eng. transl. by Purcell, J., Watzman, H. (2014).
Reich, D. (2018) *Who We are and How We Got Here: Ancient DNA and the New Science of the Human Past.*

Humanity's Global Dispersal

Cavalli-Sforza, L. L., Cavalli-Sforza, F. (1995) *The Great Human Diasporas: The History of Diversity and Evolution*, transl. by Thomas, S.

Fagan, B. M., Durrant, M. (2016) *People of the Earth: An Introduction to World Prehistory.*

Time-Travel

Gleick, J. (2016) *Time-Travel: A History.*
Rothman, M. (1988) *A Physicist's Guide to Scepticism: Applying Laws of Physics to…Pseudoscientific Claims.*

Three Novels of Time-Travel

Adams, D. (1979 and later) *The Hitch-Hiker's Guide to the Universe,* five-novel sequence.
Niffenegger, A. (2003) *The Time-Traveller's Wife: A Novel.*
Wells, H. G. (1895; and later reprints) *The Time Machine.*

Time-Out: I—Meditating

Time for a pause? Not everyone likes reading through a whole book sequentially. Some prefer to dip in here and there. Or to go back over sections several times before moving on. That's all fine.

This book was written consecutively—and it can certainly be read that way. But it also invites readers to think about Time. Which is not an easy subject, nor one that is the subject of many good jokes.

So it's fine for readers to find their own ways of tracking through these pages. And, as a help to voyagers, this point in the journey could be a good moment for a Time-out.

Pause. Think of a good song about Time (The Beatles' *Yesterday*? Aretha Franklin's *Ever-Changing Times*? Or Bob Dylan's *The Times They Are a-Changing*? Or a hymn-like *Morning Has Broken*? Songs about Time can be found in every culture). Then hum the tune. Sit back, eyes closed.

Listen closely to the silent sounds of Time passing. Don't worry about all the urgent tasks awaiting attention. Meditate. Pause, meaningfully. Pause again.

Then…take a deep breath and come back to the journey. Time has passed. All are older. But Time is still here. It's still inside everyone, and outside too. Beckoning for further attention… Back to reading and thinking…about Time.

Part 2
Scanning the Stars

Chapter 6
Dwelling in Time-Space

Chapter 6 examines what humans have learned about the nature of Time, and its linked-partner Space.

Understanding Time

Time is the pulse-beat of the cosmos—let's repeat it once more. Also known as temporality, Time is a mighty power, which pervades everything. It is invisible, though its handiworks are everywhere visible. It is unknowably grand, although its impact is universal in small things as in great. And—no doubt because it is so grand but elusive—there are very few good jokes about Time.

That said, humans have long speculated on its nature and meanings. Time is much referenced by poets and philosophers as well as much marked by physicists and percussionists and by everyone else in between. What has been learned to date?

Paradoxically, the answer is: both a lot and a little. People can and do measure the passing of Time with fine accuracy, in both the long- and short-term.

Yet, strikingly, there is no scientific formula to define the nature of temporality. No summary states that T = … There is nothing else in the cosmos quite like it. Therefore, Time can't easily be identified by direct comparison or analogy.

For these reasons, temporal power has been dubbed the 'familiar stranger'. The phrase is well chosen. Time seems familiar because all people experience its impact daily. As already noted, young children can be taught to 'tell' its passing. Yet, Time is also strange and its strangeness is hard to put into words. That point was made long ago by St Augustine of Hippo, the fifth-century Christian philosopher, who hailed from North Africa. His verdict remains one of the single most famous statements on the entire subject. Asking rhetorically: *'What then is Time?'* He answered himself: *'Provided that no one asks me, I know, [but] if I want to explain it to an enquirer, I do not know'*.

One major point, however, is clear. Time is as old as the cosmos. If the universe began with one 'Big Bang', as many scientists believe, then the temporal flow began at the same instant. Alternatively, a minority of physicists argue that there is a deeper steady-state, in which first one cosmos expands and then dies, then followed endlessly by another, and then yet another. In that case, Time also appears, ends, and then restarts.

Meanwhile, the temporal flow within each cosmos has the self-sustaining power to renew itself from day to day. Little wonder that it is hard to define in a single formula. Its elasticity also impacts upon human sensibilities. Thus *Tempus fugit*/T*ime flies*…but also T*ime drags*. One visionary Londoner, William Blake, once penned a great testament to its subjective mutability. His *Auguries of Innocence* (c.1803) included the sublime capacity to 'Hold Infinity in the palm of your hand/And Eternity in an hour.'

Historians and scientists are more prosaic. But at least they are not short of evidence to assess. After all, temporality is not hidden away. Its unfolding can be seen daily in the rising and setting of the sun. Light is followed by darkness, which is followed by fresh light, all in a consecutive timespan. So, while Time is tricky to define, it is nonetheless 'hiding' in full sight. So humans have collectively accumulated a significant set of insights, which, when assessed and put together, prove to be illuminating.

Representing Time

Temporality incorporates regular change within a constant unidirectional framework. 'Past', 'present' and 'future' are held together within its embrace—those being the terms which humans use to define its sequential unfolding or 'flow'. Accordingly, representations of time commonly focus on movement.

Wings suggest a graceful airiness and a rhythmic beat. They are powerful, yet natural. Numerous classical Greek and Roman depictions of 'Chronos' show the god of Time as a majestic figure, with huge wings. A partner figure was envisaged as the youthful 'Kairos'. He represents the immediate moment of 'Now'. So he is primed for instant action. He has great wings on his shoulders and small, light ones on his feet. He moves fast. Thus the power of Time, whether viewed in the short- or long-term, is able to soar effortlessly above mere human concerns.

In traditional Persian imagery, by contrast, a great horse represents the might of temporality. The charger is richly decked and it, too, has four strong wings on its back. Or an alternative depiction shows Time as a Sun God, riding high across the skies. In this case, it is the chariot that has wings. The image is urgent, pressing. So the seventeenth-century English poet Andrew Marvell famously urged his coy mistress not to postpone their passionate love-making: [for] *'at my back I always hear/Time's wingèd chariot hurrying near'*.

Flowing water offers another potent image of ceaseless temporal change. 'Time, like an ever-rolling stream/Bears all its sons away', as Isaac Watt's sonorous Christian hymn declares. This imagery was particularly apt since one of the oldest known human devices for marking Time's passing was operated by harnessing a regular flow of water. And such water clocks can still be seen today. Berlin's Europa-Centre has a particularly fine example (installed 1982).

Indeed, clocks of all sorts, as well as watches, hourglasses, egg-timers, sundials, and other temporal markers, are often taken as proxy images for Time itself. For example, sands, falling grain by grain within an antique hourglass, constitute another metaphor for the steady passing of the seconds and minutes. All these ingenious and often beautiful devices are signs of humanity's earnest desire to 'keep' and to 'mark' Time, while encouraging people not to 'waste' it.

Another stratagem is to humanise the abstraction. In Western culture, *Old Father Time* represents the passing of the years. He usually carries a scythe, symbolising death or the 'grim reaper'. Often his silhouette appears aloft on weather vanes. Meanwhile, at traditional New Year festivities, a venerable bearded man, dressed as Father Time, is habitually paired with a very young baby, handed into the room at midnight. The newborn is a symbol of the year's renewal. Time brings hope and life as well as endings and death.

Traditional Chinese culture, furthermore, offers a variant personality. A benevolent god is known as Shouxing [壽星] or *Old Longevity*. He carries the staff of life and, with it, a peach, signifying vitality and good fortune. Figurines of this kindly figure represent hope. *Old Longevity* thus represents the capacity to live long and well within Time's inexorable embrace.

Other imagery is rendered in abstract terms. Time is an avenger. Or it is a healer. Or an innovator. Or perhaps it is a trap or a prison. Or a thief. Or a mighty destroyer. It can help or hinder human ambitions. All these variants acknowledge the potency of Time. And a similar message, expressed in different terms, came from the creative American inventor Thomas Edison. He remarked that: 'Time is really the only capital that any human being has'. Short versions of this perception recur in many cultures: 'Time is money'; 'Time is gold'.

Perennial reminders to use this valuable commodity productively have generated countless self-help manuals. *Take Time by the forelock*, as an English sixteenth-century proverb urged. Use it, don't waste it!

And, above all, don't underestimate it. So the blunt-speaking cultural pundit of eighteenth-century London, Dr Johnson, explained crisply that: 'He [or she] that runs against Time has an antagonist not subject to casualties'. In any competition, temporality will not run out of puff or momentum. On the contrary, Time always wins, because, however visualised, it has truly cosmic staying power.

Understanding Space

Space seems much easier to understand, especially in the familiar form of local place. It has an instant physical manifestation, in all its three-dimensional glory. Of course, Outer Space or 'Deep Space' seems (and is) undeniably remote and 'alien'. Yet, on 'starry, starry nights', its nearest sparkling manifestations are fully visible and almost companionable. Indeed, great feats of human navigation have historically been undertaken with the help only of the sun and stars.

It is not easy to feel personally attached to the impersonal and fleeting power of Time. Similarly, too, the abstract concept of 'spatiality' is not in itself deeply lovable. Yet, immediately 'Space' is translated into a particular place or set of places, the result is totally different. Recognition of a familiar and loved location can produce a deep inner warmth and satisfaction. Human thoughts may well fly free, but unaided bodies don't. Life experiences happen in physical locations. These provide for many people warmly valued 'roots'.

Homage to particular places takes a myriad of forms. The works of artists, photographers, and film-makers provide memory-triggering images. Novelists, poets, and playwrights regularly invoke places, both generically and specifically. In addition, people often have their own personal souvenirs and mementoes.

Emotions at times become mixed. People may treasure specific locations yet hate unwelcome innovations that are changing an ambience for good. Songs convey such lamentations well. So the plangent verses of *I Remember Dublin City in the Rare Ould Times* (written in the 1970s) at once applaud its urban magic and mourn the spread of the 'grey unyielding concrete' which is blurring its special qualities. (All planners and developers ought to hear this message.)

By contrast, a rather different song of urban criticism is *Dirty Old Town*. Written by Ewan MacColl, it evokes industrial Salford in Lancashire, where he was born and raised. The lyrics convey a grim affection: 'I met my love by the gas works wall/Dreamed a dream by the old canal/I kissed my love by the factory wall/Dirty old town/Dirty old town…' Here past pleasures are remembered in a decrepit but vividly real urban geography.

Place, in other words, has an immense pull on human thoughts, emotions, and memories. Responses range from affection to boredom, and even to hatred. Certainly, too, shared attachments form bonds between friends and neighbours. As a result, appeals to a collective homeland often appear in emotive mass politics. Such attachments can unite people of all ages and backgrounds. The family-based terminology of 'Motherland' or 'Fatherland' shows how deep such sentiments can run. Equally, too, specific venues are central to religious pilgrimages, to festivals, to fairs, to special sporting occasions, and to tourism of all kinds.

Not only do people often warmly love places that they know well but they also enjoy journeying to see new ones. The characteristic human propensity to travel (as noted in Ch. 5) has not been halted by the long-term growth of settled communities. Of course, in every generation, there are always 'stayers' alongside the 'movers'. But humans as a species are travellers, regularly seeking new scenery, new resources, new encounters, and new life options. Sometimes the trips are short ones, returning soon to the home-base. Others are longer migrations, either chosen or forced by adverse circumstances.

Many, many songs salute 'Moving On!' and the lure of the unknown. Some suggest that it's other people who should do the leaving: 'Hit the road, Jack, and don't you come back/No more no more'. Or the singer may repent: 'Baby Come Back!'. The idea of moving can be anything from exciting to anguishing. But it is never represented as impossible. For youngsters, indeed, some exploration may almost be seen as a stage in growth into adulthood: 'How many roads must a man walk down/Before you call him a man?'

Human interest in the physical universe, both at home and far away, is accordingly intense. This world is not only explored from every possible angle (as already noted) but it is closely studied. And scientists equally probe the wider cosmos. Knowing where terrestrial locations are 'placed' around the globe, and where Planet Earth is 'placed' in the solar system, form absolute bedrocks of human knowledge.

Imagine waking up and not knowing one's location. Pretty scary but it can happen: (*say*) after illness or a very bad hangover. But imagine then discovering that no one else, for miles around, has any idea either, and that no one knows how to find any locational bearings. The disorientation, verging on panic, would be great. Ordinary living would be impossible.

Far from being 'lost', outside all sense of location, humans are three-dimensional beings, who all live in a three-dimensional Space. Not only does the power of temporality hold everything together, but so does that of spatiality.

Outside the physical specificity of Space, humans, along with everything else, would disintegrate. Little wonder that astronauts, on their travels from Earth, regularly marvel at their new perspectives on the cosmos. And little wonder, too, that their distant prospect of the tiny 'Blue Planet', which constitutes the human home, sparks strong emotions of affection and concern for its planetary well-being.

Spatiality is the form in which the cosmos—both near and far—is manifest. And that perception raises an obvious further question…

Yoking Time with Space

How then do Time and Space, both so potent, fit together? At various moments in the past, there was some intellectual jousting between geographers and historians as to whether spatiality is more basic to the cosmos than temporality. (Or *vice versa*.) Is everything really ruled by Space? Or by Time?

Those arguments, however, have now gone. They were resolved in the early twentieth century by Einstein's updating of traditional physics. Space and Time are not separate and rival powers, he realised. They are yoked together seamlessly. They form one continuum. The proposition is so fundamental that it bears repeating. Space, with its interlocking dimensions of height, length and breadth, co-exists with Time. Each one presupposes the other.

Reflecting on the new physics post-Einstein, the German mathematician Hermann Minkowski, Einstein's intellectual ally and former tutor, declared poetically:

Henceforth, Space by itself, and Time by itself, are doomed to fade away into mere shadows, and only a kind of union of the two will preserve an independent reality.

The implications are huge. It means that core propositions about Space affect core propositions about Time. And *vice versa*. Why so? Because (to repeat) Space and Time form a continuum. These great formative features of the cosmos are, of course, not the same. Yet, they are intimately and perennially united. Space is the physical manifestation of Time, which is the dynamic power which gives duration to Space. The evidence is all around.

Therefore, if asked to visualise the yoked powers of Time and Space, it's enough to look at the cosmos—whether near, in a grain of sand—or far, in the distant stars. Everything is the joint product and manifestation of Time-Space.

Incidentally, conventional usage, post-Einstein, generally refers to Space-Time. However, a minority of analysts, myself included, prefer to reverse the formulation. Time-Space seems a more logical sequence. The dynamism of temporality powers the tandem. Yet, the hyphen continues correctly to yoke the two into one continuum. (So anyone unhappy with the formulation of Time-Space in this book is welcome to read it throughout as Space-Time).

Uniting Time with Space gives their joint formation its framework stability. As already noted, temporality does not suddenly jump across centuries or zig-zag to and fro between different eras. Similarly, places in Space don't suddenly get detached from one location in order to re-appear intact elsewhere, before dodging back to their original home or moving somewhere else entirely.

Coherence is supplied by the temporal-spatial continuum. They are as one. Thus, the specificity of Space is the sheet anchor against temporal randomness.

It supplies physicality. Hence, it is Space that constitutes the Chronology Protection Agency as theorised by physicist Stephen Hawking (noted at the end of the previous chapter). And *vice versa*. Time's unidirectional unfolding similarly holds Space firmly together.

There is, therefore, a matching Spatiality Protection Agency in the universe. And that Protection Agency is Time. To take an imaginary case, the lively inner-urban area of Northcote Road in southwest London (UK) can't suddenly swap places physically with the lively inner-urban suburb of Northcote in northeast Melbourne (Australia). They remain fixed in Time-Space, a global distance apart. Without such framework stability, daily life would be impossible.

Of course, it remains true that the cosmos is not physically a static environment. Astronomers track both slow and sudden movements of comets, planets, stars and entire galaxies. Yet, their movements remain subject to the laws of physics. Sudden elements of randomness and shock factors (as explored in Ch. 9) operate within, not outside, the dynamic framework of Time-Space.

To take another example, this time on a cosmic scale: it is calculated that, in about four and a half billion years from now, the entire Andromeda Galaxy will collide with the Milky Way, which is the shimmering galaxy in which Planet Earth is located. The abrupt convergence of so many brilliant stars will be devastating, if visually stunning, sending shock waves across Space. Nonetheless, the Earth and its future inhabitants cannot simply miss the big crash by moving the whole planet beforehand to a new address, in a far-different galaxy. Both history and geography have locked the Earth within its given place in the cosmos.

Einstein's physics has, moreover, established that the fabric of Time-Space is not entirely even. Very massive objects exert an extra-strong gravitational pull that has a warping effect. The speed of objects moving within their vicinity is accordingly affected, which in turn impacts Time measurements.

This phenomenon is known as 'general relativity'. At higher speeds, there is a process of Time dilation (or expansion). It's particularly noticeable as moving objects approach the speed of light. As they accelerate through the three dimensions of Space, they experience a concomitant slowing in the dimension of Time. And the outcome is detected by fractional variations in temporal measurement. The physics of relativity, it should be stressed, update rather than destroy earlier concepts within traditional Newtonian physics. Time and Space, as identified by humans in their daily lives, are not abolished.

Relativity does, however, offer a much more sophisticated model of their yoked workings. 'Absolute' Time and 'absolute' Space are rejected as false notions. They don't exist alone. They tug at each other. So it is instead 'absolute' Time-Space that reigns supreme. Everything that happens is embraced within that yoked and dynamic continuum.

Some processes therein are undeniably intricate. They are 'relational' (dependent upon changing relationships within Space and Time) or, as Einstein chose to name them, 'relative'. So, for example, Time dilation (expansion) can be triggered by gravitational warping. That effect is produced by upheavals in Space, such as when two Black Holes collide. Or Time dilation can be produced by relative velocities. Clocks within objects travelling at ultra-high speeds measure time fractionally more slowly than clocks in an observer's stable home-base. Those are dramatic examples of measurable relativities.

Certainly, these propositions are counter-intuitive. Yet, they have been upheld by repeated testing. And their meaning can be simply stated. Relativity theory reveals that the cosmos is a complex system with internal strains and stresses (as well it might be, being held in high tension between the dynamics of Time and the physicality of Space).

As an analogy (it's no more than that), the different forces and speeds within Time-Space can be envisaged as operating rather like tides in great oceans. Under the common surface, there swirl hidden forces. Throw a large log of wood into the sea and it won't move at the same speed in all circumstances. It may bob around, going nowhere, in the shallows. Or it may surge away from land, carried by an invisible rip tide. By analogy, the cosmos too contains hidden variables, which are apparent in different circumstances according to speed and the pull of gravitational power.

Hence, the workings of the cosmos are undeniably tricky—though they are not beyond the wit of humans to study. Relativity theory shows impressively how operative variables within the whole can be detected physically, as well as explained theoretically.

Furthermore (in case anyone asks: *what is the use of relativity theory?*), such knowledge has practical applications. For example, when scientists coordinate the invaluable Geographical Positioning System (GPS), they compare Time measurements from accurate atomic clocks on the ground with those from clocks in over thirty moving satellites. The system, however, works only because the scientists are able to calculate and allow for the relativistic variations in the said measurements. Armed with such knowledge, they can provide a super-accurate positioning system, available for all Earth-bound humans when navigating, tracking, mapping, or determining precise locations.

Significantly, then, understanding the tensions and forces within the cosmic system provides practical help at home, as well as offers a theoretical understanding of macro-changes 'out there'. It shows that scanning the stars can bring home the bacon (to use very mundane phrasing).

When asked to give a simple explanation of his work, Einstein allegedly offered the following example: 'When a pretty girl sits on your lap for an hour, it seems like a minute. [But] when you sit on a hot stove for a minute, it seems like an hour. That's relativity'. Well, that comment (which was almost certainly polished by a journalist) is insightful about human subjectivity. Mighty thrills, as in great sex, can seem particularly timeless, quite outside the ordinary workings of the world. (Yes, yes, says D. H. Lawrence.) But recognising human subjectivity and interest in sexuality is no help in understanding the mathematics of relativity theory (Sorry, Einstein).

Dizzying as are the scientific details, the core point is not. Time and Space form one dynamic continuum, and their joint working can be measured, tested and used in numerous practical applications.

And here is a poetic vision of their yoking, which was penned in 1650—obviously long before Einstein. It's by Henry Vaughan, a Welsh poet and physician. In *The World*, he offered a rapt account of viewing Time in the light of eternity. He wanted to know how everything held together. And he saw, non-stop Time, 'like a vast shadow', bearing with it the cosmos. Vaughan's hypnotic words certainly do not explain the physics of relativity. Yet, they do celebrate the unity of Time-and-the-world in motion:

> *I saw Eternity the other night,*
> *Like a great ring of pure and endless light,*
> *All calm, as it was bright;*
> *And round beneath it, Time in hours, days, years,*
> *Driv'n by the spheres,*
> *Like a vast shadow mov'd; in which the world*
> *And all her train were hurl'd.*

Looking within the Sub-Atomic World

Physicists had barely finished debating and testing relativity when a new and yet more extraordinary field of enquiry began to be explored. Beyond the daily sight and touch of humanity, there lurks a sub-atomic world. Its workings are elucidated within a new field of knowledge, known as quantum physics. And its insights are totally surprising, and beyond verification by direct human experience. Indeed, the new field of study was sufficiently challenging that Einstein himself expressed concern over its deeper philosophical implications.

Simply put, there is a truly microscopic world of sub-atomic matter. It lies within the apparently solid materials of the physical universe. And the sub-atomic world is filled with 'quanta'. Each one constitutes the minimum amount of smaller-than-microscopic matter that is needed to produce an interaction with another micro-unit of matter. This quantum state is one of constant flux. Its core units are forces of probability, rather than certainty. And their indeterminacy is resolved only when the quantum state is measured.

Viewed theoretically, this probabilistic world poses questions for the orthodoxies of both Newtonian and Einsteinian physics. How does the uncertainty of the sub-atomic microcosm—seething with embryonic potential—mesh with the certainties that can be detected within the macrocosm?

Scientists grapple with the quest, as yet unachieved, for a unifying Theory of Everything. The current working answer is that one set of physical laws prevails in the macrocosm and another in the sub-atomic microcosm. In lay terms, it amounts to a two-tiered system. The microcosm stores micro-energies, within the macro-energies of the observable world.

(Non-scientists are certainly allowed to be impressed with the skills of scientists both in detecting and then in studying this invisible sub-atomic reality.)

There is, meanwhile, another crucial point to note. Within the seething sub-atomic microcosm, not everything is unstable. If everything was in total flux, there would be no yardstick against which to measure fluctuations. But the German physicist Max Planck spotted that, among the variable sub-atomic quanta, there is one tiny stable unit. Today, it is named after him in tribute. Measured in metre-kilogram-second units, Planck's Constant has a value of exactly $6.62607015 \times 10^{-34}$ Joule seconds in SI [International System] units. The number is hardly memorable, to put it mildly.

Nonetheless, the role of Planck's Constant is clear. It constitutes the basic 'quantum' or unit of an electromagnetic action. It is used thus to measure a photon's energy in relation to its frequency (a photon being a tiny particle of light). Hence, the sub-atomic flux is great but not total. And the intricate fluctuations of electromagnetic power can be precisely measured.

People sometimes wonder why they need to know such details. And the answer is that for most purposes, they don't. Scientific knowledge is highly specialised. Its detailed formulations are, fortunately, not propositions which are required to trip off the tongue daily.

Nevertheless, it is still important to understand in general terms what this scientific knowledge reveals. The grand cosmos held together in Time-Space contains multiple forces, which, for the most part, remain in balance, if subject to turbulence.

Overall, then, the combined powers of Time and Space are sufficient to contain the fluctuating microcosms at its heart. Yet, that restless sub-atomic world is simultaneously part of the whole. Again, to use an analogy (and again it's no more than that), each sub-atomic particle is like a vibrating packet of energy. To find an applied example, consider the immense inner power that was released when atoms were split in deliberate anger, in the form of the atomic bomb. That intense 'punch' should be no surprise.

Compressed within a yoked power as dynamic and remarkable as the Time-Space continuum, there must be huge amounts of coiled energy at its heart. This point is fundamental. The cosmos is constituted by Time, yoked with Space. And the whole dynamic system runs on energy, lots of energy.

Summary Next Step: Grasping the Dynamic Unity of Time-Space

What next, then? It's essential to grasp that Time-Space constitutes a dynamic cosmic system in which sentient life has emerged. It's a truly amazing story. It encompasses both the huge macro-cosmos and the seething sub-atomic micro-world. And all its variegated aspects are open for investigation—from the largest gaping Black Hole through to the smallest and lightest element in the world (that being the hydrogen atom, which has only one electron and one photon).

So the next stage of this journey sets out to clarify the key dimensions that combine to form the dynamic unity of Time-Space. In other words, the focus falls not upon either temporality or spatiality alone, but upon the whole integrated system.

Readers are invited to come *rambling through the avenues of Time* (to borrow a great phrase from a parodic song), only the target is now to investigate the inner dynamics of Time-Space. Humans are, after all, prime witnesses. They all observe and live within a cosmic system, moving with *the wings of Time…the rolling stream of Time…the sands of Time…* And they generate and study evidence from history, biology, sociology, geography, geology, physics, and astronomy.

Unfolding Time is unidirectional, and therefore, Space must also travel in the same direction. Temporality provides their conjoint motor power. But what of the qualities of Space? It is multi-dimensional. Does that not suggest that there may similarly be multiple dimensions within Time, which are then welded together in Space?

Try reading the next chapters to see if the following longitudinal dimensions strike a chord: a mix of continuity (persistence), micro-change (evolution), and rapid change (turbulence/revolution). No one of these three dimensions triumphs over the others. Instead, they cohere. And as a good start: how about scanning the stars (on a cloudless night)? Written large in the skies is a pattern that reveals day-to-day continuity—alongside slow changes over long eras—occasionally buffeted by shock factors, such as when entire galaxies collide. So there are multiple dimensions to explore within the majestic *march of Time*.

Representing Time and Space

Fisher, R. (2023) *The Long View: Why We Need to Transform How the World Sees Time.*

James, W., Mills, D. (eds) (2005) *The Qualities of Time: Anthropological Approaches.*

Peuquet, D. J. (2002) *Representations of Space and Time.*

Studying Space

May, J., Thrift, N. (eds) (2001) *Time-space: Geographies of Temporality.*

Tally, R. T. (2013) *Spatiality.*

Time Studies

Mermin, M. D. (2005) *It's About Time: Understanding Einstein's Relativity.*
Rovelli, C. (2016) *Reality Is Not What It Seems: The Journey to Quantum Gravity.*

Quest for the Theory of Everything

Hawking, S. W. (2002) *The Theory of Everything: The Origin and Fate of the Universe.*
Nicolaides, D. (2020) *In Search of a Theory of Everything: The Philosophy behind Physics.*

Chapter 7
Identifying Continuity

Chapter 7 highlights the often underestimated dimension of deep continuity, which provides crucial ballast in Time-Space.

Assessing Deep Continuity

Time is basic. It can't be overlooked. 'As Time goes by/The fundamental things apply…' So sings Dooley Wilson, musing memorably on love and heartbreak in the classic film *Casablanca* (1942). It's splendidly evocative. Yet, what precisely are those fundamentals?

People are characteristically liable to disagree, on this as on many other subjects. Nonetheless, there are a range of constant factors that can be detected, both close at hand and in the wider cosmos. (The human propensity to dispute everything being one of them: *lumpers? splitters? A plague on both your houses?*)

Elements of continuity are typically quiet and non-flashy. The longitudinal framework sameness of temporality is one non-surprising dimension of the cosmos, which is shared by all. Time is always Time, come what may. Measured moments change, from minute to minute, from hour to hour…from century to century, from millennium to millennium. Yet, as long as the cosmos lasts, so, routinely, does Time, and hence Space.

A capacity for long survival, while incorporating continual elements of change, is outwardly paradoxical yet practically highly effective. It confers upon Time an imperturbable mightiness (Such terminology is reminiscent of the persistent authority attributed to a major deity). Deep continuity's long-term survival provides cosmic ballast, throughout the life of the universe. Hence, as already stressed, separate temporal eras and distinctive spatial regions do not suddenly detach themselves from one another and fly around randomly.

Nonetheless, there are internal tensions. The longitudinal dimension of deep continuity is constantly part-challenged part-accompanied by the dimensions of change. Such invisible tensions are integrally part of the whole. The same point applies to the physical form of the cosmos. There are stresses and strains everywhere. So it is not surprising that the local manifestation of Time-Space, in the form of Planet Earth, has its own dynamic tensions too.

Deep continuity in Time, therefore, contributes to the 'elastic framing' of the cosmos. It retains the basics while incorporating changes. And it holds firm for immensely long periods. Moreover, the push-and-pull between deep continuity and multiple forms of change gives the temporal system its intense dynamism.

By way of analogy, an example of 'elastic framing' applies, at a mundane level, to all living humans. Each body daily grows and changes, while its cells renew themselves constantly. Yet, such processes are contained within each individual's unique genetic blueprint which remains unchanged for a lifetime. Outward flux, in other words, is underpinned by underlying continuity. When the power of persistence finally collapses, at the end of either human or indeed cosmic lifetimes, decomposition ensues and the whole system disintegrates.

Naming Deep Continuity

Specifying the dimensions of temporality has spawned an inventive set of terms, ranging from the grand to the homely. Close at hand, for example, a number of personal names have connotations of Time. So *Khalid* and *Khalida* [Arabic] mean 'everlasting'; and *Amaranth* [Greek] means 'eternal, unfading'. And there are lots more, including *Hisako* [Japanese] indicating 'longevity' and *Elam* [Hebrew] signalling 'forever'. Needless to say, such names provide no shield against physical death, but they mark parental hopes for their children's spiritual endurance—as well, no doubt as simple pleasure in attractive names.

When considering the history of survival, in both human and cosmic affairs, the thought-provoking Russian cultural theorist, Mikhail Bakhtin coined a variant usage. He defined the very long term as *Great Time*. For him, its supreme power was redemptive. 'Nothing is absolutely dead', he wrote: 'Every meaning will have its homecoming festival'. Temporal continuity thus offered a form of consolation. Its power can triumph even over death. Any grand cause, however apparently defunct, might return at a future date.

Bakhtin's faith, however, remains unproven. Many dead causes and 'meanings'—such as defunct languages—remain well and truly dead (so far, at least). Thus, while *Great Time* conveys grandeur, it has connotations from Bakhtin which not all endorse (The phrase also sounds like students recalling a fun party held the night before). Hence, *Great Time* remains a specialist usage.

After all, a persistent continuity that does not encompass some change could convey not a happy but a melancholy message. Hence, T. S. Eliot mused, poetically: 'If all time is eternally present/[Then] All time is unredeemable'. That is, there would be no options for spiritual or personal redemption. (Thoughts about deep Time frequently have religious parallels, since religions also probe the fundamentals of existence.) In this cosmos, however, continuity cannot simply be equated with an eternal present. Time-Space is not static but incorporates various forms of change (as probed in the following chapters).

Continuities, moreover, may work in slippery ways. Upon occasion, they twist intended innovations back into 'more of the same'. An acute awareness of that possibility prompted a classic dictum from a French journalist, named Alphonse Karr. Having witnessed the abortive revolutions across Europe in 1848, he quipped a year later that: *Plus ça change, plus c'est la même chose [The more things change, the more they stay the same]*.

Of course, Karr was not entirely right either. Fundamental changes do happen, both gradually and rapidly. Innovations do not invariably revert to 'the same old...' Nonetheless, efforts at transformation do sometimes fail. They may be thwarted by their own weaknesses or by the countervailing pull of deep continuities, embraced by campaigners for no change.

Here one further point of definition is worth noting. The power of deep continuity is not the same as the political philosophy of 'conservatism'. It is true that the latter ideology often seeks to gain support by appealing to people's desire for the former. But political conservatism is protean and takes many forms. It can embrace a gently nostalgic support for cultural tradition. Or it can take a militant stance, seeking to return to an idealised past, often by trying to combat perceived 'enemies within' or by excluding 'alien' newcomers.

Yet, there are other variants too: some forms of conservatism are future-orientated. They hope to build upon old ways to encourage new dynamism and (often) new wealth. In that way, they seek to resolve social problems, such as those generated by poverty, without re-ordering the social hierarchy. All in all, these permutations mean that conservative political movements cannot simply be equated with the through-Time power of deep continuity.

Very much the same point applies to the concept of 'conservation'. It has an appeal that looks back to the past and invokes an ideal of continuity. Yet practical plans for conservation and, still more, for restoration involve making choices about which parts of the past are to be conserved or restored.

An example is provided by a small river in south-east London, with the splendid name of Quaggy. It had meandered through marshland towards the Thames for many aeons before unsentimental Victorian engineers enclosed it in a drain. Recently, conservationists have liberated the Quaggy, too much local approval. But its new open course is now being managed to create a flood plain and a wildlife reserve. All very admirable. Yet, the restored river is not the freely meandering Quaggy of old.

Conservation work always requires making choices. Which specific era of the past, out of many different possibilities, is being restored? This question applies universally, whether to the conservation of the countryside, wildlife, art, architectural heritage, towns, antiques, saving minority languages, or any other aspect of humanity's complex inheritance.

No easy name thus springs to mind for the power of Time-Continuity (T/C). It is too majestic to be trivialised by giving it a familiar nickname. Or by being domesticated into the daily realities of political conflicts.

All the same, humans are well aware of this remarkable longitudinal dimension of Time, and are not averse to appealing to it, when convenient. So positive references are made (with varying emphases) to the dogged power of: the 'good old days', continuance, constancy, endurance, persistence, tenacity. Alternatively, negative terms dismiss: inertia, paralysis, stagnation, torpidity, dead-wood. Or plainly put: the dimension of deep continuity through Time.

Praising Constancy or Blaming Inertia?

Responses to this grand phenomenon are clearly mixed. Is deep continuity a sustaining power to praise or a detrimental drag-anchor, which should be blamed? (By the way, mariners remind landlubbers that all forms of anchor have a positive role in navigation. No one should sail any distance without one. But here the 'drag-anchor' plays a metaphorical role).

On the positive side, customs and popular traditions are often appreciated warmly within communities and across generations. They are enjoyed on their own account and as links with 'olden days'. Similarly, many like to view ancient monuments, historic towns, and traditional landscapes. These have the reassurance of familiarity, as well as the beauty of collectively accepted icons.

Yet, public reverence for antiquity is highly selective. Not only do personal preferences differ but there are deep cultural shifts, which ensure that some ancient customs, once accepted, later become rejected. So there is no twenty-first-century rush to celebrate or to re-enact the severity of former punishments, which have since been abolished on humanitarian grounds—such as, in the UK, whipping vagrants, branding felons, and executing blasphemers.

Much the same applies to the human quality of constancy. Staunch fidelity to a cause or a person is generally admired. It is an attribute that mimics the apparent solidity of the natural world. A true supporter is *a rock*. People who keep changing their minds and cannot stick to a project are seen as *lacking backbone*. By contrast, someone who is *as constant as the northern star* (Shakespeare again) is another natural prodigy, to be admired.

However, there is, again, a negative side. Blind commitment to a belief, which is proved to be erroneous, or blind devotion to an individual, who is proved to be utterly unworthy, can become a dangerous, even fatal, obstinacy.

Hence there are many warnings against excessive inflexibility in thoughts and emotions.

Writing scornfully of his political opponents in 1780, the Irish-born political theorist Edmund Burke noted that: 'They defend their errors as if they were defending their inheritance'. It was a pointed analogy. Some people do adopt a venerable cause as a personal legacy which must be defended to the death. Not for nothing are such ultra-supporters known as *die-hards*.

Critics are, therefore, ready to denounce an undue reverence for continuity. Individuals who resist innovations are 'dinosaurs', 'moss-backs', 'fossils', 'old fogeys', 'stick-in-the-muds', or relatively kindly, mere 'fuddy-duddies'. A celebrated howl of rage came from the revolutionary theorist and activist Karl Marx. In 1852, he denounced 'the tradition of all the dead generations [that] weighs like a nightmare on the brains of the living'.

Adding to the complications, meanwhile, there are often question-marks over the actual antiquity of ancient customs (whether for praise or for blame). A goodly number turns out to be of relatively recent origin. Indeed, some apparently ritual-encrusted traditions, apparently dating from *Time Immemorial*, have actually been invented at specific moments to fill a need.

Given the overlaps between continuities and changes, wits were quick to spot the paradoxes. If the cosmos itself is always in a state of transience, then to what exactly can loyal individuals remain faithful? Where is the firm terrain, in which to plant their standard? 'The world's a scene of changes', sang England's royalist poet Abraham Cowley in 1656. 'And to be/Constant in Nature were inconstancy'. So it could be argued that, in this ever-mutable cosmos, it is unnatural to stick to just one love—a great charter for philanderers.

Paradoxes, moreover, run deeper still. In a world of chronic change, some prudent adaptations might even be needed to preserve the essence of the old ways. In Giuseppe di Lampedusa's alluring novel *The Leopard* (1958), the progressive young aristocrat in Italy's deep south argues subtly that, in turbulent times: '*If we want things to stay as they are, things will have to change*'.

An example in real life may be seen today in the way that many hereditary monarchies, surviving within democratic societies, rightly relax the strictest old-style court etiquette in order to preserve the principle of a hereditary head of state in a changing world. But, but, but…what if apparently minor modifications become the *thin end of the wedge*? Perhaps continuity might, after all, not be saved but instead betrayed and lost.

Detecting the basic realities—and assessing whether they are matters for praise or blame—are then perennial challenges. Another of life's constants? Certainly, some thinkers assert strong human links across the generations. In classical Greece, in the first century BCE, the poet Hesiod of Ephesus declared, lyrically, that: 'This world [is] the same for all; it always was, and is, and shall be an ever-living fire'. Hence, all people share a fundamental unity: 'living and dead, awake and asleep, young and old, [all] are the same'.

Others have shared that insight. Robert Herrick, one of England's finest seventeenth-century lyric poets, was equally emphatic: 'Nothing is new; we walk where others walked'. (Britain's civil wars prompted much thought about change and also about things that persist… Life is about more than just hustle and bustle, mused John Milton: *'They also serve who only stand and wait'*.)

Detecting Through-Time Constants

Fundamental continuities are not rigidly segregated from other aspects of life, as already noted. Appearances may deceive. Things that outwardly look the same may not always be so. Conversely, too, changing outward forms may conceal inner persistence. Investigators need to keep alert, with their eyes 'peeled' (a macabre formulation, even if a suitably vivid one).

Time-invariant features in the physical universe have been identified in the form of numerous basic laws of physics and chemistry (Human understanding of those laws is far from constant, but that is a different point). A prime example is the statement that 'nothing can travel faster than the speed of light in a vacuum'. That proposition is the same the world over, and it remains the same throughout Time-Space.

Even within the micro-turbulence of quantum physics, there is one tiny invariant factor, known as Planck's Constant. Its role has already been noted in the previous chapter. It is one of the smallest known constants in the physical universe. And esoteric as it remains for everyday purposes, this tiny marker confirms an element of order within the cosmos. Without it, quantum changes in the sub-atomic world could not be measured. All would be seemingly chaos.

Another example of an area of structural constancy can be seen in the rules of mathematics. These are not the same as 'laws'. They are human conventions, which are collectively developed as a specialist non-spoken 'language' used both for mental calculations and for precise quantitative representations of physical realities. As a result, while there are cultural variations in styles of mathematics—studied today under the label of 'ethno-mathematics'—the core principles and rules are everywhere the same. To put things at their most basic, the addition of 1 + 1 everywhere makes 2. And the same pan-global consistency applies to all other calculations, from the simplest to the most complex.

Interestingly, too, mathematics as an intellectual construct has not emerged through any official policy. Instead, it has been communally generated, with multiple inputs from people from many different cultures, over successive generations. And it has done that within a set of unchangeable framework rules, which persist even as expert practitioners undertake ever more sophisticated calculations. Hence, using a different terminology, humans are mathematical 'lumpers', with one universal numerical system for calculating one world.

Meanwhile, cultural 'splitters' and ethno-mathematicians also study variable applications in different parts of the world. On the strength of that, they find fruitful new ways of teaching the subject, thus giving it human specificity to overcome its aura of abstraction. Examples include finding the mathematics within the ratios, patterns and symmetry in Japanese *origami*/decorative paper folding. Or deciphering the formulas behind the beauty of *fractals*, which are the never-ending patterns in traditional African designs. Uncovering universals within specifics is a great strategy for revealing one world within variety. It's especially helpful in encouraging participation among those who struggle with abstractions.

Spoken and written languages offer an instructive counterpart. Constantly shared oral interchanges encourage daily updating and many micro-adaptations in the ways that humans communicate linguistically with one another. There are constant variations within all 'living' languages.

Nevertheless, each one also keeps its basic grammatical structure and conventions of word sequence (known technically as 'syntax'). Those hardly change at all. Indeed, some experts argue that there are universal principles of grammar, which all humans are hardwired to understand.

Whether all things linguistic are quite as precise as that still remains a point of debate. Nonetheless, skills of verbal and then written communication, once developed by generations of *homo sapiens*, have spread everywhere and not atrophied. Humans have an innate capacity for basic linguistics. They can expertly decipher meanings from successive sounds and words by following shared syntactical rules. 'No at make purely random all sense words', which, unscrambled, declares that: 'Purely random words make no sense at all'.

Equally, successful humour depends on a shared ability to catch the joke. Word-play requires a mutual recognition of verbal games. Question: 'How did Benjamin Franklin come to understand the power of lightning?' Answer: 'It just struck him'. Well, it's not wildly funny. But its mild humour stems from recognising that both new ideas and lightning from the skies can suddenly strike an individual. *Aha!* (But explaining a joke always tends to kill it dead.)

Disentangling the mix of deep continuity and changes, some of which are slow and gradual, remains a recurrent challenge. The same problem applies when considering the 'natural' geography of Planet Earth. That familiar environment is the home for which all global beings are biologically adapted.(The phenomenon of 'Space sickness' among astronauts has already been noted.) Hence, one great constant for all terrestrial life, large or microscopic, is the overriding eco-importance of Planet Earth's survival as a suitable habitat.

Geography has its own power, aided by the emotions of affection felt by humans for particular land and townscapes. Yet, the undoubted significance of geography can, again, be taken too far, if is claimed as the deep determinant of all history. For the distinguished French historian Fernand Braudel, spatiality was all-important. He detected an underlying stasis, which he termed *l'histoire immobile*. Short-term events were, for him, simply 'capricious'. They were 'froth' on the surface of 'geo-history', as he termed geographically-determined history. And, by way of example, Braudel noted perceptively the impact of 'perennial' French geography upon the French sense of national identity.

And yet... The 'natural' environment faces upheavals as well as continuity. After all, France and Britain were physically linked for many millennia by a high ridge of chalk, stretching from Dover across to Calais. It was 'only' some four hundred and thirty thousand years ago that this ridge was destroyed by an inundation of glacial meltwater. Hence, France in its current form is a relatively recent arrival in global history. Put another way, geography, however stable it seems, is not always 'immobile'. So, while it's vital to spot deep continuities— it's equally crucial not to override evidence of co-existing changes.

Finding Routines in Daily Life

That said, unacknowledged continuities are everywhere. In daily life, human behaviour is commonly (except in the midst of great upheavals) structured by customs and past practices. Household routines are followed semi-automatically, without needing much thought. They can be changed, if need be. (But then people often find, forgetfully, that they are automatically doing things in the old way.) Moreover, if changes are introduced, they in turn settle into new routines. It would be far too time-consuming to rethink daily everything from scratch.

Traditions and customs play a somewhat similar role in the social life of communities. They provide reassurance and social 'glue'. And they also save time, in that the format of customary practices (celebrations, civic gatherings, religious ceremonies, funerals) do not have to be reinvented from scratch.

Generally, people are completely unconscious of the extent to which their daily lives are dominated by cultural norms. Conventions dictate which foods are acceptable to eat, and which are not. An unwritten dress code also specifies broadly how people should dress. *Avant-garde* fashions can be adopted at certain times; but it takes an exceptionally bold or troubled individual to flout all communal assumptions (Imagine walking naked along the local High Street on a sunny afternoon, when there are plentiful crowds in circulation).

'Custom, then, is the great guide of human life', as Scotland's sage philosopher, David Hume, noted in 1749. As a result, when deeply ingrained norms are suddenly challenged, many respond with outrage. Conventions bind monarchs at the 'top' of society as much as or, sometimes, more than they do beggars at the 'foot'. As a result, custom amounts to an 'unwritten Law/By which the people keep even kings in awe', as the Restoration poet Charles Davenant explained. (How often do monarchs, dressed in full regalia at formal events, dream of escaping to run, barefoot and free, along a sandy beach?)

Provisos, however, still apply. Traditions are not all equally old. Nor are they equally unchanging, as noted already. Some are very venerable with unknown origins; others grow slowly by accretion of ritual; others are consciously invented at specific times; and all are liable to repeated updating. In that spirit, the insightful Edmund Burke once ventured the seeming paradox (forestalling the author of *The Leopard*) that: 'A state without the means of some change is without the means of its conservation'. Conversely, it is also likely that some traditions, if never adapted to meet the needs of new generations—let alone the exigencies of new technologies—will wither and die.

Famously, an example from American history illustrates the stubbornness of customary behaviour and its capacity to resist the might of government. In 1920, the policy of Prohibition was enacted via the 18th Amendment to the US Constitution. The sale, manufacture and transportation of alcohol were totally banned. Yet, discreetly at first, and then increasingly boldly, mass disobedience followed. Upright citizens, as well as bootleggers, found countless ingenious ways of flouting the law. And Prohibition was quietly repealed in 1933. The human custom of drinking alcohol was/is not one easily to be dismissed.

Conversely, however, controls or even bans on disputed drugs can work when public opinion is broadly supportive. The demise of cigarette smoking in many countries worldwide is a counter-example to the case of alcohol. Yet, in that case, the procedures were very different. Bans on smoking followed as well as further encouraged changes in public attitudes, which were being increasingly influenced by medical evidence. So continuity in cultural customs can be overcome, but not simply and not *just like that*.

Underlying everything, there are also detectable through-Time elements within human biology. The globe-trotting species of *homo sapiens* has settled widely and sent probes into space. And it has done such deeds on the strength of its staple characteristics.

Humans are gregarious, large-brained, mind-conscious, language-speaking, tool-wielding, rule-making (plus rule-breaking), versatile, omnivorous, restless, bipedal mammals, with a species-unique capacity for shared joking and laughter. They have a common stock of blood groups, and a set of genetic coding (the genome), with many variants. Generally, too, many (though not all) humans have a strong sex drive, engaging in sex for recreational pleasure as well as for reproduction. (Yes, yes: again D.H. Lawrence agrees.) However, it should be noted that they are not as sexually active as the bonobos (close simian cousins) who have sex daily.

With their intriguing mix of traits, humans are outstanding as both problem creators and problem solvers. Their capacity for conflict can be one major generator of troubles—and great enmities can last for centuries, being passed on from generation to generation—while the human capacity for cooperation is regularly tested by the need to resolve troubles, not least those of their own making (These qualities are further explored below, in Ch. 13 and 14).

So the quest for universal and simply-defined characteristics has not proved successful. Claims that all humans are dominated by selfish aggression are made but do not convince. There are variations between individuals, as well as between cultures. So the Austrian expert on animal behaviour, Konrad Lorenz, took a common but not universal trait too far. Conversely, a hopeful faith in universal altruism and an innate love of peace is equally one-sided.

Grand generalisations aspire to decode the intricacies of human behaviour. Yet, there are always too many detailed exceptions within a broad set of general characteristics. Thus, the stereotypically dominant Stone Age males, breeding freely with stereotypically submissive Stone Age females, do not match with the range of actual human character traits (as noted already in Ch. 5). And the same problems apply to other studies that strive to explain all forms of human sexuality—from rape to anal sex—in terms of evolutionary strategy. Instead, humans display a characteristic of experimentalism and diversity in their sex lives, and those qualities have not harmed their collective rates of reproduction.

Biology provides a broad template rather than an overly specific design whether applied to individuals or groups of individuals. The same point applies to the once influential but now increasingly disavowed 'racial' science. It sought to specify the physical, mental and cultural traits of separate 'races' within the human family. The core task was inherently tricky. There was a constant risk of building open or inadvertent observer bias into the classification.

More centrally, however, the basic task was—and remains—ill-conceived. Racial theorists never agreed upon the number of 'races'. Many criteria for classification were advanced, from skin colour to hair quality, to cranial shape, and so forth. Yet, no consensus emerged, chiefly, because the very long history of migration and intermarriage has produced pronounced genetic variations within as well as between all genetic clusters within the human family.

'Racial' science thus proved to be an intellectual wrong-turning. It was an example of how trial and error—a constant method in research—can produce apparent outcomes which are often strongly believed but are later found to be erroneous. That result does not stop the persistence—but not ubiquity—of fixed beliefs about different 'races'. The constant testing of ideas does, however, open doors to fresh thinking and, eventually, to changing attitudes.

Alongside, the sense of sub-divisions there has long been an alternative humanist tradition that asserts a common solidarity. In classical Rome, a character in a play by Terence stated that in a much-repeated dictum: *Humani nil a me alienum puto [I regard nothing that is human as alien to me]*.

Similarly, in early eighteenth-century Naples, Giambattista Vico, the subtle historian-philosopher, gave a resounding affirmation of the power of empathetic in-species comprehension. Anything done by humans can eventually be understood by fellow humans, he asserted.

Again, that task too is complicated. It needs a good awareness of historical and cultural diversities, as well as of changing pressures in different eras and climes. Yet, human framework continuity offers the chance of a fellowship of understanding (though not necessarily endorsement), as Vico had hoped.

Everything? Really? 'Splitters' snort with derision. But the answer is: Yes, which mortal beings can best understand if not fellow humans?

Summary Next Step: Appreciating the Role of Continuity within Time-Space

There are some celebrated acknowledgements of the power of persistence. One much-quoted phrase comes from the Biblical preacher Ecclesiastes: *'There is no new thing under the sun'*. He thunderously dismisses surface fripperies as mere distractions from the basic verities of religious faith. Anything else is but vanity. So he exclaims roundly: *'Vanity of vanities; all is vanity!'* Punchy rhetoric but not enough to dissuade people from admiring innovations.

Thought about the cosmos should not, however, be divided between two binary alternatives. There's no need to opt between *either* all continuity *or* all innovation. People sometimes grumble: 'Nothing ever changes'. Or at other times, they complain: 'Nothing ever stays the same'.

Both statements are demonstrably erroneous. Time itself manages to change, while remaining the same. There is more going on in the world than can be summarised by two binary statements.

Instead, the cosmos (and all humans within it) experiences an intricate mix of persistence and transience. Those framework dimensions are part intertwined, and part opposing, as further explored in the following chapters.

Lastly, then, Time-Continuity (T/C) remains a mundane but necessary dimension of Time-Space. It is not glamorous. It is sometimes criticised as pure 'inertia'. Yet through-Time persistence ballasts the entire cosmos. So don't underestimate the potency of *long-lasting, long-term, long-in-the-tooth Time!*

Continuities in Human Affairs

Duhigg, C. (2012) *The Power of Habit: Why We Do What We Do; and How to Change.*
Hobsbawm, E., Ranger, T. (eds) (1983) *The Invention of Tradition.*
Shils, E. (1981; 2006) *Tradition.*

Constants in Physics

Barrow, J. D. (2002) *The Constants of Nature: From Alpha to Omega.*
Penrose, R. (2016) *The Road to Reality: A Complete Guide to the Laws of the Universe.*

Rules of Mathematics and Language

Boeckx, C. (2010) *Language in Cognition: Uncovering Mental Structures and the Rules Behind Them.*
Ifrah, G. (1998) *The Universal History of Numbers: From Prehistory to the Invention of the Computer*, transl. by Bellos, D., *et al.*

Fundamentals in Human Biogeography

Harcourt, A. H. (2012) *Human Biogeography.*
Thornton, W. (2017) *The Human Body and Weightlessness: Operational Effects, Problems and Countermeasures.*

Fundamentals in Geography

Lai, C-C. (2004) *Braudel's Historiography Reconsidered.*
Wolch, J., Dear, M. (eds) (2014) *The Power of Geography: How Territory Shapes Social Life.*

Chapter 8
Spotting Slow Change

Chapter 8 draws attention to the dimension of very slow change, which provides regular momentum within Time-Space.

Assessing Gradual Change

'*Time goes slow*', sings the lead singer with the Canadian instrumental band, BadBadNotGood (Their name masters the art of understatement, clearly not seeking to over-hype their output). Such discretion plays well as an evocation of the dimension of slow change within cosmic Time-Space. Gradual evolution has an intrinsic capacity for incremental adaptation. But it does not hurry.

Such a long-term momentum, within temporality, enables the system to update regularly from day to day. This news is no secret to humans. They measure Time's steady calendrical unfolding with ever-increasing precision. The basic momentum is signalled at the rate of one second per second; one minute per minute; one hour per hour…and so on.

All experiences on Earth (and elsewhere throughout the cosmos) are attuned to that steady rhythm. Its expansive momentum furnishes the system with elasticity. Thus, integrally entwined with Time-Continuity (T/C) is the dimension of Time-Evolution (T/E).

For humans, their relationship with this unfolding phenomenon is full of subjective variety. People's thoughts are not necessarily attuned directly to calendrical Time. So just as they do not automatically remember precise dates, they can mis-gauge the passing moments: *Goodness, is that really the time?*

Busy people who are completely absorbed in what they are doing—from intensive work to intensive play—from love-making to climbing mountains to writing books—may be temporarily oblivious of this slowly unfolding dimension of Time. Or in leisure mode, its gentle momentum may seem restful and reassuring.

Yet, there are other moments when the slow drip-drop sequence of second after second seems interminable. People confined indoors, with nothing to do on a rainy afternoon, fret and yawn. Bored schoolchildren fidget and watch the clock, despairingly. (Perhaps the 'Yawn Song' will make them laugh and wake up: '*You are going to yawn before this song is over*'.). These are recognitions that Time, untouched by human wishes, unfolds relentlessly at its own pace.

Regret, even anguish, can also be triggered by this accumulative momentum. It's not uncommon for older people to realise, with a sudden shock, that the passage of minutes has amounted to a lifetime. *Where did all those years go?* In that vein, a poignant ABBA song imagines that life and love are perennially 'Slipping through my fingers/Slipping through my fingers all the time'. And, most resoundingly, T. S. Eliot—the twentieth century's great poet of temporal flux—mourned the endless slow passing of empty days:

> *For I have known them all already, known them all:*
> *Have known the evenings, mornings, afternoons,*
> *I have measured out my life with coffee spoons…*

Naming Slow Change

Human awareness of the inexorable slow progression of Time has generated an absolutely huge vocabulary. Slow, gradual, incremental micro-change differs substantially from rapid, dramatic, wholesale macro-change. These categories may and do sometimes overlap at the margins (as examined in the next chapter) but here the focus is on gradualism.

Options start, alphabetically, with: adaptation, advance, alteration, amelioration, amendment, and ascent. Then there are nuanced gradations of betterment, development, differentiation, diversification, drift, evolution, fluctuation, flux, and gradualism itself. These terms have subtly different meanings, offering excellent choices for authors, and filling dictionaries. (The English language, being a hybrid with Teutonic and Latin-French roots, has an especially wide range of alternatives.)

The list continues with innovation, modification, mutation, permutation, progression, refinement, reform, regeneration, renovation, rise, shift, switch, transition, transfiguration, transformation, grotesque transmogrification, and variation. Classical Latin also contributes the terse adverb *paulatim*, translated into English as *little by little*.

Those terms include some that refer specifically to positive change; while many are neutral and can be used to signal things changing either for better or for worse.

Meanwhile, however, there is a specific vocabulary to convey the slow coming of bad news. So there are processes of corrosion, corruption, crumbling, decadence, decay, decline, degeneration, descent, deterioration, erosion, retrogression, ruination, weakening, worsening, and—classically, of course, after decline—fall.

Furthermore, classical Greek contributes some keywords, now fully Anglicised, for the experiences of shape-changing. These processes can actually happen slowly or rapidly. And they can be beneficial—or harmful—or neutral in impact.

Metamorphosis signals a substantial shift from one form of being into another. An adult butterfly provides a natural example. It has already passed through three prior distinctive forms: from egg to larva to pupa before it emerges with its fragilely beautiful wings. Legendary cases of metamorphosis also recur in Greek myths. The god Zeus cannily switches into the form of a handsome swan to seduce an entranced young girl Leda.

Amorous divinities can, however, be thwarted. When another beautiful young maid Daphne is pursued by the god Apollo, she prays for salvation and her river godfather transforms her into a laurel tree. Drastic. And a remedy of sorts. But all such divine escapades seem tough on innocent youngsters.

Metastasis, also from the Greek, is less fanciful and more melancholic in today's most common medical usage. The term indicates a shift from one state to another. Hence, when (say) cancerous cells spread from one bodily organ to another, the condition is named as advanced or 'metastatic cancer'. Not good news. And, again, cases of such metastatic change can be either speedy or slow.

Scientists also employ technical terms in their quest for precision. Another significant concept from the Greeks is *entropy*. In physics, it refers to processes of slow transformation within a thermodynamic system (or a body of matter acted upon by energy). So the extent of 'entropy' or disturbance generated by a process, like the slow dissolving of crystalline salt into water, can be calculated and given a value. The formula of disorder and heat loss in energy exchange is known as the second law of thermodynamics (of which more below).

These acknowledgements of longitudinal slow change indicate between them how significant for humans is this key temporal dimension. While Time retains its framework continuity, it also steadily incorporates slow, incremental change: 'little by little'—'step by step' … *'Baby, take your Time'*.

Praising Gradualism or Castigating Timidity?

Matching the diversity of terminologies, human reactions to slow change are equally multifarious. One school of thought advises caution when undertaking anything new. 'Slow but sure' runs one adage. 'More haste, less speed', agrees another, putting the same message the other way round. A Latin tag equally advises: *Festina lente—make haste slowly.*

In that mood of caution, indeed, why not follow the classic example of the Roman consul Quintus Fabius Maximus? He famously avoided direct confrontation with his formidable Carthaginian enemy, Hannibal, especially when the Roman troops were in a weak position militarily. Instead, Fabius cleverly played a long game. Hence, in politics and in war, 'Fabianism' entails a wily gradualism.

Nonetheless, the slow approach should not falter. Fabianism does not countenance defeatism. It settles in for the 'long march'. 'Softly, softly, catchee monkey', as a catchphrase from the early twentieth century advised. Patience is a key virtue. 'For Fools rush in where Angels fear to tread', as Alexander Pope, the eighteenth-century master of the rhyming couplet, versified sagely.

Great enterprises need a long-term commitment. 'Rome wasn't built in a day' (Fabius would have agreed). Divine power, being eternal, can also be imagined as moving with stately majesty to achieve its ends. 'The mills of God grind slowly' as Henry Longfellow's translation of an old maxim explained. 'Yet they grind exceeding small' (Theologically, however, that viewpoint can be disputed since omnipotent power can work at any or every speed).

Historically, one favourable term for slow change, which emerged in eighteenth-century Europe, was 'Improvement'. The concept was admired by liberal optimists. By the nineteenth century, too, an even more popular and laudatory term for positive change swept all before it: 'Progress'. Its proponents were confident in its inexorable power. 'Progress…is not an accident but a necessity', explained the Victorian social scientist Herbert Spencer. For him, it was part of nature. And many endorsed that assumption.

People used to say quite commonly (and some still do): '*You can't stop Progress*'. Naturally, however, opinions often differ widely as to which specific developments come into that favourable category and which do not.

Critics of slow change, meanwhile, are equally ready to pounce. For impatient radicals 'in a hurry', gradualism as a policy risks becoming too dilatory, too sluggish, and too timid. It leaves entrenched traditions unchallenged for too long. And while setting its eyes upon eventual long-term betterment, it risks condoning dreadful conditions in the here and now.

Therefore, many activists warn against too much hesitation. 'Don't dilly-dally'; 'A window of opportunity, once missed, may never come again'; 'Strike while the iron is hot', they urge. Or more emphatic still, in advice attributed to England's seventeenth-century republican regicide, Oliver Cromwell: 'Not only strike while the iron is hot, but make it hot by striking'.

Conversely, too, pessimistic critics of change call not for more action but for much less entirely. They are not impressed by innovation. And they deplore all systemic alterations as change-for-the-worse. Things are perennially 'going to the dogs'. Or have actually 'gone to pot'. Or, worse still, 'gone to rack and ruin'. All phrases expressive of gradual disorder and disarray.

Evidently, there's massive scope for disagreement. And it's not uncommon for individuals during their lifetimes to change their own verdicts about major trends. In addition, within different societies, cultural fashions may fluctuate. Sometimes, they foster hope. But, at other times, either generally or at specific moments of disaster, communal attitudes may foster resentment and fear.

Plenty of songs express sadness about historic trends, and a few are positively doom-laden. Bob Dylan's searing imagery in *It's a Hard Rain's Agonna Fall* (1962) provides one jeremiad, prompted by his sense of then living through 'black days, of schism'. It includes a line which (it must be hoped) will not prove to be prophetic, even though today the polar ice-caps are melting: *'Heard the roar of a wave that could drown the whole world'*.

Transformations in human affairs that are fast enough to detect (some rey slow changes take millennia) tend to provoke scattergun responses. If novelty is coming too fast for the nervous and the affronted, then it's coming too tardily for the impatient and the enthusiastic.

Any upheaval can be upsetting (or 'disorderly' in thermodynamic terms) and hence passions rise. For ardent reformers, however, confidence in the long term helps to override disappointment at short-term or even medium-term setbacks. That view is voiced in Sam Cooke's yearning but ultimately optimistic American Civil Rights song (1964): 'It's been a long, a long time coming/But I know a change gonna come/Oh yes it will'. And a traditional Christian gospel song offers a powerful anthem of persistent hope, in the same vein: 'Oh deep in my heart/I do believe/We shall overcome, someday...' While a Scottish song to stoical endeavour advises simply and firmly: *'Keep right on to the end of the road'*.

Detecting Evolution in the Natural World

Long-term changes in human biology often occur in gradual style: *little by little*. Bodies and minds grow imperceptibly older. Weight is added, not always imperceptibly, to the human frame (and sometimes imperceptibly, removed). Years pass, while bodies and minds become older still. Even those few obstinate theorists, who deny the reality of Time (as further discussed in Ch. 10), are eventually confronted with death: 'Earth to Earth, ashes to ashes, dust to dust', as stated in the rolling cadences of the Anglican Prayer Book.

Moreover, not only do individuals change gradually over time, so do entire species. As the genetic inheritance is transmitted from generation to generation, subtle modifications ensue. The process is known as biological evolution, potentially affecting all aspects of life, even the most intimate. But some speculations remain impossible to answer. So (for example) has the human organism changed significantly in its physical intensity (for better? for worse?) throughout the long evolution of the species? And how might an answer be researched and calibrated? (At this point, D. H. Lawrence shakes his head and frowns dismissively.)

Skeletal evidence has, meanwhile, allowed scientists to detect two notable long-term human adaptations. Both are responses to changing environments and lifestyles. One trend is producing a slow reduction in the average size of the human jaw when compared with those of early hominid skeletons. And the second can be seen in the long-term rise in the number of adults with fewer than the average number of teeth (a condition known as 'hypodontia').

With the taming of fire and the later advent of settled agriculture, humans slowly adapted to eating 'softer' cooked food, which is more easily chewed. Massive jaw-power is no longer essential for species survival. And as average jaw sizes decline, so does the mean number of teeth per mouth, thus reducing dental overcrowding. Indeed, in some parts of the world today, about one in three people lack a third molar.

By contrast, it is rare today to find humans with an excess number of teeth. However, the trend towards reduced dentition is taking millennia—providing no relief for any of today's unfortunate individuals who suffer from overcrowded small jaws and chronic toothache.

Micro-adaptations place humans fair and square within a global picture of biological evolution that affects all living creatures, in the context of changing environments. The process is known as natural selection over time. Those adapting best manage to transmit their modified genes to the next generation, while the 'weaker' specimens are weeded out, not by conscious policy but by evolutionary biology. The long-term outcome is popularly summarised as 'the survival of the fittest'—a punchy phrase coined by Herbert Spencer in 1864.

Crucially, however, there is another variable, which is equally essential. To survive, all living creatures need their appropriate habitats to survive around them. Currently, the global loss of biodiversity is eliminating too many species. And many others are endangered. For example, even the healthiest panda cannot survive without supplies of suitable bamboo leaves, which constitute ninety-nine percent of its diet. So evolutionary success depends upon habitat survival as well as species adaptation, and global habitats can become very unstable.

Biological evolution, explaining the mechanisms of gradual changes within species, was demonstrated in the mid-nineteenth century by Alfred Russel Wallace and, almost simultaneously, by Charles Darwin. And it was his name and reputation which became associated with the new science.

Initially, Darwinian evolution was highly controversial. Many Christian thinkers, who took the Biblical account of Creation literally, rejected the case outright. And to this day, there are minority groups who teach Creation-Science in lieu of Darwinism. However, with accumulating evidence, education, and pugnacious polemics from pro-Darwinians like Herbert Spencer, the case for slow biological evolution has won mainstream intellectual support worldwide.

Indeed, some social thinkers became so excited by the idea of competition and the 'survival of the fittest' that they tried to extend Darwinian ideas to questions of social policy. Aiding the poor, for example, seemed to go against the principles of ruthless competition for survival. Yet, biological changes operate within suitable habitats. If the work environment becomes highly unfavourable, then even the very fittest cannot survive—and the 'weakest' certainly cannot.

So, for example, when economic slumps afflict very unequal human societies, those who 'fail' are not always biological 'weaklings'. Instead, they may include not only many industrious workers without capital assets, who are suddenly thrown out of work but also some venture capitalists who have taken risks that would have succeeded in happier economic times.

'Brute' biology, furthermore, contains examples of group nurturing within species as well as of internecine individual competition. Humans provide examples of both experiences. So it is unwise to reduce everything to one explanatory formula when the evidence indicates diversity.

Elsewhere within the physical world, meanwhile, there are many different cases of gradual change, with many variant outcomes. Erosion can destroy over long epochs. Mountains crumble imperceptibly through the action of wind and water. Banks of earth and sand are slowly swept away, grain by grain.

Accretion, however, has the opposite effect. At sea, coral reefs grow with steady persistence in clear, warm, shallow water, if they have an underlying calcium-carbonate mesh and a suitable supply of nutrients. In caves, stalagmites gradually extend upwards and stalactites unhurriedly reach down, as dripping water leaves accumulations of mineral deposits. Impressive examples can be admired in the Mammoth Cave in west-central Kentucky (USA) and also within the Postojna Cave in southwestern Slovenia.

Equally, sand banks and sand spits grow fractionally, grain by grain, as winds, waves and currents augment rather than erode sedimentation. Long Point, Ontario (Canada) runs for some thirty-two km+ (approximately twenty miles) into the freshwaters of Lake Erie on its northern shoreline. And the global saltwater giant is the colossal Arabat Spit (one hundred and ten km or sixty-eight miles) stretching into the Sea of Azov, just north of the Black Sea.

Given many cases of slow-moving development, a traditional maxim from classical times went so far as to declare, famously, that '*Natura non facit saltum*' [Nature does not proceed by sudden leaps and bounds]. In fact, the universalism of that verdict must also be challenged. ('Splitters' to the fore again!) There are cases of catastrophic transformations in the physical universe, which are further explored in the next chapter.

Nevertheless, gradualism still retains a powerful dimension within cosmic Time-Space. By the way, it's worth noting too that incremental changes in the physical world are not invariably directed along the equivalent of a 'one-way street'. Depending on temperature, ice gradually melts but can then re-freeze, before melting again. Water equally can boil, cool, and boil again; and so forth. Yet there is a gradualist consequence: each changing state entails some increase in disorder (*entropy*) as the second law of thermodynamics states.

Across the cosmos, such changes are infinitesimal and have an impact infinitesimally slowly. But they signal that the system is not in permanent equilibrium. Even tiny changes have effects over millennia. If the cosmos is an enclosed thermodynamic system, then it will one day reach a state of 'maximum entropy' and cease to function. But scientific 'splitters' predictably disagree.

Speculations such as these are at the frontier of current knowledge. That the cosmos is an enclosed system, in thermodynamic terms, remains unproven. Hence the ultimate death of this cosmos—although thought likely by many experts—is not a foregone conclusion. (Aptly enough: *Time will tell…*)

Recognising Gradualism in Human Affairs

Most obvious as an instance of gradual change in human affairs is the steady unfolding of infant growth, and the slow acquisition of knowledge and skills. There is much to learn. Maturing does not happen overnight. Brains grow slowly and basic know-how slowly gets wired into their systems. Because these processes happen simultaneously, there is a finite 'window of opportunity' for language acquisition by the growing young. Sad evidence is furnished by cases of feral children who, without sustained human contact during their formative years from 0–6, never learn to speak more than a few words, if that.

Consequently, educational programmes are built around accumulation, plus stimulus and testing—and then around further accumulation. It is true that there are a few *Eureka!* moments. People experience a sudden mental breakthrough. When that happens, it is exhilarating. Worth jumping out of the bath, as reputedly did the Greek scientist Archimedes. Yet virtually all learning is gained gradually, usually imperceptibly, over many years. And those who have *Eureka!* moments (not all do) not only build upon prior knowledge but also systematise their views subsequently. Not for nothing is the great adage in both physical and mental learning (as already noted): 'practice makes perfect'.

Another massive area of human experience which features gradualism is communal language growth. Of course, there are strong elements of linguistic continuity as already acknowledged. Yet, within stable grammatical frameworks, languages are continuously adapted. The process happens as speakers and writers use their mother tongues spontaneously. People invent slang. They play with vogue words or new usages, which come and go fairly quickly—though a proportion of novelties do survive.

Consider the state of English over the last six hundred years—that is, during the last twenty-four generations of English-speakers (taking the demographers' standard of count of one new generation every twenty-five years). There are notable innovations alongside the shared grammatical basics. So Chaucer's English in 1400 contrasts with Shakespeare's English in 1600, which differs again from Jane Austen's English in 1800, which differs from Zadie Smith's English in *White Teeth* (2000). The further back in time that readers go, the trickier the historic usages are to comprehend. But at least one simple query, using a basic Anglo-Saxon verb, could still be asked in all eras: *To be or not to be?*

Over very long periods indeed, humans have between them evolved some five to seven thousand separate tongues across the world. Estimates of the total vary depending upon decisions about classifying dialects, pidgins, and world-regional permutations of standard languages (such as variations between English/English; American/English; Indian/English, and many more).

At the same time, rival tongues converge as well as diverge. People freely recycle common loan words. Today, there are numerous terms which are used internationally. Examples include: 'hotel', 'weekend', 'okay', 'ciao', 'kindergarten', 'Olympics', 'pyjamas', and 'tsunami'. These eight globally well-known words are derived from French, English, American, Italian, German,

Greek, Hindi, and Japanese respectively. And there are many more sharings, especially in specialist fields of study and in common food names.

Inter-linguistic borrowings of this sort do not necessarily signal the emergence of one universal language. But it's likely that mixings will become more common, as long as worldwide contacts continue to multiply.

Incremental micro-changes, which multiply into big trends, are often hard to spot for people living through them. There are also ebbs and flows. Sometimes a trend (for example in fashion) appears to have come to stay, only to become reversed in a later generation.

Among numerous big developments which seem unlikely to disappear soon, one prime example is the spread of human literacy. In c.1700, the ability to read and write was confined to a minority, and sometimes to a truly tiny minority of male scribes and officials. Yet, appreciation of the socio-economic utility plus the cultural value of literacy is spreading slowly, in authoritarian as well as in liberal states. In 2015, the illiterate constituted no more than fourteen percent of the world's adult population, and the proportion continues to fall. Moreover, women as well as men are joining the ranks of the literate, notwithstanding local variations between cultures, religions, and world regions.

Hence, today, literacy skills seem a basic human requirement, whereas only a few centuries earlier, mass illiteracy was seen as unavoidable and unremarkable. The switch was helped by the spread of printing (providing cheap books and newspapers), plus accessible schooling, growing parental approval, and, eventually, compulsory state education (now almost universal).

True, there are still many arguments about schooling. What curriculum? What teaching methods? For which groups of students? And how is creativity to be nurtured, while keeping order but without instilling uninventive conformity? Great questions; great debates.

But these arguments broadly follow upon the trend towards full literacy. Very few individuals or groups now dispute that all should have the basic capacity to read and write. Slowly, all the global millions of illiterates, once poetically imagined by Thomas Gray, in mid-eighteenth-century England, as 'mute inglorious Miltons', are learning to read, write and do sums, even if they won't all become poets of the stature of John Milton.

Acknowledging the power of gradualism underpins the position of many moderate political reformers. They hope that by promoting changes slowly they can bring public opinion with them, without enraging opponents. Once reforms become embedded and 'normalised', they become much harder to reverse. Giving women the right to citizenship by allowing them to vote was once a proposal greeted with anger, ridicule, and even fear. Now, however, disenfranchising women is not a common plank in mainstream democratic politics, though arguments persist over female rights to a full education.

Conservative critics from time to time counter the discreet power of gradualism by issuing a rival warning. Reforms may come slowly but each modest adaptation may turn out to be the *thin end of the wedge*. (That warning mantra has already been encountered in Ch. 7) Or, to change the metaphor, a gradual fall of stones may swell into an avalanche. People may thus become gradually accustomed to innovations. Yet, it's equally true that the erosion of rights can also occur slowly. Gradualist strategies can be used in any cause, though they work most successfully when going with the epochal trends.

One significant example shows how patient advocacy and modest reforms are managing to change attitudes over the long term. Once, majority opinion in many cultures held that human slavery was permissible and acceptable—even necessary and justifiable—in specific circumstances. The first campaigners against the practice in the seventeenth and eighteenth centuries were condemned and ridiculed for their unrealism and naivety.

Now, however, worldwide opinion condemns slavery as a social evil, even though many forms of personal unfreedom and human trafficking still—shamingly—survive. No doubt, global enforcement will one day be undertaken with more rigour, and may even succeed. There is already a ringing international ban on contemporary slavery, as formulated in the 1948 International Declaration on Human Rights, Article 4.

Today's consumers who benefit, unknowingly, from the unpaid (or grossly underpaid) labour of coerced workers will at some stage discover their own part in the grim chain of exploitation, as did eighteenth-century consumers of rum and sugar from the slave plantations. And, as then, calls for effective action to end the social evil will mount.

So it can be predicted that personal slavery will, eventually, join illiteracy in being slowly eliminated. Precisely when is hard to estimate. Sadly, recent statistics suggest that there is currently (2022) an increase in the number of women and girls being trafficked into sexual slavery (though data on this illegal trade is hard to verify). It will thus take considerable extra effort by enforcement agencies to get to grips with halting this intolerable abuse which wrecks lives. Trends indeed often work in centuries, not in decades. Predicting the end of sexual trafficking is dependent upon the survival of today's liberal, if imperfect, world order. Were there to be a cataclysmic breakdown of international organisation—say, following a global climate catastrophe—then all bets are off.

Overall, there's no space here to consider all possible cases of incremental changes in human affairs. But it's clear that big trends can be detected and that, where big vested interests are attacked, there is often big opposition as well.

Gradualism, in other words, is not always invariably friction-free. One trend that is gaining momentum, especially among young people in the world today, is support for green environmental policies. At the same time, however, there is often resistance from vested interest groups—such as car drivers and frequent fliers—when they are asked to adapt their daily behaviour.

Thus, while policy changes tend to work most effectively when backed by organisational support from states and other structured organisations, there are still practical limitations when it comes to changing daily habits (say, in patterns of drinking or drug use). Slow change may thus collide with the power of inertia and will win sometimes but not invariably.

Summary Next Step: Recognising Slow Momentum within Time-Space

Abhay Kumar's *Earth Anthem* (2008) joyously hymns the *cosmic blue pearl*, at home in an intricate cosmos, and experiencing the steady momentum of slow change. Popular recognition of this process is age-old. At one point, attitudes, especially in the West, were over-confident. Changes would always be slow and always benevolent: *Onwards and Upwards!* Alas, that's too simple. But it's not axiomatic that changes are always detrimental: *Backwards and Downwards!*

A neutral term is slow 'progression'—shorn of over-hyping. All cases of gradual, incremental micro-change need to be evaluated carefully. Specifically on Planet Earth today, there is no lack of worrying ecological trends to scrutinise: deforestation, loss of biodiversity, environmental contamination, light pollution, air pollution, noise pollution, rising sea levels, and climate change.

However, the lessons of gradualism also apply to finding remedies. No doubt a range of big and probably controversial policy decisions need to be made and implemented. Yet, there is also a strong case for many accumulative micro-changes on the ground. Examples at the individual level include: planting trees, changing diets, insulating homes, reducing harmful patterns of transportation, recycling; helping to restore habitat diversity, and so forth.

Participating individually gives everyone a stake in the solutions. And such popular input will help to build support for structural eco-changes that entail painful choices. Many micro-changes make a trend.

Relevantly, one Victorian pioneer of Alpine mountaineering advised: 'Do nothing in haste; look well to each step; and from the beginning think what may be the end'. Well, there are moments when haste and large steps are needed. Yet, Edward Whymper's counsel remains pertinent: *'When taking steps on a journey, check constantly where they are leading'*.

Gradualism is unglamorous and often unremarkable. It is not the only key dimension within Time-Space. Yet, unfolding evolutionary/incremental progression is a fundamental feature, whose impact needs full recognition.

One song in 1988 was cheerfully laid-back: 'Relax, there's no hurry/Here we are/With all the Time in the world'. And yes: there is a lot of Time, viewed inter-galactically. Yet, the message of gradualism is not to do nothing, when facing a local crisis in one corner of the cosmos. Instead, measured steps offer a constructive chance of building public support for remedial action. Walk on and get others to join the journey. Keep checking the direction of travel. And keep moving onwards: *One Step at a Time…*

Ideas of Slow Change in Human Affairs

Ashley, G., Lloyd, T. (2010) *Two Speed World: The Impact of Explosive and Gradual Change: Its Effect on You and Everything Else.*

Berman, G., Fox, A. (2023) *Gradual: The Case for Incremental Change in a Radical Age.*

Language Change

Kretzschmar, W. A. (2018) *The Emergence and Development of English: An Introduction.*

Thomsen, O. N. (2006) *Competing Models of Linguistic Change: Evolution and Beyond.*

World Literacy and Illiteracy

Miller, J. W., McKenna, M. C. (2016) *World Literacy: How Countries Rank and Why it Matters.*

Biological Evolution

Bowler, P. (2007) *Monkey Trials and Gorilla Sermons: Evolution and Christianity from Darwin to Intelligent Design.*
Workman, L. (2014) *Charles Darwin: The Shaping of Evolutionary Thinking.*

Slow Changes in Geography

Poole, R. second edn., (2023) *Earthrise: A Short History of the Whole Earth.*
Termier, H., Termier, G. (1963) *Erosion and Sedimentation.*
Trudgill, S. T. (1983) *Weathering and Erosion.*

Chapter 9
Bracing for Turbulence

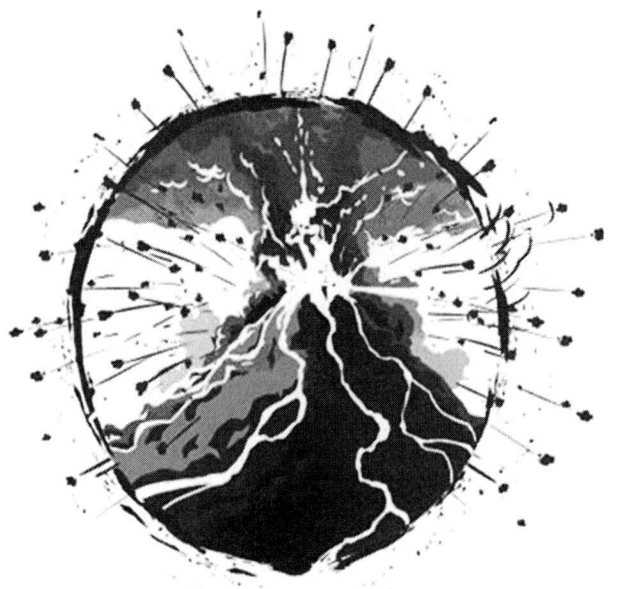

Chapter 9 takes a further step, by assessing the dimension of explosive change, whose turbulence is also integral to Time-Space.

Assessing Explosive Change

Time produces 'wrecks and scars'... which highlight the theme of cosmic turbulence. (The phrase is adapted from a poem on *King's Cross Railway Station*, by the quixotic English author G. K. Chesterton, musing in 1900 on smoke, station architecture, and changing times). Ruins and wrecks are part of history too. Irregularities, shocks, surprises, and turbulence are found throughout the cosmos; and such upheavals form an integral part of the whole.

The enduring dimensions of continuity (T/C), entwined with evolution (T/E), go far to constitute Time-Space's mix of continuance and elasticity. Yet there is more. A further dimension of rapid, explosive change adds volcanic discontinuities into the equation. Such upheavals, also known by the term 'revolution' confer massive dynamism. In other words, Time has three dimensions, the third being Time/Revolution (T/R).

Viewed at its simplest, such an explosive element explains both the birth and death of the cosmos. That scenario, however, does not preclude there being a series of universes, one after another, as some astrophysicists conjecture. (Nor does it predict any one precise form of cosmic death). Reassuringly, too, physicists calculate that the remaining life expectancy of the current universe extends for another two hundred billion years, though there is absolutely no consensus.

Simultaneously, Time's volcanic dimension is also apparent in many forms of turbulence within the natural world. Various physical indicators signal its coiled tensions. Often visible to humans are lazy puffs of smoke, emitted by apparently dormant volcanoes. And, now and then, these simmering monsters erupt to reveal a raging, fiery heart. Moreover, volcanoes provide more than spectacular fireworks displays, as they impact upon geography, ecology, climate, and human societies. They reveal turbulence and unleash more.

An even starker example comes from scientific experiments in splitting atoms. These microscopic particles are the building blocks of all solids, liquids, plasma, and gases. They are invisible to the naked eye. Yet when one atom is split by an externally applied blast, a massive surge of stored energy immediately explodes (a small-scale variant of the original cosmic 'Big Bang'?). And when trillions of atoms are split simultaneously, the result is a chain reaction which produces an atom bomb, or more constructively, their force can be harnessed to supply nuclear power.

Each explosion, furthermore, triggers long-term consequences. The smallest nuclei of the sundered atomic nucleus experience prolonged radioactive decay, surviving in what is known as their 'half-life'. In the case of some material substances, the process can take literally millennia. This phenomenon highlights the latent energy, coiled within the physical universe.

Turbulence thus remains, in one sense, abnormal. It prompts discontinuities and upheavals. Yet, in another sense, it is integral to the cosmic mix. In deep Space, turbulence follows from rare and spectacular events like galactic collisions. It also ensues when a supernova (or exploded star) implodes to form a Black Hole, which is a gravitational node so dense that no particles of matter or light can escape. Moreover, in the quantum micro-cosmos, turbulence is the norm. And, at times, upheavals occur within all human societies too.

Naming Explosive Change

Suitably enough, a huge and nuanced vocabulary offers extensive choice for naming drastic discontinuities (There is some overlap with terms for slow change, since transformations great and small cover a spectrum).

'Revolution' leads the field, partly as it offers a neat contrast with 'evolution'. There is one initial qualification to be made. In one usage, 'revolution' means turning a full circle. One familiar example is Planet Earth's yearly revolution around the sun. Another is the steady revolving of a well-balanced wheel—one of humanity's simplest but greatest inventions.

However, the context usually makes it clear whether the reference is to a neat circle, or to a drastic upheaval. A non-cyclical 'revolution' means a major case of macro-change, as in a political 'revolution', which signals a big, often bloody, overthrow of one system to be wholly replaced by another.

Other descriptive terms include metamorphosis (in its drastic sense), transformation, fundamental discontinuity, radical disjunction, and *diagenesis*. The latter is a technical term for major alterations during physical formation. Examples can be found in geology when fundamental changes occur in sediments between their first deposition and their later solidification.

Humans are good at making fine distinctions of that sort. Another useful pair of terms highlights differences between alterations in size and those in form. So 'quantitative' growth is numerical: bigger, faster, heavier. It means more of the same. But 'qualitative' growth signifies an accumulation of changes (possibly small in themselves) which lead to systemic transformation. It means more but also significantly different.

Many everyday phrases additionally name degrees of disjuncture: 'turning point', 'tipping point', 'broken symmetry', 'step-change', 'pathway shift', or 'watershed'. Satirical songs and prints in history have gleefully imagined *the world turned upside down* when horses sit in carriages drawn by humans, or kings wait at tables as beggars wine and dine.

And a cornucopia of terms indicates upheavals which may lead to major transformations: schism, caesura, rupture, hiatus, breakdown, dissolution, disaster, convulsion, seismic shock, cataclysm, catastrophe, or simply, chaos.

In the field of ideas, the American philosopher of science Thomas Kuhn defined a sharp break in thought systems as a 'paradigm shift'. An example was the scientific switch from Newton's physics to Einstein's relativity, though, of course, few individual scientists changed their minds 'at a stroke'.

Earlier, another analyst of a rapid switch in ideas was the German philosopher, Georg Wilhelm Hegel. He used the term 'dialectic', to signal drastic change through contradiction or opposition. His stress upon friction was admired by Marx and Engels. But, for them, class conflict was the motor force. Hence, Marxists define a great political disjuncture as 'a dialectical leap forward'; pithily termed by China's Chairman Mao 'a great leap forward'.

At moments of drastic discontinuity, normality seems shattered. People are disorientated. There is no firm footing. The familiar balance between the potent dimensions of continuity and gradualism has gone awry. In Shakespeare's phrase, the times seem *'out of joint'*.

Is there light at the end of every dark tunnel? Or instead (as a melancholic song from 2015 suggests) 'a tunnel at the end of the light'? Either way, humans are aware of the risks of drastic upheaval and startling outcomes, whether for good or for ill. And they are not short of terms in which to identify turmoil.

Praising or Fearing the 'Terrible Beauty' of Revolution?

All [is] changed, changed utterly/
A terrible beauty is born.

So the Anglo-Irish bard W. B. Yeats celebrated the 1916 Easter Uprising in Ireland. And mixed reactions—applause; alarm; or both—are common when individuals are confronted with revolutionary upheavals of all kinds.

Enthusiasts revel in the 'shock of the new'. *All that is solid melts into air; all that is holy is profaned*, in the gleeful words of the 1848 *Communist Manifesto*. The adjective 'new' trails its own glory. Renovation is beautiful. *Let a thousand flowers bloom*. Miranda in Shakespeare's *Tempest* is saved from her island confinement and applauds her meeting with sympathetic fellow humans in a much-requoted catchphrase: *O brave new world*.

Red, bright fiery red, emerged from the nineteenth century onwards as the symbolic hue in the West for revolutionary upheaval. Proletarian crowds in Paris in 1789 wore their *bonnets rouges*. Red roses or red tulips are symbols of radical protest. And a red flag is the standard of popular uprising.

Its colour has the resonance of cleansing fire, or more, pointedly, the spilling of blood. 'The people's flag is deepest red/It shrouded oft our martyred dead', declare the lyrics of the song of international labour, known as *The Red Flag* (1889). Its chorus proudly urges: 'Then raise the scarlet standard high!/Beneath its folds we'll live or die'. True, not all who sing these words are active revolutionaries. They enjoy, however, the appeal to battlefield solidarity. Not just commitment, but commitment unto death.

Simultaneously, however, it's worth noting that red conveys very versatile symbolism. It is associated with heat and anger but also with sexual passion, joy, and love. In many countries in the east, it betokens happiness and good fortune. People wearing 'rose-coloured glasses' may accordingly see a range of visions in red, from good cheer to revolutionary activism.

For very ardent enthusiasts for a cause, political violence may at times seem cleansing. It offers force to remove what is seen as old corruption and gangrenous rot. Dear or dying wood can all be cleared away 'root and branch'.

Aptly enough, Lenin, as leader of the Russian Revolution, favoured direct, forceful action. 'Liberation of the oppressed [working] class is impossible without a violent revolution and without the destruction of the machinery of state power', he wrote in 1917. He stressed that history does not advance smoothly. It can move by jumps and zig-zags, allowing revolutionaries to give events a hefty push. However, it is worth noting that drastic direct action can be espoused by radicals of the political right, as well as of the left.

Against such militant hopes, however, were ranged a rival chorus of doubts and fears. Beautiful fires of upheaval may destroy more than they create. Unintended outcomes may follow. *The revolution brings forth monsters.*

Ambitious plans to 'force' humanity to be free may produce not freedom from one repressive system but subjugation to new power-brokers, ruling in the name of 'the people'. In that case, the desired brightness of an egalitarian revolution is replaced by '*darkness at noon*'. That evocative phrase was coined by the Hungarian-born Arthur Koestler, as he recoiled from Stalinist tyranny.

He added sombrely that: 'Nothing is more sad than the death of an illusion'. The proposition is open to debate. Other horrific developments may be even more upsetting. Yet, it was a heartfelt statement of Koestler's own experience as he lost his youthful faith in communism. Roseate dreams may then turn into nightmares. Anguish, injustice, violence and betrayal can be the outcomes as well as the causes of great revolutionary upheavals.

Physical violence in particular can be self-defeating. It brutalises both perpetrators and victims. It teaches all parties to rely upon force, not upon the power of argument and of just policies. It creates and/or perpetuates inequality. It empowers the most violent individual or group, not the best.

Moreover, if violence is ever justified (as in a 'just war'), to prevent or halt even worse deeds, then physical force should be kept to the minimum necessary and should be exercised within reasonable bounds. That is why rules of warfare have been invented (even if not always upheld). Rules of engagement play the same role in combat sports, such as pugilism.

Otherwise, untrammelled violence may well lead not to light and hope but to darkness and death, often heightened by countervailing violence from opponents. So warned the African American poet Dudley Randall, amid urban political turmoil in 1968: he loved the transcendent hope of beauteous change-for-the-better. Simultaneously, however, he warned prophetically of the attendant dangers. Light might turn into darkness. Joy might turn into mass lamentations. No fast and easy highway leads to instant liberation for all. Instead, reformers note that changes are often made only slowly—and that gains, once made, require consolidation. Thus liberation movements should be ready, not for a headlong rush, but for a determined long march through history.

Detecting Upheavals in the Natural World

While the laws of physics remain constant through Time, they do not signify that everything within the cosmos exists in a state of calm and good order. On the contrary. The laws of physics incorporate turbulence throughout the natural world, whether viewed at the macro- or micro-level.

Birth and death are abrupt discontinuities—evidence of both creation and destruction—that apply to all living creatures. Humans need no special reminders. Entire religious systems are devoted to explaining the mysteries of their coming into being and, especially, the spiritual significance of their eventual physical departure.

Countless works of literature, drama, poetry, and philosophy also meditate upon the natural forces of creation and destruction. Arrivals can be risky. 'My mother groaned! My father wept/Into the dangerous world I leapt', as William Blake in 1794 imagined his own advent. Every day thereafter is a subsequent rebirth, suggests the Colombian novelist, Gabriel Garcia Marquez, provocatively: 'Life obliges [individuals] over and over again to give birth to themselves'. It's a positive mantra of constant self-renewal.

Sexual pleasures for humans also contain an element of joyous turbulence. An orgasm is sometimes termed the *little death* (not the cheeriest terminology but indicating a supreme sensation, beyond all daily cares). Of course, there are also subjectivities here. Not everyone manages to climax successfully during sex. And even when lovers do experience ecstasy, it is impossible to know whether they are feeling identical sensations. (*Stop pontificating and get on with it!* D. H. Lawrence again interjects with rising irritation).

Then there is physical mortality itself. In Samuel Beckett's pointedly named *Endgame* (1959), the chief protagonist is Hamm (perhaps a theatrical heir to Shakespeare's philosophically questing Hamlet?). The Beckettian universe is bleak. Hamm sees multiple mini-deaths before the final departure: '*We breathe, we change! We lose our hair, our teeth! Our bloom! Our ideals!*'. In fact, people generally tuck the knowledge of their eventual demise into their mental recesses. Daily routines take priority. In that spirit, Hamm later offers a key message: 'The end is in the beginning—and yet you go on'.

Counter-balancing powers of creation and destruction pervade the cosmos. Time-Space has many 'bonding' features, yet it also has explosive potential. This cosmos probably began with a Big Bang. And it is likely to have a similarly dramatic ending, either as a hypothesised Big Crunch (implosion), Big Freeze (heat death), or Big Rip (chaotic final explosion). After that, a new Time-Space may start to unfold again. But that would be, as they say: *another story…* and these matters are still being debated by cosmologists.

One authenticated moment of macro-upheaval remains locally pertinent to all humans. Some 4.54 billion years ago, a powerful coalescence of swirling gases and interplanetary dust came to constitute Planet Earth. In the greater scheme of things, this event, occurring one-third into the estimated lifespan of the cosmos, is a sideshow. Locally, however, its importance is paramount.

Furthermore, shortly after that epic moment, there was a significant collision. The young Earth was hit by a passing planetoid. Materials dislodged from both bodies coalesced to form a chunky satellite, known as the Moon. Its subsequent environmental effect was crucial. Not only does the reflective satellite shed a luminous light at night but its gravitational pull augments the tidal rise and fall of the Earth's surface oceans, giving them a dynamic churn and preventing stagnation.

More too. The moon's co-gravitational interaction has helped to slow the Earth's initially very rapid rotation. The globe's slower pace works to support a broadly more stable atmosphere and an associated ecosystem (though it is still liable to notable variations). The partnership between the 'blue planet' and its only satellite is an unequal one. Yet, the lunar counterweight still plays a vital role. *'Moon River…wherever you're goin', I'm goin' your way…'*

Intermittent collisions with passing meteors continue, triggering changes on Earth of varying magnitude. And global forces also engender their own range of drastic upheavals and turbulence. These include earthquakes, tsunamis, volcanoes, avalanches, tempests, blizzards, floods, fires, heatwaves, droughts, famines, plagues, pandemics, and extinctions.

Of course, not all 'disasters' are equally disastrous. Long-term powers of renewal can prompt recovery. Forest fires clear undergrowth to make room for new saplings. Floods leave fresh alluvial deposits to improve soil conditions. And so forth. Nonetheless, great disruptions are by definition stand-out-events. And they cause much more than normal wear and tear.

Even within the generally show-changing world of evolutionary biology, there is also an omnipresent possibility of drastic discontinuity. Outright extinctions of entire species are irreversible. Earth's history has already witnessed a number of drastic cases. The disappearance of the dinosaurs some sixty-five million years ago is but one example.

Terrifyingly, too, humans are today living through another phase of major species loss, partly triggered by human-made climate change and partly by adverse human encroachment upon plant and animal habitats. Eroding Earth's current biodiversity will have incalculable consequences.

Coiled tensions and the potential for turbulence apply throughout the cosmos. Even within the micro-world of sub-atomic particles, matter itself is revealed as unstable and potentially fissile. Particles release and absorb energy, not in a regular flow but in discrete bursts. They are hard to detect because tests that reveal (say) the wave properties of light, conceal its particle properties, and *vice versa*. The conventional rules of Newtonian physics are superseded by a counter-intuitive world with strange, though still identifiable, characteristics.

Looking into an atom is like looking into a micro-moment of Time-Space. Within, there is turmoil. As already noted, 'splitting' the nucleus of an atom unleashes a great blast of power. Yet, ordinarily, the sub-atomic world coheres. Electromagnetic forces attach electrons to matter, while a mix of 'strong' and 'weak' nuclear forces hold protons and neutrons together. Cohesion thus still applies within the turbulent micro-cosmos, very much as forces of gravity and inertia bind the turbulent macro-cosmos together.

Dangers, however, may lurk everywhere. W. B. Yeats in 1919 was again thunderously melodramatic: 'Things fall apart; the centre cannot hold;/Mere anarchy is loosed upon the world'. Nonetheless, cosmic instability should not be over-estimated. One interpretation, known as 'Chaos Theory', measures the multiplying impact of even minor perturbations upon the bigger picture. The flapping of a butterfly's wings might, in specific circumstances, trigger a chain reaction leading to (say) a disastrous tornado.

Yet, Chaos Theory does not assert a permanent state of crisis. After an upheaval, some form of equilibrium returns (Millions of butterflies flap their wings daily, without unleashing constant tornadoes).

Restless nature is thus not always malign. Not all surprises are bad ones. But older claims about the intrinsic benevolence of 'Mother Nature' cannot be upheld either. For humans, their understanding of the damaging effects of dwindling biodiversity and the current climate emergency—and their knowledge of the system's ultimate cohesion—gives them grounds for hope that, if sufficiently motivated, they can take effective remedial action.

Indeed, in 2020, there was an unexpected 'anthropause' or weakening in the adverse impact of human activities. Social Lockdowns in densely populated cities, in response to the Covid pandemic, led to a marked reduction in car and air travel and consequential pollution. It was a sign.

Coping with Turbulence in Human Affairs

Upheavals in human affairs are not generated purely by fellow humans. One example of turmoil generated by 'natural' forces is the havoc wrecked by epidemics arising from spontaneously generated viruses and contagious diseases. Indeed, until recent advances in preventive medicine, one of the chief regulators of the global total of humans has been the changing incidence of killer diseases, like plagues and smallpox.

Because there are so many potential sources of turbulence, in both the human and the 'natural' world, great disruptions do not occur within orderly timetables. There are eras of calm as well as periods of turmoil. But neither alternative is readily predictable. For that reason, long-range forecasts become increasingly problematic, the farther into the future they reach.

Being members of a species which is assertive and competitive as well as gregarious and convivial, humans themselves also contribute to making or worsening upheavals. Sometimes, they respond erratically or unhelpfully to natural crises, such as droughts and famines. It often takes time for the full scale of a calamity to become understood. And in some regrettable cases, there have been major disasters produced by dogmatic government policies. One example was the 1958–61 Chinese famine when Chairman Mao's Great Leap Forward failed to generate the desired economic improvements. Millions of excess deaths (above the norm) ensued, though the precise figure remains uncertain.

Sources of friction between people are legion. Warfare between rival nations and/or religions is no surprise, historically speaking. And there are also civil wars within homeland communities, where good neighbourliness is supposed to prevail. All fighting tends to generate distrust and subsequent bitterness. Yet, civil wars *between brothers* leave especially fraught legacies. Fear spreads. Killings happen, not far away but near to home. And subsequent reconciliation is hard to achieve, though not impossible (For further thoughts on both conflict and reconciliation, see Ch. 13 and 14 below).

Civil confrontations, short of outright civil war, recur frequently. They may be prodded by intentional deeds from radical activists, or exacerbated by slow, unhelpful or punitive government responses. Or triggered, as often happens, by a mosaic of factors.

Most drastic is the push for mass revolution, seeking the overthrow of an entire political and social system. That, in turn, may be contrasted with a *coup d'état*, seeking by force to replace one set of rulers with another. A *putsch* is another term for a quick and 'dirty' (often violent) overthrow of a government. And there are other confrontations, ranging from riots to revolts, insurrections, rebellions, wars of liberation, and below-the-radar guerrilla warfare.

Any challenge to an established order has the potential for escalation. On that theme, the ever-alert Shakespeare allowed Ulysses in *Troilus & Cressida* to voice a warning: '*Take but degree away, untune that string/And, hark, what discord follows*!' Disorder, once triggered, can spread rapidly, though it can also fizzle out, or be suppressed by a greater force.

Coping successfully with protests requires the powers-that-be to show a judicious combination of firmness and a willingness to listen to grievances. The tottering regimes in financially hard-pressed France in 1789 and, later, in war-weary Russia in 1917 proved unable to respond effectively. With dramatic political consequences in both cases. The obduracy of the old regimes—combined with their ineptitude—meant that their angered and desperate subjects had no other recourse than to overthrow the old system's root and branch.

Revolutionary takeovers, however, do not always succeed. For a start, it is not easy to transform both a system of government and its supporting social structures. Entrenched vested interests frequently fight back, with counter-revolutionary zeal. Privileged people are often loath to give up their status and wealth. And as soon as any revolutionary cause encounters obstacles, it quickly risks becoming splintered or side-tracked.

Consequently, one outcome may be the emergence of a strong leader—a Napoleon, a Stalin—delivering not political liberation but dictatorial power. The higher the original radical hopes, the greater the risk of failure to deliver. Thus, anguished cries of 'betrayal' often punctuate the history of major political upheavals, as initial supporters experience later disillusionment.

Nonetheless, political revolutions can provide grand symbolic moments of purgative liberation. The fall of the Bastille in Paris on 14 July 1789 remains a world-historical monument to the power of an outraged people. And some positive outcomes can follow. Yet, revolutions also fail, abort, halt, recede, fudge, diverge, transmute and/or provoke counter-revolutions. The varied outcomes of the communist takeovers, inspired in the twentieth century by the predictive historical philosophy of Marx and Engels, make that point practically, as well as theoretically.

Meanwhile, commentators generally tend to overuse the term 'revolution'. It suggests something 'big' and 'new'. Yet, it has by now become blurred in usage. There are references not just to political revolutions but also to 'industrial revolution', 'transport revolution', 'agricultural revolution', 'commercial revolution', 'financial revolution', 'cultural revolution', 'feminist revolution', 'gender revolution', or (today) a 'digital revolution'.

Can one catch-all term helpfully define all these macro-transformations? In fact, it's most productive to keep 'revolution' for big, fundamental and often bloodily contested attempts at overthrowing entire political systems.

Hence, it's best to use some permutations of macro-transformation or radical discontinuity for other great disjunctures. For example, Britain's long-term industrialisation in the eighteenth and nineteenth centuries, often known as *the*

Industrial Revolution, certainly fostered epic changes. The economy shifted from one based upon human- and animal-power to one reliant upon fossil-fuel-powered mechanised industry. And Britain's society shifted from one that was predominantly rural to predominantly urban. Yet, its technological macro-changes depended not only upon big radical innovations but also upon many incremental alterations and repeated testing, in the spirit of 'trial and error'.

Rather than one instant 'revolution', these cumulative changes—some rapid, some slow—amounted to an epic macro-transformation, a huge step-change in human history, with an impact which is still unfolding economically and environmentally.

Similarly, big but generally peaceful cultural turning points in human affairs also need different descriptive terms. Was the advent of experimental science in the seventeenth and eighteenth centuries the same sort of change as the 1789 socio-political upheaval in France? Both led to epic transformations. But they were different processes, with different timetables.

It took centuries for the full impact of the so-called 'scientific revolution' to unfold, with eras of rapid innovations, interspersed with eras of relative consolidation. Einstein for one was happy to identify the 'evolution' of physics as a discipline. That term may be too modest for the great rethinking, undertaken by astronomers and physicists in the era of Galileo and Newton. Yet, creative humans should be able to find varied terms for the varieties of drastic change.

Was there really just one 'sexual revolution'? And if so, when? Just one 'learning revolution'? And, if so, taking what form? And so on.

Interestingly, some radical reformers today, who oppose the mass production of ultra-cheap clothing by exploited labour, are calling for a new 'fashion revolution'. But their excellent aim would be more incisive with a call for *Fashion Justice.*

That said, many people will probably still recycle the catchy word 'revolution' (Such is the power of linguistic continuity). One consequence is that there can be no general theory of 'revolution' as long as the term covers so many disparate forms of upheavals. But it can be agreed that most forms of drastic change do trigger drastic reactions, whether of praise or blame.

Turbulence may often follow turbulence. Or as John Milton specified sadly in his epic *Paradise Lost:* '*Confusion [is] worse confounded*'. Yet, there are countervailing dimensions of cohesion, cooperation, and continuity, in the cosmos as well as within human life on Earth.

Summary Next Step: Bracing for Turbulence within Time-Space

Trying to anticipate the unexpected twists and turns of events is good mental training. That point is made with an amusing coda in Oscar Wilde's play *An Ideal Husband* (1895). A surprise lady caller is shown into the drawing room as the butler has been instructed by the master of the house. 'How thoughtful of him!' she purrs: 'To expect the unexpected shows a thoroughly modern intellect'. Yet, the joke is improved by the fact that the surprise visitor is not the longed-for lover after all. The butler obeyed orders but the new arrival was the 'wrong' lady. There are shocks within shocks, as the truly astonishing requires.

Confronting unexpected crises is not an easy art (or science), to restate the obvious. However, the scale of turbulence should not lead to an attitude of fatalism or despair. Cosmic workings—generally and locally—can be studied. Living in a dynamic but unstable world requires no less than constant vigilance.

Successful answers to macro-problems may well require radical macro-solutions, as well as sustained micro-contributions. All permutations must be considered, without forgetting the ballasting role of continuity. In the midst of today's global eco-crisis, there is certainly scope still for a greener, less polluted world to emerge. While much in the great cosmos is beyond human control, people are not entirely powerless, within their own homestead of Planet Earth.

Thus whenever there is scope for action, there is also scope for meaningful choices… And in the tensions between creativity and destruction, humans can strive to pluck 'beauty' from revolutions, without unleashing 'terror'.

There's certainly no respite from the dimension of revolutionary turbulence (T/R). Deep within the cosmos, there is *Timeshock!* People should always be ready to brace themselves. True, not all in the cosmos is chaos. Nor is everything in a state of constant upheaval. But…all the same, no one should underestimate the turbulence within temporality. It's a dimension with a hidden potential for great ferocity. In boxing, naïve people are said to be caught out by punches that they don't see coming. In life, such a lack of caution is seriously unwise. One thing not to ignore is the *mighty punch of Time*.

Political Revolutions

Krejči, J. (1973) *Great Revolutions Compared: The Search for a Theory.*

Varieties of Cultural Transformation

Kuhn, T. S. (1962) *The Structure of Scientific Revolutions.*
Skinner, C. (2018) *Digital Human: The Fourth Revolution of Humanity Includes Everyone.*

Chaos Theories

Eve, R. A. (et. al) (eds) (1997) *Chaos, Complexity and Sociology: Myths, Models and Theories.*
Gleick, J. (1987; 1990) *Chaos.*

Turbulence in the Natural World

Davis, L. (1993) *Encyclopaedia of Natural Disasters.*
Ward, P. D. (2007) *Under a Green Sky: Global Warming, the Mass Extinctions of the Past, and What They Can Tell Us about Our Future.*

Cosmic History

Lago, M. T. V. T., Blanchard, A. (eds) (1998; 1999) *The Non-Sleeping Universe*
Parsons, P. (2018) *The Beginning and the End of Everything: From the Big Bang to the End of the Universe.*

Chapter 10
Experiencing Time-Space in all Its Dimensions

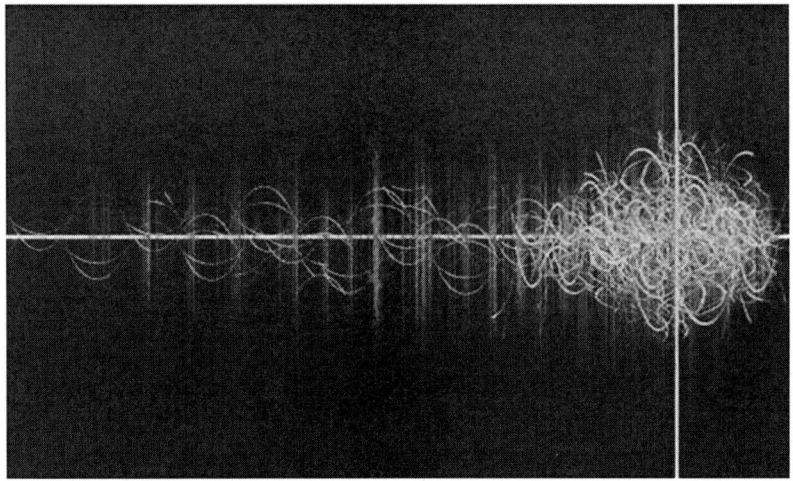

Chapter 10 brings the journey to an interim staging-post, exploring how everything is experienced within multi-dimensional Time-Space and therefore rejecting Time Denial.

Co-ordinating in Time-Space

Time is rhythm…brain ripple, breathing, the drum in my temple… These evocative words were penned by the Russian Vladimir Nabokov, the author who left his homeland to reside in Germany, the USA and Switzerland in turn. They show yet again how varied descriptions of Time can be. It's both mighty, yet intimate. Impersonal, yet personal.

In this case, Nabokov was referring to the sense of inner temporality, pervading the body. It is something that can be experienced by all living beings. *We breathe…*

As has been argued in previous chapters, Time's fuses a potent mix of the three interlocking dimensions of continuity, momentum and turbulence (T/C ×

T/E × T/R). And temporality simultaneously embraces and enables Space, with its own dimensions of height, length and breadth.

Together, they fuse to form the cosmos. Time is, therefore, much more than a simple 'fourth dimension', added onto the standard three dimensions of space. (Theoretical physicists today debate the advanced Superstring Theory. It envisages a cosmos of ten dimensions, each one representing a facet of the whole. But—no surprise—there is as yet no consensus).

For purposes of daily life—and of getting to grips with the steady unfolding of past, present and future—the core parameters are fewer in number. Space's three dimensions are formed and 'placed' within Time's own longitudinal three. The formula is more than three plus three; or even three times three. It's more like three to the longitudinal power of three. The result is certainly unique. Time-Space is thus unidirectional, intricate, and dynamic.

Making Music/Marking Time

Making music is one ubiquitous human means of saluting temporality. Combining sounds and beats in meaningful sequences is an audible way of *marking Time.* Most people manage to find some form of music that pleases them. And even those with unresponsive 'tin ears' (or actual hearing disorders) understand that music provides a deeply primal means of communication.

Music is, after all, completely steeped in Time. And it builds upon the basic temporal mix of continuity, momentum, and turbulence. Music readily embraces forms of continuity, with repeated or embroidered rhythms, tunes, and (when applicable) words, which aid recognition and appreciation. Music also has momentum, telling stories, evoking variable moods, and proceeding in stages. And it can depict and embrace turbulence.

Even the gentlest and most melodious musicians at times use shock tactics to jolt audiences into attention. Beethoven (never a simple composer) provides numerous great examples of musical surprise. His Eroica Symphony (no.3) mixes bold strokes of *fortissimo* with delicate hushed melodies, driven with repetitious rapid beats. Even after many hearings, this music can still amaze. (Try listening to the 2015 rendition by the *Deutsche Kammerphilharmonie Bremen*, conducted at a rattling pace by Paavo Järvi.)

Plus, in the mid-twentieth-century, a new musical genre was invented, featuring harsh, jangling, randomised noise. It's called 'stochastic' music, based upon randomness, not order. 'Pretty' tunes are eschewed. It was rough music for an era of mass global warfare and the atomic bomb. One key exponent, the Greek/French composer Iannis Xenakis, sought to convey a 'sensual shock', like hearing 'a clap of thunder' or looking into 'a bottomless abyss'.

Paradoxically, however, the human brain and ear can assimilate such discordant clamour into a pulsating anti-harmony. Continuity fights back. (Listen to *Metastasis* (1955) by Iannis Xenakis, conducted impeccably by Ajtony Casba in 2012: people will respond variably but the cacophony can be heard, after a bit, as a jangling, mesmerising aural continuum, which imposes a sort of order on the whole.)

Musical pleasures are widely enjoyed by humans, both in solitude and in company. Making music together can help rival groups to overcome even deep-seated rifts. It forges community. Furthermore, music's elemental power and rhythms are also effective as a means of reaching out to sad cases of people with mental disorders, as already noted. And music may possibly help the tiny number of ultra-disorientated patients with severe brain injuries, who struggle to gauge the passing of Time (a malady known as 'dyschronometria'). Tapping into temporal rhythms is a very fundamental way of tapping into temporality.

Human music, in all its variety, is among the quintessential sounds to be hard on Planet Earth these days. It's there, alongside the noise of winds, waves, weather, birdsong, wildlife…and the hubbub of human chatter, laughter, work, recreation, travel, and all forms of construction and destruction. Hearing sounds consecutively is a hallmark of life in consecutively unfolding Time and it's an essential skill to which human ears are attuned.

Living Unique Lives Together

People, as living entities of assembled materials originating in stardust, are without question completely Time-and-Space-specific. It's a point worth repeating. Lives are rooted. Individuals live in one specific era, on one specific planet, dependent upon one specific sun, in one specific galaxy, and in one specific cosmos.

Reincarnation beliefs do not contradict that proposition. If humans are able to live multiple lives, they do so sequentially in different epochs, not concurrently all at once. The same point about Time-specificity also applies to individuals with a considerably different and often very trying psychological condition, known as 'split-personality'. In this case, the sufferer has a seriously fractured sense of identity. Different personalities often vie for 'control'. Yet, the sufferer continues to live in one singular body, which follows the normal trajectory from birth to death, in one consecutively unfolding slab of Time.

Ultimate temporal and spatial rootedness imposes certain limitations upon human choices. Some things can't be changed. Exhortations to positive self-help do sometimes offer to teach *Ten Steps to Achieving Anything You Set Your Mind To*. The vibes are positive. Yet they don't, of course, really mean that people can achieve *anything*.

No one can stop Time or even alter its unfolding pace by a fraction. Hence, while some people might sincerely want to be younger—or older—they can't make themselves belong to an era which is not their own. There is scope for making drastic changes to one's personal image, to look either younger or older (as noted above in an earlier chapter). And some onlookers may be fooled.

Nonetheless, people still can't make themselves to have been born (say) one hundred years earlier than their actual birth-date. Or wait to be born one hundred years later, no matter how much they might prefer an epoch change.

Go-getters in today's aspirational culture may find such restrictions on Time-switching a bit irksome. But there are compensations. Temporal-spatial specificity is shared by absolutely everyone. In this matter, there is not one law for the rich and one for the poor.

Moreover, each individual has something unique. No one else can inhabit his or her specific conjunction of Time-Space. Twins, triplets and other children of multiple births come close. Yet, they are still birthed in sequence and occupy neighbouring spaces. And all other non-related people, born on the same day at the same moment of Time, still occupy their own segments of Time-Space and live separate lives. They are unlikely ever to meet *én masse*. Yet, if they did, they would quickly find that sharing a common birth-moment cannot ensure a shared outcome in terms of developing personalities and careers.

Individual life-chances do often fall into broadly detectable patterns. These can be influenced by socio-economic-cultural-ethnic circumstances, which can be identified and studied. Yet, each specific trajectory from birth to death remains unique. Thus, (for example) only one baby of all those born in the south German city of Ulm on 14 March 1879 grew up to become world-renowned.

True, some theoretical physicists take a different perspective on these matters. They speculate whether it is possible for the same mix of physical materials to recombine, at different moments and in different places across the cosmos, to form duplicates, not just of the human species, but of specific individuals. The argument, put in non-technical terms, states that: *In an infinite universe, anything that can happen will happen, and happen infinitely often.*

But is that proposition really correct? In a system where unidirectional Time is yoked with Space, there's scope for endless permutations in events that might happen. Another proto-moon might bump into Planet Earth. Yet no rule specifies that every option must happen, let alone infinitely often.

Those who speculate about exact cosmic replication suggest as an example—in the words of physicist Paul Davies in 1995—that in different eras and locations: 'There may be a trillion Albert Einsteins'. Countless physical replicas of one baby born in Ulm on 14 March 1879. What a bonus for the cosmic stock of genius. Certainly, it would be a big surprise to encounter an identical physical replica of Albert Einstein, whether at a distant point in the Milky Way galaxy—or down the road in Basingstoke. Yet, encountering a genetically identical twin is far from rediscovering one Time-Space-specific individual.

An Einstein, born in (say) the Virgo constellation at the far end of the Milky Way—or born down the road in Basingstoke—would have a different life from the baby born in Ulm in 1879. The lookalike would not have learned the same languages; would not have studied the same mathematics and physics; would not have worked as a junior official in the Bern Patent Office; would not have encountered the Swiss linguist Jost Winteler, who wrote on language 'relativity' and was a key intellectual mentor; and so on. In short, it was nurture as well as nature which turned the genetic Einstein into the famous *Einstein*.

Equally, in another place and epoch, the reception of his innovatory physics of relativity might also be quite different. Perhaps, in a future era in the constellation Virgo—or down the road at Basingstoke—the pronouncement from a genetic replica of Einstein that $E = mc^2$ would be greeted by fellow physicists with yawns of boredom and the remark: *why labour the obvious*?

While many things within this cosmos can recur (sunrise) or be replicated (photographs of sunrises), unidirectional Time-Space cannot. There was only one physicist Albert Einstein, with his own responses to his genetic inheritance, to his nurture at home and at school, and to his life experiences. Even an identical twin, born a moment before or after, would have been a different person. Incidentally, the real-life Einstein was fond of playing his violin, finding that through-Time music provided positive fuel for his scientific creativity. Rhythmic repetition can calm immediate worries and unleash deep thoughts.

All in all, Time and Space combine to offer a specific opportunity to each individual. *'It's your road…and yours alone…'*, as the Buddha once remarked. *'Others may walk it with you, but no one can walk it for you'*. Does that fate give grounds for optimism or pessimism? Either way, it's unavoidable.

A reminder of the specificity of unique lives does not, however, endorse a philosophy of untrammelled individualism. On the contrary. People are deeply located both physically and mentally, within their families, communities and wider networks. Those factors are equally Time-and-Space-specific.

Physically, each person constitutes one variant of the collective human genome, inherited at birth. Each child carries a genetic combination conferred by two parents. After that, individual bodies are affected by whatever upheavals, accidents or illnesses befall them, offset by whatever medical help is available. Some dramatic changes are productive (giving birth) while others are adverse. Between them, individual experiences can generate major and lifechanging outcomes, while other ailments may leave only minor scars.

Additionally, people have to cope with their personal 'microbiomes' or bacterial ecosystems in the gut (as scientists explain, unromantically). These inner worlds are affected by diet, contagious diseases, and each individual digestive system's capacity or inability to cope, which may potentially trigger major or minor allergies. People thus develop their own micro-biological destinies within a world of seething viruses, microbes and bacteria.

Surprises vie with predictabilities. Each human body is a historical construct, forged through Time. Each expresses how it is feeling via its body language— and uses facial expressions (as well as words) to signal directly.

Mentally and psychologically, too, individuals face all sorts of unexpected as well as expected experiences. And they process these with their own mindsets which have grown since childhood. As they develop, people are influenced by those who nurture them; by those who teach them; and by friends, families and communities around them. All operate, furthermore, within wider societies with their own traditions of moral, social, religious, political and legal expectations. (Which can be upheld or disputed). The result is that unique individuals, coming from a sociable species, grow within entire societies which have, in parallel, their own highly specific trajectories in Time-Space.

No baby can survive to adulthood without having received some nurturing care from others. That applies even to the small number of individuals who become, in later life, great loners. They were not always so. Incidentally, too, monasteries and other retreats for spiritual contemplation carefully set aside time for sociability as well as for silent prayers.

Many studies confirm the dense networks of social care that are required to raise a child successfully. As shown earlier in Ch. 2, deep mental, physical and psychological harms are caused by enforced isolation and a complete lack of appropriate mental stimulus and physical care. And the reverse holds good too. Growing humans need daily access to fresh air; natural light, especially sunshine; a balanced diet with lots of fresh produce; secure and warm housing; regular physical exercise; sustained mental stimulus; congenial company; freedom from anxiety; and the confidence of being loved (Shamingly, it's still a challenge to provide such basics for all).

These human requirements are stunningly obvious and are confirmed by millennia of experience. The upshot is that people are all individuals, with their own place in Time-Space. Yet, they do not grow in isolation. Hence (to adapt slightly a famous sermon by the seventeenth-century Anglican clergyman John Donne): *No one is an island, entire of itself. Everyone is a piece of the continent…*living in the same unidirectional Time-Space. As a result, it can be stated that: *Each individual is as unique as Einstein! But none grow alone!*

Rejecting Time Denial

At this point, it is worth pausing to confront a minority view among philosophers and physicists. It denies the existence not of Space but of Time. Instead, it urges that everything occurs within one 'tenseless' state, in which past, present and future coalesce. All things remain present: in an eternal here-and-now.

Here a crucial distinction needs to be made. There are religious and lifestyle teachers who urge people to experience moments of peaceful contemplation *as if* Time does not exist. That approach—found in many versions of Buddhism as well as in therapies of 'mindfulness'—seeks to set the mind free and to banish the fret of humdrum daily preoccupations.

Apparently simple systems of meditation and related exercises provide immensely helpful therapeutic techniques. And scientific research has identified an impressive range of personal benefits: from reducing stress and anxiety; to promoting well-being; improving attention spans; reducing blood pressure; and possibly reducing age-related memory loss. *What's not to like?*

So the following criticisms of Time Denial are not directed at the exponents of meditation. Far from denying temporal reality, they acknowledge its huge capacity to generate fret and anxiety. Their remedy is to provide physical and mental exercises which help people, psychologically, to step outside the pressures. In that way, practised meditators return to the busy world refreshed.

They are not denying Time but transcending its pressures. (Interestingly, too, rival styles of mindfulness embrace either slow or super-fast techniques. The customary pathway is slow and gentle, but a quick, short time-out, taking in and holding deep breaths, can also clear the head significantly. Either way, to repeat, people who meditate successfully are not denying Time but coping with it—a very different matter.)

Meanwhile, a very different viewpoint is held by a small number of speculative physicists and theorists. They hold Time itself to be an illusion. (T = zero) They do accept that there is a persistent and general belief, among most humans, that there is a process of temporal change. Yet, these critics deny its reality (*Arch-splitters!*).

The veteran British quantum physicist Julian Barbour is one who challenges normal assumptions. In *The End of Time* (1999), he argues that each nano-second is separate from all others. That is, Time is nothing but a staccato set of fragmented moments. The Swedish-American cosmologist Max Tegmark agrees but with a distinction. 'Time is not an illusion', he decides. 'But the flow of Time is. So is change. In Space-Time the future exists and the past doesn't disappear'. Each moment remains in an ever more capacious present.

Similar temporal scepticism was also voiced by some literary postmodernists (as noted in Ch. 4). Indeed when unfolding events generate major shocks—as did the fall of the Berlin Wall in November 1991—it's not uncommon for some onlookers to extend their surprise to query everything. Is the cosmos basically orderly? Or is it totally fragmented and in chaos?

Even in epochs of upheaval, however, it is interesting to note that many things continue as normal. 'Old-fashioned' clocks, calendars and diaries are not thrown aside but are still regularly bought and sold. And new-fangled technology in the form of mobile phones, with built-in timers, stop-watches, clocks, alarms, personal planners, and the capacity to film and replay through-Time videos (and more), continue to gain customers worldwide.

Most vocal of the temporal sceptics in the later twentieth century was Jacques Derrida, the intellectually impish Algerian-French literary scholar with a following on the USA campus circuit. For him, time has no independent reality. It is an idea, he declares, which 'belongs entirely to metaphysics' (That verdict was clearly not intended as a compliment).

What's more, Derrida boldly offered an alternative cosmic model. People live, he argues, not in Time but in an atemporal spatiality. By which he meant, an eternal present. People's thoughts about Time are, therefore, in his view, purely subjective and personal. These may have meanings for individuals but do not relate to any independent reality.

Derrida's alternative envisages a cosmic state of Space-without-Time. This perma-state is able to catch and filter information and ideas from all sorts of sources. And it then sifts through them to generate meanings. Thus impressions of other epochs can be gathered. But those other eras are nonetheless still illusory.

Adding specificity to his eternal Space-without-Time, Derrida named it *Khôra*—a term, borrowed from the Greek, meaning a space or site. Historically, it was used to indicate the extra-mural territory of a city-state. But, in philosophy, it was used by Plato to imagine, cryptically, a 'form-less' state between being and non-being. Possibly, an inspiration for the later Derridean model?

Then, in 1986, Derrida was challenged to be more specific. In response, he drew a quick sketch of a huge sieve-like grid. It would be lifted to the skies, like a giant radio receptor, collecting and filtering data to generate knowledge (The formlessness of Plato's *Khôra* was forgotten).

Impressed, an American architect, Peter Eisenman, offered to create a physical model of Derrida's vision. It was to be displayed in a Parisian public garden. But, alas for good intentions, the project to render philosophy visible was not completed. What's more, had the model been built, it would have eventually shown signs of weathering, acquiring moss and pigeon-droppings as well as perhaps graffiti—in other words, exhibiting the handiwork of Time. So Derrida's *Khôra* remains unconvincing—and architecturally elusive.

Denying the role of Time does, after all, fly in the face of the physics of Newton (who saw Time as an absolute) and its updating by Einstein (whose relativity theory yoked Time to Space in one absolute continuum). Spatiality needs a temporal medium in which to appear and to survive. So the Time-Space continuum cannot be un-coupled simply by saying that Time has been shattered.

Ordinary life experiences provide practical evidence. If temporal moments were not linked seamlessly, people could not listen to music unfolding sequentially (*Ta-ta-ta-tah!*). Sounds in fragmented Time would be and sound purely fragmented (*Bang! Silence*). Furthermore, if listeners, themselves exist only fragmentarily, they would have no through-Time hearing capacity; nor could fragmented musicians play sequentially. Non-Time entails non-music.

Nor could fragmented people be able to speak in unfolding sentences, let alone paragraphs. In a split-second, the only possible message would be a cry of *Oy* or *Help*, or some monosyllabic sound like *Aaaargh*. Moreover, within fragmented moments, there'd be no chance of getting even the briefest reply. All communications, and not just between humans, depend upon seamlessly flowing sequential temporality (The problems of understanding caused by disrupted mobile phone signals make the same point with a practical example).

Countless other instances spring to mind. Sexual encounters happen through-Time. Even the briefest of couplings (parodied as *Bang, Bang/Thank you ma'am*) take more than a single instant. And satisfactory sex generally requires people to 'go with the flow', to surrender to the ecstasy, and to build rhythmically towards a climax (Yes, yes, agrees a smiling D. H. Lawrence).

Furthermore, all other events in human life, trivial or significant, occur within unfolding Time. Birth, growth, ageing and death are the supreme instances. All these experiences apply to temporal sceptics as much as to everyone else. Death makes no special exceptions for Time-deniers.

Only by arguing that absolutely everything is an illusion can the Time-Space continuum be, theoretically, made to vanish. Yet, in that case, Algerian-French philosophers arguing for *Khôra*, must be illusory too. Total scepticism should logically yield the answer: *Don't know*. And even that verdict should be given with due hesitation: *Possibly*.

By the way, note that some Time and cosmic changes have elapsed even while writing and reading about these issues. Stepping off the world to halt everything is not an option. Demolishing Time is no easy matter, even in contemplation. There are a few jokes on that theme (some funnier than others). *Why did the shark eat the clock? Answer: Because it wanted to kill the time.* Hmmm... Neither the would-be humourist nor the shark believed in *Khôra*.

Instead, humans are stuck with Time and in it, while it inheres within them too. It is constantly unfolding and takes everything in Space with it. And it has already been doing just that for millennia, throughout the lifespan of this cosmos. Here an old Chinese dictum gives wise advice to stop fretting and to try a different perspective: '*Enjoy yourself! It's later than you think...*'

Embracing Temporal Complexity

Returning to re-examine the key dimensions of temporality, it is instructive to see how they interlock and interact. As already noted, Time does not just have one characteristic which it always presents to all humans. It's intricate. Cue song: *'It's tricky to rock a rhyme, to rock a rhyme that's right on time'*. Yet, the major characteristics of temporality can be identified.

Continuity provides underlying ballast. It gives staying power and cohesion to the entire Time-Space continuum. When disruptive events occur, all cosmic operating systems do not automatically shatter. Depending on the precise circumstances, elements will regroup and try to restabilise. So it will take something truly epic to end the existence of the entire cosmos. Continuity thus provides a significant default factor, but it does not operate alone.

Just as Space's three dimensions of height, length and depth combine seamlessly, so do those of Time. Hence, in certain circumstances, continuity blends into very slow micro-transformation.

Evolutionary and small incremental changes of all kinds provide steady temporal momentum. But it can always be asked: how slow is slow? There is no hard-and-fast rule. Context is all. Hence, the slowest of very slow changes can sink back into apparent deep continuity, as just noted.

Nevertheless, at the other end of the scale, accelerating micro-momentum can eventually become something much more drastic. Tectonic plates provide an apt geological example. The San Andreas Fault stretches for some one thousand two hundred kilometres (seven hundred and fifty miles) close to the California coast in the USA. It marks a geological process known as 'a transform'. To the west, the Pacific Plate is moving slowly northwards; and to the east, the North American Plate is shifting south. The contradictory movements are in tension along the entire fault line. Its greatest upheaval to date occurred in 1857 when the Fort Tejon Earthquake in southern California produced eight hundred and eighty cm [twenty-nine feet] of movement in one jolting moment. All seemed calm but then many micro-movements made one colossal Earth-jump.

Within human societies, revolutionary upheavals and radical disjunctures may similarly appear to come unexpectedly 'out of the blue'. But they too almost invariably have long pre-histories of escalating tensions. That state of affairs does not apply in absolutely all cases. The vulnerability of Planet Earth to cosmic shocks (such as meteor strikes) means that some great upheavals happen stochastically—that is, with a purely random probability. In other cases, however, internal upheavals spring from prior internal tensions, which may explode to generate revolutionary upheavals.

Such drastic moments of accelerated transformation may well have a colossal long-term impact. Yet, their fever-pitch is hard to sustain. And the powers of continuity and micro-change immediately rally to restore some form of order, after even the most seismic of upheavals.

Revolutionary turbulence does not, then, bring a halt to the powerful dimensions of continuity and micro-change. Yet, equally, continuity and gradualism do not have the capacity to banish drastic upheavals. All these different dimensions combine, making a 'braided' cosmic history of many interlocking strands.

Thus is formed what physicists call the 'non-sleeping universe'. The ever-adapting and omnipotent mix of continuity (T/C), evolutionary momentum (T/E) and revolutionary turbulence (T/R) provides cohesion *and* onward movement *and* inner tensions, all at once. It produces a state of affairs that is both utterly surprising and utterly normal. *'Time marches on', with its own inner tensions and dynamism. And with Time, in constant step, goes Space…*

Summary Way Station to End the Journey's Second Stage: Experiencing Time-Space in all its Dimensions

Here then is the great cosmic framework of linked temporality and spatiality within which all human experiences occur—both individually and collectively.

Metaphorically, the dynamo of Time can be interpreted as something akin to a form of super-energy. It began (in this history of this universe) with the cosmic Big Bang. And now it propels everything onwards, working out the explosive afterlife of that initial seismic event. The whole constitutes a cosmic moving system, with an overall coherence but with a distinctly bumpy ride.

Understanding the changing yet interlocking combinations of the dimensions of continuity, slow momentum and revolutionary turbulence throws key strategic light upon the overall journey, as well as illuminates many staging posts along the way.

Needless to say, cosmologists and students of Earth history often criticise one another and are criticised in turn. Yet, their continuing research and debates are vital for the collective journey. It's not a good idea for humans to navigate through the complexities of Time-Space with faulty maps and erroneous information.

Really so? Yes: Time-Space is no illusion. Temporality unfolds steadily from past to future, taking cosmic spatiality and all human life with it. Survival in a turbulent universe is a serious business. Breathe deeply…scan the stars…study the way ahead…tread carefully…experience life to the full…and heed the rhythms of continuity/change/turbulence, within what the classical Greeks imaginatively termed: *the music of the spheres.* Humans are in Time-Space for the long haul. And they are travelling within a moving system: *'Tomorrow, and tomorrow, and tomorrow/Creeps in this petty pace from day to day/To the last syllable of recorded Time'.*

Unique Lives in Time-Space

Davies, P. (1995) *Are We Alone? Implications of the Discovery of the Extraterrestrial Life.*
Green, J. (2023) *The Possibility of Life: Searching for Kinship in the Cosmos.*
Unger, R. M., Smolin, L. (2014) *The Singular Universe and the Reality of Time.*

Time Transcendence

Fontana, D. (1992) *The Meditator's Handbook: A Comprehensive Guide to Eastern and Western Meditation Techniques.*
Tunis, R. (2017) *The Handbook of Meditation: Discovery of Internal Happiness.*

Scientific and Philosophic Varieties of Time Denial

Barbour, J. (1999) *The End of Time: The Next Revolution in Our Understanding of the Universe.*
Hodge, J. (2007) *Derrida on Time.*
McTaggart, J. M. E. (1908) 'The Unreality of Time', *Mind,* 17, repr. in his
Broad, C. D. (ed) (1927; 1968) *The Nature of Existence*, Vol. 2, Ch. 33.

Arthur, R. T. W. (2019) *The Reality of Time Flow: Local Becoming in Modern Physics.*

Smolin, L. (2014) *Time Reborn: From the Crisis in Physics to the Future of the Universe.*

Time-Out: 2—Laughing

Time for another moment of Time-out? The journey goes in stages, so it's worth having a rest now and then, to recharge batteries.

Laughing is another great way of stepping temporarily off the treadmill of Time and being-busy. Expressing mirth aloud works as a mechanism for filling the body with feel-good serotonins and it relaxes all sorts of tensions of which people are often unaware.

It's especially good to share laughter. Try the 'laughing game', when safely away from work and serious business. Find a friend or group of friends. Sit round in a circle. And, without speaking, try to make everyone laugh.

It can take more than a few moments to get going. But, once launched, the laughter is contagious. Everyone rolls around, forgetting that the laughter is about nothing in particular. Just pure good laughter.

And if no friends are handy for joint laughing, try laughing aloud when alone—and listening seriously to the noise. It's a strange thing. Laughing people release their breath in short gasps. And they aspirate with each breath. Ha-ha-ha-ha-ha!

Then, if people grimace and move the voice up the scale, it comes out as: he-he-he-he-he! Or open the mouth widely in a large O, so that it comes out as a belly laugh: ho-ho-ho-ho-ho! Or even try a sardonic put-down sort of laugh, when indicating superiority about someone else's blunder: that needs a slow emphatic laugh, in a jeering style: har-har-har!

Most oddly, too, the mouth can be kept almost closed, and the sound is produced from the lowest vocal register. Hurh-hurh-hurh-hurh-hurh! (Once, when having breakfast in a quiet hotel, I turned in surprise at the sound of a low growling from the table behind me. Were some wild animals on the loose? But no. It turned out to be a large family, who were all giving the same exceptionally low, growling laughs. It set me wondering whether laughing styles run in families. A great topic for future research…)

Feeling better now? This exercise has no deeper meaning than to distract people from the passing of Time, in order to regroup energies. But now's the moment to get back to reading…while bearing in mind that sharing laughter is a special human attribute which can be used to laugh at people as well as with them. Ha-he-ho-har-hurh!

So laughter can be kind, jolly and pleasant—or, at times, unkind, sardonic and unpleasant. That marked variability is part of the trickiness of humans and their relationships. Things are not always straightforward, to say the least. …So attention now turns to exploring the strategies that people have devised to map together the human journey through Time.

**Part 3
Mapping the Journey**

Chapter 11
Coping with Deceptions

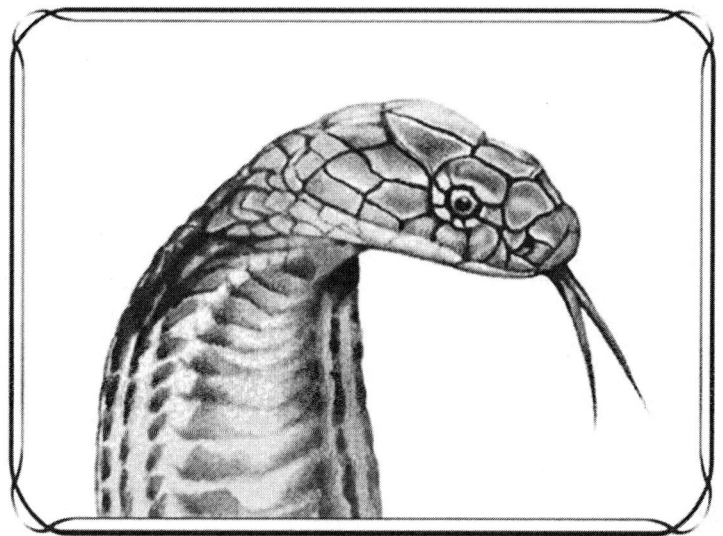

Chapter 11 starts the final stage of the journey—which focuses on tracking the human story—by spotting both obstacles to knowledge and mechanisms for coping

Taking Nothing for Granted

Time is the pulse-beat of the cosmos (*again!*) Yet simultaneously, Time is deceptive: *it flies; …no, it drags; …it keeps its secrets; …no, it always tells… What does it all mean?* Tracking the human story successfully through the turbulence of Time-Space is necessary for securely continuing human survival. Yet, the route to knowledge has many pitfalls. So attention now turns to the challenge of finding and interpreting good evidence to understand what is going on. How can truth be detected among the potential for errors and deceptions? It's a great question, and not just for scientists, historians, detectives, lawyers, fraud investigators, explorers, navigators, and moralists, but for everyone.

Of course, it's worth recalling that not all errors are equally erroneous—or equally malicious in intent. Some 'polite lies' are offered for social convenience (as discussed below). And some outright 'untruths' may be well-meant. As a result, words, even if spoken or written with the greatest solemnity, cannot always be taken absolutely literally.

People collectively are ingenious, crafty animals. Moreover, the capacity to deceive is not confined to *homo sapiens*. One animal tactic is to feign dead (*play possum*) to avoid catching the attention of predators. Another option is to use decoy strategies, trying to lead aggressors away from a nest. Or there is a bluff. Some animals try to appear more physically alarming than they actually are. 'Startling' actions include bright displays of warning coloration or skunk-like unleashing of unpleasant smells. These mechanisms are instinctive attempts at deceiving or deterring enemies in the interest of survival.

Among humans, lies and deceit are used with great versatility. They can be deployed in self-defence, for example, to deceive an enemy in warfare. Yet they are also used, consciously and aggressively, in daily life—whether to gain an advantage over fellow humans—or simply to enjoy the fun of a successful hoax. Fakers have a long and lively history. They take advantage of the human capacity to be deceived, through misplaced trust. Yet, fakery also engenders the countervailing human capacity for critical scepticism.

Getting to grips with the human story therefore means staying alert at all times (to stress again this crucial point). Witnesses may lie or be confused. Ask lawyers and judges. Venerable objects presented for sale may be fraudulent mimics. Ask any reliable antique dealer. Unanticipated offers of money, no matter how slickly presented, need to be double-checked. Ask the victims of confidence tricksters. Financial returns can be manipulated or concealed. Ask the Fraud Squad. The 'obvious' clues at a murder scene may be red herrings. Ask detectives or crime mystery-writers. An apparently ardent lover may be an unrepentant two-timer. Ask divorce lawyers and angry ex-partners.

A degree certificate may be phoney. Ask officials who try to close down fake universities. Plausible but erroneous information circulates daily. Ask professional fact-checkers. A pretend-sincere politician may daily lie and deceive, in order to gain political advantage. Ask the voters. In sum, not everything is as it seems. Ask any good magician or card-sharper.

Therefore, whenever anything significant is at stake, everything should be tested. Nothing should be taken for granted. One great constant is the human capacity to add to 'turbulence' by lies and deceptions. Yet, another equally great countervailing constant is human scepticism, and the capacity to build, test and confirm secure foundations for knowledge.

Being Aware of 'Sweet Nothings' and 'Polite Lies'

It's no surprise to learn that not every spoken and written word is intended to be taken absolutely literally. Conventional salutations are not made on oath. They have evolved to ease the flow of conversation, without requiring deep thought. The greeting 'Good morning!' expects a reply like: 'Good morning!' or 'Hi there!'. It would be considered excessive to respond, even if truthfully: 'No, it's an absolutely dreadful morning. I'm deeply in debt; my dog is seriously ill; my partner has just run away with my best friend; and my planet's on fire!'

So people normally recognise and follow the conventions of their communities and their era. They know that not all letters signed 'Yours sincerely' are necessarily sincerely meant and that not everything within a missive signed 'Yours truly' is automatically true.

These provisos apply to all written documents whether from past or present times. Human communications include elements of conventionality, which are taken for granted on all sides. Literalist interpretations in all circumstances can be seriously misleading.

Even when political/social attitudes are fast changing, many people continue to speak and write in traditional terms, especially if there is a system of censorship. A few radicals may publicly canvass alternatives. Yet many people cautiously express support for existing ways until they collapse. It's called paying *lip service*. That practice means that unpopular rulers can be shocked and surprised by the arrival of a serious political challenge. They had been sheltered from the changing tide of opinion by conventional usages. People were constrained by fear and/or caution from expressing their views frankly.

Another restraining factor is the desire not to hurt someone's feelings. That kindly impulse can lead people to state something that they do not really believe. Such deceitful statements are known as 'polite' or 'white' lies; while 'little' lies are known as 'fibs'. In the idle talk of lovers, these imprecisions are also termed 'sweet nothings': they may sound sweet but cannot be relied upon. Indeed, in the words of an American ballad, a false-hearted lover *'will tell you more lies/Than the cross-ties on the railroad/Or the stars in the skies'*.

All untruths, viewed strictly, constitute moral lapses. Yet, 'polite' lies are usually given social leeway because the motive is not to cause harm to another. If someone asks, with a joyful smile: 'What do you think of my new hat?' or 'my new sneakers?', the questioner expects to hear 'Terrific', not 'Terrible'. And when a love-partner, after energetic love-making, asks tenderly: 'How was it for you?', it's clear that a shared affirmation is expected (*Mmmmm*... (appreciatively)), not an impartial critique: 'Well, your kisses are a bit sloppy and your breath smells...'

There is thus a considerable grey area, especially in spoken language. Sometimes half-truths or concealment by omission are acceptable in a specific context. They form part of the subtle variations of language use, where corrective cues are also provided by vocal tones and body language.

Moreover, humans often convey oblique messages via humour, irony, puns, and sexual innuendo. The word-play is part of the fun. In response, those on the receiving end of oblique messages may laugh, or groan noisily, or purse their lips with disapproval...or just look bewildered.

Other notable forms of non-literal communication include rhetorical exaggeration, bluffing, strident complaints, or over-the-top threats. In these cases, words can be used for wooing, deceiving, distracting, and/or acting aggressively. Working out how seriously to take them is hard enough at any given moment—and even more so when applied to historical evidence.

Context is always vital. To take an example from medical practice, doctors are trained in interpreting requests for advice from patients who ask: 'Doctor, I'm not going to die, am I?'. If the case is not immediately terminal and/or if the question has been asked many times already, it can be fine to reply: 'There, there, don't worry; we'll look after you'. Conversely, it's not helpful to state curtly: 'Well, yes; everyone dies sooner or later'. So doctors and healthcare workers have to make constant judgement calls. When is soothing reassurance needed or when is truth required, to be delivered with appropriate tact?

Philosophically and morally, it can well be debated whether it ever right to tell a lie. In daily life, meanwhile, it is very difficult to survive for many years while speaking and writing only the absolute and literal truth. That observation applies to even the most shiningly honest person. Some imprecision and prevarication are unavoidable. Thus many stoic people say 'I'm fine' when they aren't. And polite people say 'Good to meet you' even when they don't mean it.

Matters, however, become difficult and even dangerous when humans step beyond social conventions in order deliberately to take advantage of others. Conscious deceivers appear in all societies, although they are probably never in the majority. Annoyingly, however, their lies and frauds are most likely to succeed when they closely mimic normal good behaviour. For that reason, really polished liars are very hard to spot.

The upshot (to repeat yet again!) is that people should stay alert. They should check to see when minor 'white lies' have escalated into something more serious. Beyond a certain point, fraud becomes a matter for the law; and, theologically, for repentance, though hardened offenders are usually slow to see the errors of their ways. Most songs about lying take the victim's viewpoint but a few celebrate perpetrators. So the Rollins Band's unrepentant *Liar* (1994) ends cheerfully: *'I'll lie again and again/And I'll keep lying/I promise'*. But, confusingly, a liar's vow cannot invariably be relied upon either. *Vigilance!*

Spotting Historical Fakes and Forgeries

Evidence from the past, whether of recent vintage or from long ago, can also be faked or forged. All who study the collective human story go to great lengths to check the validity of all doubtful information and its sources.

Accuracy is paramount. When, therefore, professional historians do make public mistakes, there is an instant furore. In April 1983, Hugh Trevor-Roper initially verified as genuine the fake *Hitler Diaries/Hitler-Tagebücher*, before later changing his mind. Such a blunder from a former Regius [royally appointed] Professor of Modern History at Oxford University caused genuine shock. The satirical magazine *Private Eye* quickly renamed him 'Hugh VeryRopey'. And it updated his noble title from Lord Dacre (pron. Daker) to 'Lord Facre'. His mistake was a matter of public as well as academic interest.

Worse still, there are sometimes cases of professional researchers who themselves consciously perpetrate fraud. Such actions are outlawed in absolutely all fields of study. Whenever professionals in positions of trust are discovered to have behaved fraudulently, then public confidence in all forms of professional qualification tends to be undermined. Can anyone be trusted?

An extraordinary case in 2002 led to an unexpected denouement. One 'Stephanie Harvey' referred in print to a previously unknown 1862 letter from an 'up-and-coming' Russian novelist Fyodor Dostoevsky. In it, he detailed his London encounter with the eminent author Charles Dickens, then at the height of his fame. No one knew that the two had ever met (And, in fact, they never did). The literary world was all aflutter with piqued surprise and interest.

Nevertheless, one scholar remained unconvinced. And in 2013, after dogged detective work, Eric Naiman, an American expert on Slavic language and literature, revealed that 'Stephanie Harvey' was the pseudonym of a freelance researcher named Arnold (A. D.) Harvey (b. 1947). And there was more. Harvey's invented reference to Dostoevsky's letter was but one foray in a career of writing under invented names. Using different pseudonyms, he both praised and attacked the works of A. D. Harvey. In other words, he created his own media buzz. Harvey seemingly felt himself to be an academic outsider and he enjoyed trying to fool the experts. For a time, he did. Yet the world, eventually, was totally unamused; and Harvey's reputation plummeted.

Motivations for playing fast and loose with historical evidence are very varied. Some deceivers have personal and psychological axes to grind as, it seems, did Harvey. Others try to use forged documents or fabricated material items to bolster their arguments. Their sense of their own intellectual 'rightness' has unfortunately led them into culpable wrong-doing.

Alternative motivations include obvious ones, such as a desire for fame and/or for money. Both can potentially be gained by revealing to the startled world an apparently authentic masterpiece that is both unexpected and highly prized. Yet, historical detectives are getting cannier, and the techniques available to test the authenticity of all manner of material objects are ever more effective.

Most dangerous are those deceivers, who fabricate evidence for ideological purposes, especially when they appeal to audiences who are willing to be deceived. One prominent case is that of David Irving, a leading Holocaust denier. He was found legally guilty of forging and misrepresenting historical evidence. His crime was not his support for Hitler's political outlook (After all, various eminent thinkers supported fascism in the 1930s). Instead, Irving was found to have misused evidence to support a statement about the past which cannot rationally be upheld.

Thus, abundant records and documents, amassed by many researchers, refute Irving's case that the Holocaust simply 'did not happen'. Those who continue to make that claim are ideologues, polemicists, propagandists, and *provocateurs*— arguing against, not with, valid historical evidence.

By no means do all experts agree on the nature and details of Nazi extermination policies. There are continuing debates—and rightly so—because historical detection thrives on questioning and reasoned argument. Yet, over the long-term, a core of authenticated evidence has been generated. So the continuing scholarly debates operate within increasingly agreed parameters.

Against such accumulating evidence, it was striking that David Irving was prepared to undertake costly litigation (including an appeal against the first verdict against him) to protect his research reputation. He really wanted the badge of historical validity for Holocaust Denial. His failure was accordingly a momentous occasion. A boundary had been publicly drawn.

After all, there are qualitative differences between historical research and imaginative fiction. Holocaust Denial has been shown as falling into the latter category. People *én masse* cannot test all surviving evidence from the past. Instead, they rely upon reputable experts. So it is vital that false ones be unmasked.

This specific issue became in the 1990s a matter for some discussion between historians and their postmodernist critics (introduced earlier in Ch. 4). It took a grim slice of real history to test the theory. Postmodernist thinkers stressed the subjectivity of writings about history. Yet, they did not wish to align themselves with Irving and his followers. There are, after all, grounds for stating that one version of history is more reliable than another one. And for deciding, after consulting the evidence that some versions are fabricated.

Taking a stand against Holocaust Denial did then (and does today) imply therefore that accounts of the past are not *purely* subjective. They are not created solely by individual researchers' whims and wishes. Though the task is challenging, humans can and do study past and present human trackways over the long term; and they can and do establish reliable knowledge.

That said, very ingrained beliefs, in all fields of study, can persist for very long periods (The power of continuity). Thus, persistent flat-Earthers can still ask physicists whether the sun doesn't really revolve around the Earth. And creationist supporters of 'Intelligent Design' can always ask biologists incredulously whether humans are really descended from ape ancestors.

Yet, experts don't spend too much time refuting arguments already refuted many times. Debates move into new territory as evidence accumulates, and old debates fade, though not necessarily quietly.

Above all, issues that arouse strong emotions and beliefs (whether political or religious) often prompt lengthy controversies. Thus, disputes over the causes and outcomes of wars and civil conflicts often simmer for years (as further explored in Ch. 13). Such controversies offer special scope to practitioners of disinformation and fakers of evidence. And they are aided by the readiness of partisans to welcome all apparently authentic support for their causes. The message therefore remains, in life as in historical debates: *Vigilance!* (*Again!*)

Uncovering Factoids/False 'Facts'

Complications are further multiplied when some apparently long-established nuggets of truthful information turn out, when cross-checked, to be deceitful 'factoids'. That useful noun was coined in 1973 by the American author Norman Mailer. He was then writing about Marilyn Monroe, the incandescent American film star about whom myths and legends continually gather.

Factoids are false 'facts' which have gained, over the years, the appearance of truth. They may have been created by outright invention or, more subtly, have gained plausibility via repetition. People who recycle factoids are thus not knowingly spreading lies, even if, inadvertently, that is what they are doing.

Knowledge is thereby being pushed in the wrong direction. In the most immediate sense, the damage done is relatively minor. But factoids, which often encapsulate familiar and culturally-embedded ideas (about social classes, different ethnic groups, and the so-called gender divide), still need to be identified and errors corrected.

Take one example from mid-eighteenth-century England. In September 1752, there were, allegedly, popular riots when calendar reform was implemented. The current dates had become out of synchronisation with the seasons. So parliament decreed a collective update of the calendar, to achieve an accurate alignment. In 1752, the dates jumped directly from Wednesday, 2 September to Thursday, 14 September. Cue popular complaints: *'Give us back our Eleven Days!'*. Time had been stolen. It sounded plausible. Some later historians even described the riots in graphic detail.

But, in reality, there was no civil disorder. Popular grumbling, yes. However, intensive research in local archives across the entire country found no evidence of calendar-reform riots. They were purely mythic, based on later assumptions about how the 'ignorant' masses would surely respond. And then the myth, through repetition, became a factoid, encouraging a condescending attitude towards the ignorant 'plebs'.

It follows that, if people are asked to explain or to respond to some surprising nugget of intriguing information, they are always well advised to ask first whether the said nugget is actually true. Or whether it is being circulated by someone with a vested interest? No point in explaining or responding to something that is not true. There is a lot of misinformation and disinformation around, especially on the worldwide web. Some items are circulated with intent to deceive; but many are also casual errors, gaining respectability by repetition.

For example, another factoid, in this case relating to women's history, has gained a very long afterlife, even though it has repeatedly been exposed as false. In 1784, a German historian declared that almost nine-and-a-half million witches had been put to death in Europe and colonial America, during the years of the so-called 'witch craze' from the sixteenth to the early eighteenth centuries. And, over time, the figure was familiarised as a neat nine million.

Actually, the true figure of witch-burnings is not known with any precision. Witch-prosecutions varied from region to region, and from year to year. Record-keeping was also patchy. Nonetheless, careful investigations by many researchers suggest a more plausible total of between forty thousand to a hundred thousand trials at the height of the 'craze', bearing in mind that only about half of all trials ended in actual burnings. Well short of one million, let alone nine.

Animosity against women (and a relatively smaller number of men) accused of witchcraft was undoubtedly vehement. Yet, it was also episodic. And, gradually, popular belief in the literal role of 'black magic' was abating, which helps to explain why the European witchcraft trials eventually came to an end.

Does it matter that the nine-million factoid long held sway and is sometimes still repeated? In the first place, having more accurate information permits a more reasoned assessment of the persecution of alleged witches. And secondly, wild exaggerations make such procedures appear as a standard part of social life. One pioneering American feminist in the nineteenth century, Matilda Gage, embraced the nine-million total as evidence of the perennial victimhood of women, and, for good measure, as a sign of male assault upon female pagan powers of sorcery (Men accused of black magic were omitted in this version).

Thereafter, the nine-million factoid was cited by many feminists, though Gage's celebration of female paganism was quietly sidelined. In the later twentieth century, for example, the radical American feminist Andrea Dworkin added her authority to the view that all nine million tried as 'witches' were women and that every prosecution led to an ignominious death.

Exercises in comparative victimhood (the *most persecuted group ever*) are not helpful, especially when based on inaccurate data. The factoid can be cited to encourage women everywhere to feel aggrieved. And it can also be invoked to downplay criticisms of twentieth-century genocides (*not as bad as the witch-burnings*).

Absolutely all persecutions, however, must be unequivocally deplored. There should be no hierarchy of victimhood. Furthermore, today's campaigners on the ground, who try to stop continuing accusations of witchcraft in some parts of the world, argue strongly that real understanding, not lurid rhetoric, provides the best hope of spotting and defusing the underlying social tensions.

When factoids are weaponised, they can be dangerous. They appear to carry with them the weight of history, making a nugget of information to be thrown at all unbelievers.

Various other factoids arrive, flourish briefly, and then disappear. Many persist modestly for long periods until they are refuted. But their numbers are continually being augmented—despite the best efforts of fact-checkers who try to debunk them. As a result, it's not possible to track the global stock of factoids. New myths enter circulation as fast as old ones die or are disproved.

Again, the moral is *yet more vigilance!* If some nugget of information seems too exaggerated, or too 'convenient', for some argument, then its veracity should immediately be challenged. It may be a factoid, claiming to be part of 'common memory' but actually being a fraudulent or accidental mis-memory.

Summoning that critical spirit, the great Victorian spinner of detective tales, Conan Doyle, put a wry warning into the mouth of his super-detective, Sherlock Holmes. If something seems too utterly straightforward for words, then be sceptical and cross-check before simply ratifying: '*There is nothing more deceptive than an obvious fact*'.

Noting also Practical Limits to Deception

Creative imagination, constructively used, is a wonderful human attribute. It contributes to the making of knowledge, especially when interwoven with the cool rational faculties that also characterise the 'thinking ape'. However, creativity, when misapplied to propagating serious lies and calculated deceit, becomes socially as well as morally and legally problematic.

True, there are exceptions such as when disinformation is used as a valid tactic in a just war to mislead a dangerous enemy. There is a greater good at stake. Deception can also be used to spring a surprise upon opponents or to lure them into making a false move themselves. Such manoeuvres have affinities with the canny feints and dodges during card games and competitive sports.

Generally, however, serious lies and chronic deceits harm the normal workings of society. They undermine mutual trust. There's thus a collective social loss when criminal fraudsters don't put their undoubted ingenuity and persistence to better and more constructive uses.

Practical limits, however, do operate to provide some protection against malefactors. Ordinary life could not function if all people and all organisations lied systematically at all times. Social trust would not just be undermined, it would entirely evaporate. For that reason, criminal gangs enforce strict rules upon their own members. They need to be able to trust one another (Summarised by the old adage: 'Honour among thieves').

Liars and fraudsters, in fact, rely upon general conventions of social honesty, which they twist to their own ends. On one occasion, I remember teasing a telephone cold-caller, who offered a large sum of money, if, in advance, I supplied full details of my address, passport and bank account. Usually, I halt such calls at once. But, on this occasion, I gave random answers in a serious tone. After a while, the caller said, reproachfully: 'Wait a minute, you are lying to me'. I agreed but asked what was wrong with matching lies for lies. The fraudster immediately ended the call (I lost my notional 'millions').

Interestingly, that exchange reminded me of a dictum by Niccolò Machiavelli, the Italian theorist of political deceit and *Realpolitik*. He once remarked that: 'It is a double pleasure to deceive the deceiver'. In fact, my brief exchange with the fraudster did not give me much pleasure, though it has yielded an amusing anecdote.

Nonetheless, this encounter helps to make an important point. Fraudsters expect everyone else to behave honourably. They are parasites within normal society. They don't want to change the customary ways that things are done or to subvert all morals. On the contrary. They seek instead to gain personal advantage by relying upon everyone else to follow the social rules and norms. And, fortunately for social cohesion, criminal fraudsters are a minority of the total population, even if an annoying one.

Further to underline the practical limits to universal lies and deceit, imagine a world in which all shopkeepers deceitfully charge the wrong prices for goods; all bartenders serve the wrong drinks (or serve none at all); all bus drivers advertise that they will drive north but then, without explanation, drive south; all umpires lie about the results of sporting contests; all map-makers deliberately bodge their maps; all police officers arrest citizens indiscriminately; all cars signal that they will turn right but then drive left or straight ahead; all tax officials issue erroneous tax assessments; all bankers refuse to release funds from bank accounts and decline to honour credit cards.

And (continuing the fantasy) all teachers teach outrageous errors as truth; all surgeons are told to amputate the wrong limbs; all patients give doctors false information; all doctors issue fake prescriptions; all lawyers regularly lie to clients; all juries deceitfully free the guilty and condemn the innocent; all religious leaders profess beliefs that they do not hold; all weather forecasters invent their predictions; all official news bulletins are knowingly deceitful; all lovers are unfaithful; and…all politicians lie.

Well, any or all of such behaviours *might* happen. Sometimes, obviously enough, some do.

However, if all those malicious and deceitful actions occur all the time, not only would ordinary citizens be tearing their hair but entire communities could not co-exist successfully. Social order is predicated upon a modicum of routine trust. The greater the breakdown in people's confidence in their fellow humans, the more chaotic, ill-disciplined and dangerous their society would become (*Trust is a great communal capital good*).

Summary Next Step: Becoming Ever More Vigilant!

Not for nothing do laws, customs, cultural expectations and religious/moral injunctions stress the importance of honesty, reliability and good faith. And not for nothing are there enforcement mechanisms, both legal and societal. Those forces cannot halt all criminal deceit and misbehaviour. They do, however, express the strong human need for a prevailing framework of order.

Similarly, laws and social conventions stress the importance of accurate exchanges of knowledge. Again, fraudulent errors and undetected factoids will at times remain lurking within the whole. But every deviation from accuracy has the potential to cause harm.

Humanity's expanding stock of knowledge provides the road-map that tracks the collective human journey from past to future and furnishes the information that is needed along the route. And since the elements of turbulence will always spring surprises, there is no knowing in advance precisely what know-how will be needed and which errors will matter.

Travelling with flawed data is like navigating with a faulty map and compass. Immediate mistakes may not be noticeable. Yet, before long, problems will multiply.

Hence, the a constant need to detect and reject fake knowledge. And to improve the quantity and quality of what is known for sure. Knowledge is not only passed down the generations but is also constantly accumulated/ tested/ revised/ updated/ and expanded.

Sometimes commentators claim that humanity is now living in an age of *post-truth*. Is that actually true? The answer is NO. There has to be a core of truth in order to be able to categorise some things as lies.

Today, people are certainly witnessing the circulation of disinformation and misinformation at unprecedented rates of velocity, thanks to social media. Accordingly, vigilant citizens have to become: *ever more vigilant! If in doubt, double-check! If still in doubt, then treble-check!* Since some tricky humans are prone to lies and deceptions, it's essential that societies are equally primed to take countervailing action. Expect turbulence! Look at the stars…but also watch your steps closely! *Checking the route map throughout the journey is never a waste of Time!*

Deception in the Animal World

Edmunds, M. (1974) *Defence in Animals: A Survey of Anti-Predator Defences.*
Mitchell, R. W., Thompson, N. S. (eds) (1986) *Deception: Perspectives on Human and Non-Human Deceit.*

The Spectrum of Lies

Leslie, I. (2011) *Born Liars: Why We Can't Live Without Deceit.*
Saul, J. M. (2018) *Lying, Misleading and What is Said: An Exploration in Philosophy of Language and in Ethics.*

Fraud and Deception

Park, R. (2000) *Voodoo Science: The Road from Foolishness to Fraud.*
Thomas, D. (2014) *Beggars, Cheats and Forgers: A History of Frauds through the Ages.*
Whaley, B. (2007) *Stratagem: Deception and Surprise in War.*

Holocaust Denial

Jensen, O., Terry, N. (2017) *Holocaust and Genocide Denial: A Contextual Perspective.*
Lipstadt, D. E. (1994) *Denying the Holocaust: The Growing Assault on Truth and Memory.*

Chapter 12
Generating Shared Memory-Markers

Chapter 12 examines a parallel feature of human behaviour, offsetting potential deceptions by generating shared memory-markers, which underpin wider grids of knowledge.

Relying on Shared Information

Time is constructive...it lays good foundations...it builds... Well, not always! Yet, despite obstacles, people generally rely on stable points of reference in their daily lives and share those with others. Such knowledge markers provide continuity. They work to offset the disruptive impact of turbulence. And both formal and informal grids of shared knowledge provide a pool of stored resources, upon which people can draw and to which they can contribute.

In that context, current technological advances are increasing the chances that high-speed cooperative computing can greatly enhance the power of human cognition and, with that, creativity. It's another big step in the human pooling of knowledge and skills for collective survival. But…as already argued, every big step needs to be matched by big steps in appropriate surveillance and communal control. Techno-advances thus need to be matched by ever-greater advances in techno-vigilance.

Collective knowledge grids are supplied and reinforced from many sources. These include family training and values; book-learning throughout the educational process; craft-lore, learned by watching and doing; religious and moral teachings; local community and peer-group attitudes; and each individual's experiences. These components mesh (and sometimes contradict each other). They are learned throughout a lifetime and are sometimes forgotten too (as acknowledged above in Ch. 2 and 3).

Various categories of information that persist through Time have already been noted. They include the principles of mathematics; the laws of science (about which humans can always learn more); agreed calendars for counting the days; and established languages, which combine their constant grammatical structures with flexibly changing usages.

Here attention turns not to the sum of all human knowledge (an impossibly mammoth task) but to the creation of basic markers, such as agreed names and dates. These not only locate people in Time-Space but are mutually exchanged with fellow humans. Sharing a grid of familiar data about everyday living makes community living possible. The cosmos is huge but locally not unknowable. Cue many songs: '*Reach out of the darkness…*'

Noting Stability in (Most) Personal Names

Names of people provide one major source of continuity. Of course, these can be changed, officially or unofficially. And names are frequently embellished, with nicknames and diminutives. But it is not customary for nomenclature to be changed often. And, new names, if adopted, are not expected to be revised again in a hurry. The social presumption favours continuity.

People are supposed to be who they purport to be, yesterday, today and tomorrow. No one remains without a personal identifier. And most people accept their names as utterly familiar accompaniments to daily life.

Hence, in historic cases, where captive people's identifying nomenclature was abruptly changed by their captors, the process exacerbated the culture shock of sudden bondage. And the effects were dramatically worsened when imposed renaming occurred in the context of brutal physical relocation, as happened to millions of captive Africans who were transported to the New World between the seventeenth and early nineteenth centuries. Little wonder that shock waves from this great upheaval continue to ricochet through history.

Personal or 'given' names are gifted to babies by others. There are rich variations in global traditions. In some countries, 'impious' or unacceptable names are legally banned. Plus, in some other cultures, names are updated with extra descriptive terms, to acknowledge stages in the individual lifecycle. So parents don't have a completely free hand, but naming their children is one matter over which they can exercise some choice.

Overall, the great majority of people stick with what they get, whether they secretly like the name or not. After all, it is something that they have known since their earliest childhood. In aggregate, the world's stock of personal names is following a rising trend but its expansion is nowhere as rapid as the rate of population growth. Habit is powerful. Many people have affection for traditional names—excluding the very few which become notorious.

Unusual monikers, when invented by parents, can become accepted with tolerable equanimity (if at times with concealed laughter). But children don't always appreciate eccentric names. One 'amusing' variant was invented in 1971 by British pop icon David Bowie. His son was known for his first twelve years as *Zowie Bowie* before rebelling. Now he is identified by his real first and last name as *Duncan Jones*. Years later, however, the son revived the idea. His own daughter (b. 2018) is named *Zowie Jones* (her adult response as yet unknown), as once startling innovations become history in turn.

The stock of last names or surnames also shows great stability. Over time, the range of options has increased. But at nothing near the rate of global population growth. Thus, in 2018, the world's most common last name was Wang (meaning 'King' or 'Prince'), with almost one hundred million people in China sharing this identifier, full of historic meaning.

Again, multiple factors, including loyalty to family, plus the power of familiarity, and the weight of inertia, discourage people from shedding their inherited surnames. A few do so, especially if the name is ignominious or embarrassing. Yet, they are unusual. One further factor that discourages random name-changes is the extent of legal formalities required. Nation-states like to know the identities of their citizens. And, while governments did not invent the conventions of individual naming, they certainly find the custom useful.

All personal identifiers have relevance, not just for the individuals concerned but for friends, families, societies and states. As a result, when new surnames are adopted, notably by women marrying under specific legal/religious jurisdictions, the transition is conventionally marked by a special wedding ceremonial. These days, however, numerous married women do *not* change surnames, indicating that conventions are mutable.

Other reasons for changing names may include adopting a new religion and a new name to match. Or people wanting a new starry public persona take a new identity to play the role: Norma Jean Mortensen becomes *Marilyn Monroe*; Greta Lovisa Gustafsson becomes *Greta Garbo*. Numerous literary figures also enjoy writing behind a pen-name. America's Samuel Langhorne Clemens emerges as *Mark Twain*; and Chile's Ricardo Basoalto as *Pablo Neruda*.

Furthermore, it was not uncommon in the nineteenth century for women to find boldness by choosing a male pen-name. And a recent literary sensation has reversed the syndrome when it was revealed that Spain's best-selling author *Carmen Mola* is actually a fictitious female 'front' for three male script-writers.

Name-changes can be made both unofficially and by official legal processes. And such renaming usually gain public acceptance. All the same, close friends and family often find that the force of habit makes it hard for them to use the new names spontaneously.

Yet, if and when false identities are assumed for purposes of criminal deception, then public acceptance quickly evaporates. And if government officials in the police or secret services use fake IDs to impose upon and deceive private citizens, there is great public indignation.

Living a lie is emphatically not 'fair play'. It breaks very deep-rooted conventions. As a result, people who have the misfortune of being duped often find that shocking revelations of long-standing false identities seriously undermine their confidence in the world around them.

Incidentally, too, it is stressful for those double-dealers who are maintaining two or more public identities at the same time. One person, one through-Time name. It is absolutely not a law. Yet, it is a global custom, which is not only useful but is also internalised into people's own sense of self.

Acknowledging Longevity in (Many) Place Names

Common labels for physical locations also show great through-Time longevity. For the same reasons of familiarity and habit, let alone convenience. What's more, place names long outlast individual lifetimes. As a result, the terms for identifying locations, in towns and countryside alike, constitute a rich historical legacy. And, if names are revised, sometimes after controversy, the new variants eventually become absorbed into history in turn.

Moreover, in countries with waves of settlement by different peoples at very different dates—Australia being a prime example—diverse languages and cultures sustain parallel names for the same places over long periods. There is also some cross-fertilisation. Thus, while numerous indigenous Australian placenames survive tenaciously, others are adopted or adapted by English-speakers.

Significantly, too, there has been one case of name-doubling in the service of ecumenical goodwill. The majestic sandstone rock outcrop in Australia's Northern Territories, known since 1873 as *Ayer's Rock*, was in 1993 given the joint English/Anangu name of *Ayer's Rock/Uluru*. Later, in 2002, the sequence was switched in tribute to antiquity. It was renamed as *Uluru/Ayer's Rock*. The dual name commemorates convergent histories that both meet in one place.

Elsewhere, less elevated reasons have led to other renaming. Some old terms, which later generations find embarrassing or comical, have been quietly dropped. In the East Anglian capital city of Norwich, a historic thoroughfare known as *Cockey Lane* (a Saxon term for a sewer or watercourse) was upgraded in the early nineteenth century to become the much smarter *London Street*. And in the British capital, the crudity of the old *Pissing Alley* was replaced by the genteel *Little Friday Street* (now part of Cannon Street).

Nonetheless, the power of custom has saved many apparently 'rude' names. In the English-speaking world, the Old English term for a broad valley floor was, graphically, a 'bottom'. It did not refer to the human posterior, though that is the word's most common meaning today. The power of affectionate familiarity means, however, that, despite some unkind sniggering, local residents still determinedly still keep the old name from *Foggy Bottom* (Washington, D. C.); to *Peach Bottom* (Pennsylvania, USA); *Pratt's Bottom* (S. E. London); through to *Scratchy Bottom* (Dorset); to mention just a few.

Political interventions also at times produce revisions. Some newly independent nations, for example, seek to shed their colonial legacy, by renaming major roads and buildings. And some former colonial powers also try to 'sanitise' their past by erasing references to contentious links. However, it is always best, in such enterprises, to gain public support. Otherwise, people's stubborn memories mean that old usages are likely to persist, perhaps covertly.

One classic case was seen in Hungary's capital city, Budapest. After World War II, its grandest avenue, *Andrássy út*, was renamed by its new communist rulers as *Stalin Street* [*Sztálin út*]. During the 1956 Hungarian Uprising, it briefly became the *Avenue of Hungarian Youth* [*Magyar Ifjúság út*]. Then, once their authority was restored, the communist rulers tried the less provocative: *People's Republic Street* [*Népköztársaság út*]. Yet, in 1989, when Hungary's peaceful 'system-change' [*Rendszerváltás*] took the country out of the Soviet bloc, the name *Andrássy út* was immediately restored, by general consent (In 2002, the avenue became a UNESCO World Heritage Site).

Evidently, place names are far from immutable. Yet, there is considerable public resistance to random chopping and changing. Unlike the postmodernist view, that Time is fragmented (see earlier discussion in Ch. 4), people are accustomed instead to living within a continuously unfolding Time.

Stability in place names provides an antidote to many forms of turbulence which may disrupt daily living. In practical terms, they provide invaluable identifiers, in both towns and countryside. No need to make up names for everything from scratch. They exist. And they are shared with others.

Think, too, of the exhaustive efforts that humans have applied collectively to identifying geographical features. There are names for every point on Planet Earth, from polar ice-caps to submerged trenches under the deepest oceans. Names for all features on the moon that are visible to humans. And names for many bright stars and constellations in the night skies (objects out of sight being known by numbers).

All this shared nomenclature is produced by humans who like to wander (and to stay put), who look around as they go, and who simultaneously like to identify their habitat, and to lodge the information in a shared grid of stable knowledge. Cue thousands of songs about specific places, from *Africa Bamba* by Santana to *Zimbabwe* by Bob Marley and the Wailers.

Sharing Significant Milestone Dates

Dynamic markers are equally appreciated, sharing information about Time's passing. They help to give people a good sense of temporal location. So milestone dates are often occasions for special celebrations. Options include both significant moments within the annual cycle of the seasons and notable points within much longer-term timetables.

Recurrent birthdates can be celebrated as individual Time-markers. Customs in this regard vary greatly from culture to culture; and within those, according to personal preferences. The emphasis is usually upon festivities with family and close friends. And the greatest fun is usually aimed at children, characteristically taking the form of parties, presents, cakes and candles. It's a cheerful way for them to learn that they get steadily older, year by year.

Many other communal festivities are linked to the annual cycle. Their prime focus may be either religious or secular, including nationally decreed holidays. Traditional dates have often emerged to mark seasonal turning points: midwinter, spring, high summer, autumn, and back to midwinter. Other chosen moments are those with specific meanings for local communities.

Classic commemorations take the form of fairs, festivals, firework displays, fetes, feasts, parades, pilgrimages, fasts, tournaments, sporting contests, and community walks/runs. In all, there are multitudinous ways to 'mark' communally the passing of Time. One notable combination of worshipful meditation with rejoicing is the Islamic fast for the holy month of **Ramadan**, which is then followed by the three-day Eid Festival (*Eid al-Fitr*), devoted to special prayers, family visits, and gift-giving. The cycle expresses penance, followed by spiritual elation and concern for others.

Crowded secular gatherings can become highly convivial, at times verging on the bacchanalian. Above all, the big annual fairs were traditionally great places for young people to get together, relatively unsupervised. Bawdy songs accordingly sang about the crop of newborn babies, produced precisely nine months later (Mythology, of course, was/is not quite the same as daily reality).

As well as very ancient festivals, there are also relatively more recent inventions. In Ireland, the small town of Tullamore (Co. Offaly) celebrates annually its urban recovery from disaster. In 1785, a crashed hot-air balloon (exemplifying the perils of the latest new technology) caused a massive fire and extensive damage. Today, the town's emblem is, appropriately, a phoenix rising from the ashes, and its celebration is named the Phoenix Festival.

A completely different frolic takes the form of the Boryeong Mud Festival in South Korea (first held in mid-July 1998). The event proved a surprise hit.

And today uninhibited crowds attend, to bathe, wallow, wrestle, watch fireworks, and mock-fight in the mineral-rich local soil: *Mud, glorious mud.*

How far individuals participate in such events is a matter of choice. In close-knit communities, there can be pressures to conform to conventional rituals. Nonetheless, people can keep aloof, if they wish. They can side with Charles Dickens's Ebenezer Scrooge, who derided Christmas good cheer by snorting: *Bah! Humbug!* But commemorative events don't, in fact, require unanimity (rare among humans except in dire emergencies). Instead, they offer options and reminders, even for non-participants, of Time's passing.

Alongside the cyclical year-in-year-out festivities, there are also countless one-off special celebrations. These mark key staging posts in the long-term unfolding of the human story. They are reminders, both personal and communal, that the progression of Time occurs not just moment by moment but over years, centuries, and millennia.

Major generators of milestone dates are the world's great religions. Historically, they have helped to forge community patterns of work and worship. And they generally inculcate a long temporal perspective, looking back to the faith's first foundation. In that context, special anniversaries, jubilees, festivals, pilgrimages, and/or visits to holy shrines, in any combination, all help people to place the fleeting present into a greater timetable.

Similarly, secular powers have had a large impact, not least in recent centuries. They too celebrate jubilees and centenaries. Rulers like to underline their historic legacies. And the people are usually willing to join the fun. Moreover, these days many civic organisations, both national and international, are ready to sponsor their own commemorative events.

Notably, too, the sporting world has, relatively recently, begun to develop a regular timetable of global competitions. These combine sport with an element of collective celebration. For example, the four-yearly international Olympic athletic competitions, since their revival in 1896, are managing to get global participation, global audiences and (a tribute to their organising vigilance) global mechanisms to prevent organised cheating.

And on 31 December 1999, the media showing of fireworks displays from around the world created a highly unusual international sharing of one major calendrical turning point. There were also countless local celebrations, both religious and secular. Not everyone watched. Nor cared. Very far from everyone shared the Christian teachings that defined this moment as the two-thousandth anniversary of the birth of Christ.

But that was far from the sole point. The shared millennium festivities were top news items almost everywhere, as shared global festivities rather than purely or even chiefly as religious markers.

Firework displays, first invented in ancient China under the Song dynasty, have now become an internationally-known component of communal festivities. And their global use at these end-of-millennia celebrations marked a special moment of calendrical consensus for a species which has long displayed a concern for telling the Time, and 'marking' its key moments.

Raising Special Monuments to Memory

Special monuments are also created, to 'place' memory-markers at specific sites. It's a way of harnessing human spatial awareness to trigger the power of remembrance. *See! Think! Remember!* (Just as many mnemonic systems use visualisation as a means of recovering stored memories).

Moreover, such monuments, great and small, help not just to remind individuals but to crystallise civic emotions. Those may be feelings of reverence and faith. Or pride in secular triumphs. Or emotions of grief and solemn remembrance. Or as in the case of battlefield monuments and war memorials, a special mix of both pride and sorrow (as further explored in Ch. 14).

Highly unusual, too, there are a few rare public monuments to the glory of human sexuality, as represented by the erect male phallus. (To date, however, there does not seem to be a similar public celebration of the female vulva and clitoris.) Those curious to inspect the evidence, and to share Lawrentian joy in the male member, should forthwith visit Haesindang Park [해신당 공원], also called Penis Park, south of Samcheok in South Korea.

Meanwhile, various primeval sites bear witness to the antiquity of the human interest in creating monuments, by arranging giant stones into distinctive patterns. Even if the precise functions of places like Stonehenge in Wiltshire (England) or the Standing Stones at Carnac in Brittany (France) are unknown, their monumental impact is clear. They were shared venues for people to visit and learn, and to stare and wonder.

State powers in more recent times also sponsor monumental art, generally to impress but sometimes also to intimidate. Secular monuments range from statues to triumphal arches, ornamental plazas, obelisks, towers, through to tombs. Some edifices are gigantic. Today, the world's tallest statue is located near Kevadiya in Gujarat (India) and celebrates the Gujarat-born lawyer and protagonist of Indian Independence, Vallabhbhai Jhaverbhai Patel, known as Sardar. Standing one hundred and eighty-two metres high (almost six hundred feet), the colossal monument is known as the Statue of Unity, and its political message is unequivocal.

Recently, too, there have been some moves to 'democratise' the range of people (either individually or in groups) who receive homage in the form of a public statue or plaque. And there are also campaigns to remove past monuments to individuals who have subsequently become controversial—a development which can itself stoke rather than end controversy. These things matter.

Religious memory-markers are equally historic and widespread. Some are relatively small and local, like wayside shrines. But others include large statues personifying deities, saints, or holy teachers, as well as ornamental tombs and memorials to specific individuals. One celebrated example is the serenely beautiful marble mausoleum at Agra (India), known as the Taj Mahal. It houses the tomb of Mumtaz Mahal, favourite wife of the Mughal Emperor Shah Jahan, who in 1632–43 raised the edifice in her honour.

Some monuments trigger awe at their sheer scale. Today, the world's second tallest statue (built 1997–2008) commemorates the Buddha. Located at Fodushan, in Lushan County, Henan (China), the figure stands at one hundred and twenty-eight metres (four hundred and twenty feet). And, with its massive plinth, the entire monument reaches a height of over two hundred metres (six hundred and fifty feet). Glittering in cast copper, it is a staggering sight.

However, religious monumental art also has the power to divide as well as to unite. Clashes between faiths at times include iconoclastic attacks on visible symbols of the hated or feared rival. A relevant case was the destruction in 2001 of two colossal sixth-century cave statues of Buddha in Bamiyan (central Afghanistan) by the fundamentalist Islamic group known as the Taliban. For its activists, the move was a blow against idolatry. Yet, instant condemnation followed, not only from Buddhists everywhere but also from global admirers of historic art and artefacts. The deed was resented as trying to erase history.

Diverse attitudes to religious monuments here stand revealed. The Islamic faith specifically bans physical representations of the deity and the Prophet Muhammad. It does, however, encourage prayer at specific holy sites. These include the Mosque of the Prophet (Al-Masjid an-Nabawi) in Medina, Saudi

Arabia; the Al-Aqsa Mosque in Jerusalem's Old City' and the holy of holies, the Kaaba [Arabic ٱلْكَعْبَة; Romanised *al-Ka'ba*] at Mecca in Saudi Arabia. That sacred building provides the direction of prayer for all Muslims. And they are expected to make a holy pilgrimage (*Hajj*) to its site, at least once in an adult lifetime. In addition, the Shia branch of Islam accepts a further range of holy shrines and mosques as venues for prayers and pilgrimages.

Specific locations thus become readily associated with deep meanings as well as deep emotions. Consequently (and unsurprisingly), disputes are likely if rival groups simultaneously focus their competing expectations upon the same physical location. A well-known case is Jerusalem's Temple Mount. It has spiritual significance for Jews, Muslims *and* Christians; and today constitutes a veritable political hotspot. However, the principle of mutual respect between global religions is clear enough, even if the practice is subject to turbulence.

Generally, meanwhile, there is considerable consensus among people of virtually all faiths and cultures to respect monuments to the dead. Indeed, most national legal systems apply severe penalties to anyone who desecrates corpses and/or vandalises graves. Such unsavoury crimes do happen. But the global expectation is that due reverence be accorded to all burial grounds, tombs, mausoleums, memorials, gardens of commemoration, and holy riverside sites, such as those where Hindus hold their rituals of cremation.

Incidentally, too, recent excavations confirm the antiquity of the practice of paying respect to the dead. In the Panga ya Saidi Cave in S. E. Kenya (south of Mombasa), there is evidence of a child burial, dating back some seventy-eight thousand years. The fragile body, which lies in the foetal position, rests its head on something akin to a pillow. Nothing else is known but the respectful intent is evident.

To be sure, some of the grandest funerary monuments do attest to worldly power as well as remembrance. Massive buildings indicate the investment of huge sums of money and immense physical labour. The great pyramids of Egypt, especially those at Giza (close to Cairo), entombing the pharaohs and their retinues, remain some of the largest monuments ever constructed by humans.

Close by, too, is the Great Sphinx. Its stylised lion-body supports a massive human head, with a famously blunted nose. It was probably built to guard a temple, which no longer survives. The whole magnificent complex, dating back to the third century BCE (now a World Heritage site) was a testament to lasting grandeur. It now has the additional poignancy that these memory-markers have long outlasted not only their builders but even the historic cultures that first sustained them.

Great investment is, however, not always required to honour the dead. There are also *ad hoc* memorials, which are created spontaneously, Thus at sites of fatal accidents (whether natural or human-made), local people may mark the site by bunches of flowers. Or by other symbols, such as toys to mark the death of a child.

Such tributes are purely unofficial. And they often honour complete strangers. So there are some on-the-ground memorials to victims of aircraft disasters when crews and passengers fall from the sky to die far from their homes. And in the same spirit, there are coastal plaques and monuments to those who lose their lives in maritime disasters, at sea far away. All these local memorials signal collective solidarity with fellow humans who died abruptly and painfully.

Governments at times also provide monuments to special disasters, especially when the deaths were heroic. One moving testament is the Ukrainian tribute to the fire-fighters at Chernobyl (near Pripyat, north of Kiev, by the Belarus border). They died while dousing the fires after the nuclear accident and preventing a major crisis from turning into a global cataclysm. The 'Monument to Those Who Saved the World' is also dedicated to all the later helpers who, at some personal risk, cleaned and secured the site in the following years.

Today, the ghost city of Pripyat offers a *de facto* underlining of a well-known message. Techno-vigilance is required for every known technology. And, notably, the huge Exclusion or 'Alienation Zone' around Chernobyl (Ukrainian: Chornobyl), now uninhabited by humans, has a new local ecology. Wild animals congregate there and biodiversity flourishes. Monuments to human deaths may bring scope for different lives to flourish—a stark global message, not to be ignored.

Summary Next Step: Generating Shared Knowledge

Basic items of information about names, places and dates, are just that—basic. Yet, humans build upon basic information to create and share knowledge collectively. What is known is not necessarily always precise. Nor are all individuals equally well informed. However, having access to shared knowledge helps to root everyone simultaneously within Time-Space.

Errors do creep into the knowledge stock, as already noted. But humans continue to test and check—and to maintain a sufficient common store of know-how for collective survival. Were all global names of places and people to be changed daily, then utter confusion would ensue. (As already noted, the unexpected loss of familiar 'moorings' can leave people, who are abruptly and unwillingly exiled, with an acute sense of shock, alienation, and even existential terror, until new bearings are established.)

Over the very long-term, there's no doubt that many of even the greatest communal memory-markers have been adapted, updated, and even disrupted or lost completely. Entire historical cultures have disappeared. An imaginative awareness of vanished glories is expressed in a great poem (1818) by the English 'Romantic' P. B. Shelley. He depicts the forgotten ruin of a huge statue, discovered by a traveller in the desert sands. Nothing around remains. Only the following words are legible on the statue's pedestal: '*My name is Ozymandias, king of kings;/Look on my works, ye Mighty, and despair!*'.

Magnificent testimony to the transience of supreme power. And yes, empires rise and fall. Entire people can be scattered. Yet, ordinary humans continue. They generate and share stocks of knowledge that enable them to live successfully within Time-Space (to date).

Generating shared knowledge is always work-in-progress. But not all information is constantly in flux. *What's in a name?* After all, '*That which we call a rose/By any other name would smell as sweet*'. Yes, Shakespeare. Elegantly phrased. But a rose must remain a rose, not for its smell but for effective human communication. Grids of basic information establish some things beyond doubt. And people then expand, test, and continually debate, a growing corpus of knowledge. It's the essential bedrock for the human journey *through the Avenues of Time…*

Knowledge Networks

Batten, J (*et al.*) (1995) *Networks in Action: Communication, Economics and Human Knowledge.*

Bedford, D., Sanchez, T. W. (2021) *Knowledge Networks.*

Naming Practices—People

Ainiala, T., Östman, J-O. (eds) (2017) *Socio-Onomastics: The Pragmatics of Names.*

von Bruck, G., Bodenhorn, B. (eds) (2006) *The Anthropology of Names and Naming.*

Naming Practices—Places

Randall, R. R. (2001) *Place Names: How They Define the World—And More.*
Whitaker, E. A. (1999) *Mapping and Naming the Moon: A History of Lunar Cartography and Nomenclature.*

Significant Dates

Baker, B. A. (*et al.*) (comp) (1999) *Holidays and Anniversaries of the World: A Comprehensive Catalogue…*

Public Monuments

Dickenson, C. P. (ed) (2021) *Public Statues across Time and Cultures.*
Kerrigan, M. (2007) *The History of Death: Burial Customs and Funeral Rites from the Ancient World to Modern Times.*

Chapter 13
Encountering and Judging Conflicts

Chapter 13 confronts human hatred and warfare, and examines how societies cope with containing/resolving/understanding and judging conflicts.

Being Combative

Time is a mighty warrior...and it guards ancient grudges. Humans too know how to fight and they can nurture long hatreds. Their global success today (in numerical terms) has not come about without extensive turmoil and bloodletting. While people are good at mutual cooperation (see Ch. 14), the human species is also notably combative. Sometimes to the extent of physical fighting, not just on *ad hoc* occasions but also in organised armies. So human aggression has long-lasting effects on human actions and thought patterns.

Throughout the animal world, there are countless examples of one species preying upon another, lethally. Usually, the motive is the quest for food. Meanwhile, lethal violence between members of the same species is much rarer. Of course, there are exceptions. When two stags fight in the rutting season, seeking sole access to the herd's females, it's not unknown for one or even both combatants to be wounded fatally. However, their aim is mating dominance. If the loser decamps, the victor does not follow to kill him off.

Overall, biologists observe that some sixty percent of mammal species do not deliberately kill their fellow-members. Using lethal violence is not an obligatory *rule of the wild*. Yet, that observation does leave forty percent of mammal species which do sometimes kill fellow-members. Australian black-tailed prairie dogs under pressure for resources will, for instance, bite and decapitate the young of even close family. However, even highly combative animals do not spend all their time fighting. It wastes energy and it's risky.

Among the most aggressive to their own kind are the large-brained mammals known as Primates. They have prehensile hands that can grab and grapple (Humans use them to wield weapons). Primates are very social and territorial, which can lead to conflict if interests clash. But again, there's no universal rule. Bonobos are almost wholly peace-loving, while chimpanzees are chronically combative. When seriously enraged, the most common form of primate belligerence takes the form of killing the young of a rival (infanticide).

Humans thus stand out, among the apes, for their capacity to kill fellow adults as well as offspring. In that respect, they rank with fighting carnivores, like wolves, lions, and hyenas. However, humans go further. They combine into armies of fellow belligerents, who are trained to kill designated 'enemies' (and who at times kill non-combatants too, causing 'collateral damage').

That said, a readiness to fight varies greatly between individuals and between global cultures. Wars and violent conflicts between organised groups, like nation-states and religions, are thus not inevitable. Yet, they do recur.

This notable human combativeness, furthermore, not only plays a big role in history but also affects how humans view their collective story. Just as lies and deceit can warp rational judgments, so can hatreds and conflicts. Animosities can be transmitted through successive generations and can and sometimes do last, literally, for centuries. Societies thus grapple not only with short-term turbulence but also with long-term hatreds and grievances.

Experiencing the Spectrum of Hatred

Hatreds have, of course, a parallel history of human love (And, at times, the twin emotions can intersect, as noted below). Hatred can be burning, passionate, eager and 'hot'. Or 'cold', dark, brooding, vengeful. In both cases, it is usually intense. It differs from mere dislike, which is much more common.

People in a lifetime have many shades of engagement and disengagement with their fellow humans. It is common to have many varied likes and dislikes. But it is comparatively unusual to sustain for long an intense hatred of another person, though it does happen. Many people hate rather theoretically. Some, however, express their negative feelings in physical violence or even homicide. Generally, victims of hate-killings are known to their murderers. And, in cases when people are killed by complete strangers, the killers' motive often turns out to be articulated as a generalised hatred of humanity.

Adding to the intricacies, emotions can get tangled. In close relationships, couples may for brief moments—or perhaps for long periods—find themselves experiencing love-hate. Feeling strong but conflicted emotions can be tormenting. So Catullus, the poet of classical Rome, announced in his verse couplet: '*Odi et amo*' [*I hate and I love*]. Many novels, plays and films find that theme irresistible. (Great actors also revel in the chance to convey mixed emotions by the slightest nuances of expressions and body language.)

Expressions of strong hatred may conceal parallel emotions, which add to the intensity. Perhaps secret guilt at having earlier harmed the hated individual or group? Or secret and hardly-admitted admiration? In such circumstances, conflicted haters may end up hating themselves. Negative feelings frequently eat inwards. Hence hatreds may be more complicated than they at first seem.

Sado-masochistic relationships, meanwhile, enjoy their own intricacies. Lovers gain sexual pleasure from the consensual inflicting/receiving of pain, within agreed limits. Playing at dominance and submission can be sexy. Erotic art and literature offer many salacious hints, providing additional titillation.

However, at times, sadistic behaviour escalates dangerously beyond the agreed boundaries. At such moments, sadists let hatred triumph over love. Some sado-masochistic sex-killers on trial have offered the defence of consensual 'rough sex'. But public (and judicial) opinion does not generally accept that individuals can validly consent to being brutally battered to death by a lover. (A reminder that society has a definite viewpoint too.)

Because of the complications of mixed emotions, there is no historical or indeed contemporary 'hate-index'. Feelings wax and wane in intensity. It is well observed, however, that hatred often becomes much stronger when it is shared by a sizeable group. A sense of communal solidarity adds increased passion and shared repetition helps the emotion to last.

Group hatred may indeed absolve haters from a sense of individual responsibility. Their shared viewpoint seems 'natural' and 'obvious'. It has communal endorsement. And a group rant, as on social media today, can help to revive passions, should they ever flag.

George Orwell, England's author of the great dystopian novel *1984*, set himself to imagine how communal animosities work. He envisaged: 'Two-Minutes Hate' sessions, organised daily by a totalitarian state All citizens participate—and are swept into a quasi-orgasmic frenzy. They bury inner qualms, in intense group-think: 'A hideous ecstasy of fear and vindictiveness, a desire to kill, to torture, to smash faces in with a sledge-hammer, seemed to flow through the whole group of people like an electric current…'

Dangerously, too, these mass emotions of hostility need collective targets. These may include a (simplified) big idea, or associated material objects. So religious conflicts can focus hatred upon religious art and statuary. Items are vandalised or defaced for their symbolic meaning; just as Orwell imagined dedicated haters wishing to smash human faces with a hammer.

Most commonly, however, group hatreds target other humans. Any set of people will qualify if they are seen as dangerously and unacceptably different. Such 'other' groups may be defined by rival religions, nationalities, political ideologies, territorial interests (competing for resources), class interests, gender loyalties, and/or rival ethnic origins. And if multiple causes for competition are aligned, then angry passions fly extra high.

Habit and custom also play a role. Group hatreds, if unchallenged, are readily reinforced by communal traditions. Enemy 'others' are disparaged not only in theoretical writings but also in causal slogans, graffiti, and snide jokes.

Some reflex hatreds, therefore, have long back-histories, lasting for millennia. One example is Christian anti-Semitism (extrapolated from the belief that Jews were ultimately to blame for the crucifixion of Christ the Messiah)—although that attitude is emphatically not shared by all Christians.

Defining a rival group as collectively 'sub-human' or even 'non-human'—a process known as 'othering'—kindles emotions of fear, competition, anger, and revulsion into a blazing hostility. And if the hatred is reciprocated (as does happen), mutual enmities become engrained. Trust is lost and remains hard to recover. Small flash-points trigger big conflicts, fuelled by past grievances. So Shakespeare envisaged, in *Romeo & Juliet,* how two warring families quickly 'From ancient grudge break to new mutiny [strife]'.

All accounts of human history need to understand the spectrum of hatred. It's also good for people to check whether they have themselves unwittingly imbibed, from their own cultural traditions, some historical prejudices. Or, alternatively, developed a reflexive guilt at ancestral misdeeds, perpetrated by earlier generations. The power of passions is sufficiently great that it's wise to ensure that they are if strongly held, authentically one's own.

Making War

Locations for all forms of overt conflict are multifarious. Households, workplaces, leisure centres, transport systems, indoors, outdoors, fields, forests, there's no limit, other than practical options. There have at times been physical set-tos within religious edifices and holy places. But fighting in inappropriate venues always prompts cultural disapproval. It also further distresses the victims, as their faith in a place of safety is betrayed.

For that reason, violence within the household is notably damaging. Private homes are meant to be intimate places, housing close families, kinfolk, and (sometimes) servants. They are all supposed to be well-wishers. Violent treatment from trusted familiars is destructive of both mental and physical health. Moreover, if perpetrators of ill-treatment are cunning enough to keep their actions secret, then victims suffer, unaided, for long periods of time. Essential trust is destroyed. Which is additionally confusing, when victims continue to love, at least at some level, their abusers.

Violence impels turbulence and negativism into daily routines. The 'family' is idealised in many cultures. It is seen as a core building block of the wider society. Family breakdowns are thus greeted with special dismay. In cultures where homes are guarded by household gods, as in Shinto Japan, there is also a spiritual reckoning when domestic shrines [*Kamidana* (神棚)] have to be dismantled. Those suffering from such upsets feel that the divine order, as well as normal social life, has collapsed.

Once viewed as a 'private' matter, violence within households is now attracting attention from police, local authorities, teachers, and charitable agencies. Eyes are being opened to the extent of domestic partner-battering, servant-beating, child exploitation, all forms of sexual abuse, including unduly 'rough sex', and psychological coercion. The historic frequency of domestic violence of all kinds remains unknown, though it no doubt varies between cultures. But everywhere a bland domestic façade may conceal a darker story.

By contrast, organised warfare is socially better understood (even while the actual battlefields are often, but by no means always, at a distance from human residences). Fighting between rival armies requires prior mobilisation of funding, logistics, and manpower. Historically, wars were fought by men; but most armies had camp followers, including women who cooked, tended wounds and provided (more or less unwillingly) sexual services for the troops.

Given such reasons, the role of organised warfare is socially known, as well as recorded in official documents. But there is no 'war-index' to tabulate its historical frequency and intensity. Still less, any tally of its global impact.

Motivations for organised warfare are often offensive, undertaken with prior rational calculation. Other combatants may, however, find that they are forced to fight defensively. Wars can then be waged in moods of 'hot' hatred or 'cold' fury. The latter tends to promote shrewder tactics than striking in blind passion. Yet, military experts advise against fighting in the grip of any extreme emotion (Albeit hard to avoid in hand-to-hand combat).

Professional soldiers are trained to adopt coolly disciplined behaviour in warfare (More than a few lapse). And in recent eras, international conventions declare that armies are committing war crimes, if they adopt particularly brutal forms of fighting (Again, more than a few continue to lapse). Because wars produce disruption, laced with strong emotions of anger and fear, participants with even the coolest of prior intentions are severely tested. Put simply, unchecked fighting lowers the moral bar in the minds of combatants.

Civil warfare produces further problems. It's a hideous shock, if and when previously pleasant neighbours suddenly turn into hostile killers. Bystanders who try to stay neutral are almost invariably pressurised into joining one side or another. Normal mechanisms of conflict resolution don't work. Routes back to social harmony are hard to find, especially after atrocities and territorial dispossessions. The abnormality of 'fratricidal' killings within one national 'family' generates anguish and bitterness, on all sides.

Genocides are extreme examples of civil strife when one section of a community tries to eliminate another, not by expulsions (traumatic enough) but by mass killings. Such actions can be organised with all the authority and institutions of a nation-state, or arise spontaneously, often with the tacit permission of local or national power-brokers.

Arguments continue as to what precisely constitutes genocide. Do Turkish killings of around one million Armenians in Anatolia, within the Ottoman Empire during World War I, indicate a specific policy of group obliteration? Or was it 'just' the exacerbation of ancient tensions into mass murders? Either way, wrong-doings on a mass scale, by whatever name, indicate severe social dislocation, requiring retrospective acknowledgement and positive steps towards reconciliation (A theme explored further in Ch. 14).

Classifying the variety of genocides meanwhile helps to highlight some common trigger factors. Mass killings are thus associated with times of heightened instability; with social fear and economic crisis; with intense competition for resources; with breakdowns in conventional moral and legal restraints; with long-held group antipathies, which have been encouraged rather than downplayed; with explicit incitement (often but not invariably) from unscrupulous leaders; and (most disastrously) with the coercive use of the organised institutions of a powerful state.

Without a healing settlement at the end of agonising 'fratricidal' killings, then hostility and bitter feelings are liable to persist. A sort of 'frozen' civil war ensues. People remain suspicious of others (and of the authorities). A tradition of negativism prevails…which requires much communal effort to undo. (For that reason, one outcome of civil warfare has taken the form of jurisdictional partitions, to divide permanently the warring combatants.)

Mass warfare between rival nation-states or religions can, by contrast, have the opposite effect. Far from dividing a community, opinion can unite against a common 'outside' enemy. War propagandists try to demonise the opponent. That stokes enthusiasm for war and makes recruitment of soldiers easier (though sometimes fighting is done by mercenaries). Interestingly, there are many brisk army marching songs, plus victory songs and lamentations in defeat. Yet, there are virtually no songs about the goriness of actual killings.

If wars then become too lengthy and costly for apparently little gain, political opponents and public discontent may start to challenge the strategy. Moreover, there are pacifist movements, both religious and secular, that oppose all fighting on principle.

After campaigns have ended, victors tend to believe that their righteousness has been confirmed by the *gods of war*. Complacency and even arrogance may follow. But tensions often arise when the civilian population has to reabsorb disbanded regiments of battle-hardened soldiers. A percentage will have physical wounds in need of healing; others have psychological ones.

Warfare is a gigantic disrupter. And the appeal to physical force as arbiter (as in political revolutions) can prompt the emergence of a powerful war-lord or autocratic ruler. Entire societies may become endemically militarised.

Losers, meanwhile, tend to seethe with resentment. They wish to avenge their war-dead. They also hope to recover lost assets and lost territories. And in the case of people who have become subjugated to an external power, a simmering resistance to conquest may persist. Leaders who have led the cause to defeat become 'betrayers'. Heroic resisters become symbols of long-term hope. Thus wars may—and often do—eventually breed further wars.

Only when one of the combatant powers has been totally routed, ideologically as well as militarily, are attitudes among the losers liable to change, especially if the victors offer a constructive peace settlement. In that way, the dials can be reset. But the process still does not happen overnight.

Collectively, all humans do not march through history united, shoulder to shoulder. Instead, they often march to rival drums. Societies face frequent costs of warfare, whether in terms of premature deaths, economic disruptions, and property destruction. Victors, however, may gain politically, economically, financially, and culturally. Empires have been founded on the battlefield (and lost there too). Colonies have been annexed by fighting (but independence campaigns similarly won). Meanwhile, others have taken up arms, unwillingly, in order to defeat aggressors (defining their resistance as a 'just war').

While armed conflicts are thus great disrupters within the collective human story, they can bring gains to specific sectors. That said, the long-term outcomes are frequently more complicated than the individuals or groups striking the first blow ever realise. The developing art of averting conflict must therefore seek not only to defuse hatreds that lead to violence but, equally vitally, to change the calculations that make warfare seem a rational option.

Memorialising Past Conflicts

One school of thought recommends briskly: *Don't brood; move on.* It is indubitably a mistake to become fixated on past experiences of violent conflict.

On the other hand, forgetting entirely precludes the chance to learn, let alone the chance to heal and the chance to administer redemptive justice. Knowledge must come from confronting the dark side of human history, as well as its pleasures.

Individuals and families often create their own memorials to remember victims of personal violence. There are plaques and *ad hoc* shrines, with flowers and messages. Communities may offer support, with commemorative vigils and special events, such as community walks. Another option, for mourners with activist temperaments, is to campaign publicly to ensure that no other victims ever meet similar malign fates.

Then there are specialist venues which display exhibits relating to horror and violence. Museums of Crime seek to shock and thrill but simultaneously to alert and warn. They update traditional 'freak' shows, once displayed at fairs. Such museums try not to glamorise murderers and malefactors. Yet, criticisms follow, if the displays appear to 'forget' the victims. It's a fine line to tread.

Dilemmas of that sort confronted Madame Tussauds Waxwork Museum in London (now an international franchise). It exhibits models of notorious criminals as well as popular celebrities. But public tastes have changed; and some waxworks had become targets of protest long before, in 2016, Tussauds closed for good its 'Chamber of Horrors', with its grisly array of murderers. Real-life killings are not 'fun' (Hence, detective stories and murder games generally feature the thrills of detecting or evading detection, rather than the agony of being murdered, whether by a false friend or by a hostile stranger).

In divided societies, which have recently known the traumas of civil war, the nature of public memorials remains highly sensitive. Triumphalism on the part of the victors is unhelpful. But so is a policy of official 'silence' about mutual killings and wartime atrocities. If people's memories about what has happened are ignored, and if reconciliation is not attempted, then resentments are liable to turn bitter and be transmitted to successive generations.

There is particular distress if those slain in sectarian killings have not been properly laid to rest, and relief when, even many years later, bodies are exhumed and given respectful burials. In contemporary Spain, the Association for the Recovery of Historic Memories [*Asociación para la Recuperación de la Memoria Histórica* (ARMH)] is undertaking precisely that task, to assist Spain's prolonged coming-to-terms with its rancorous civil war (1936–9). The same development has followed recently in Argentina, where the *Equipo Argentino de*

Antropologia Forense now offers its services worldwide as a not-for-profit professional war-crimes exhumation team.

'Healing' civil war memorials to all combatants—and museums recording the full picture of the conflict in a non-partisan style—can be socially beneficial, if they are constructed—and managed—with due sensitivity. They are certainly more positive for collective healing than separate commemorations by rival groups. Those instead foster the continuance of a 'frozen' cultural civil war, long after the actual fighting has ended.

Yet, all ecumenical memorials work best in the context of wise peace-making. Unless there is some sense of reconciliation and the delivery of justice, warring groups remain understandably resistant to the prospect of their dead being buried or commemorated next to their killers.

Lives as well as properties need to be rebuilt, after civil wars. And communal trust needs to be revived and nurtured (Never easy). Moreover, after decisive conflicts over big emotionally engaging issues, losers may have to face the loss not just of the war but also of their grand cause as well (Even more difficult).

And more complicated still, there are issues that call for legal and moral judgment. Wartime atrocities, on all sides, that remain unpunished and unatoned, generate heavy anguish and particularly unforgiving anger.

Memorials to organised fighting between people who do not live near one another are in some ways easier to manage. (Incidentally, many antique battlegrounds are by now forgotten and slumber beneath grass or sand or jungle.)

Particularly when memorials are built on sites of conflict, an ecumenical magnanimity is required. All sides lose combatants in fighting. Battlefield sites are thus places of precipitate death; and all the fallen, who often lie far from their homelands, should be respected. The same principle applies to those buried in mass commemorative graveyards.

Meanwhile, museums or displays can help to explain how specific wars began and ended. In Northern Ireland, for example, the new Museum of the Troubles and the Peace Process offers a forum where all comers can learn and share memories of the bloody community strife between (many not all) Catholics and (many not all) Protestants in the years 1968–98. It offers an appropriate grass-roots venue for shared grass-roots 'coming-to-terms'.

Reflecting on how wars should best be memorialised, the eminent German historian, Reinhart Koselleck, urged that past combatants must not be mentally categorised as either all *goodies* or all *baddies*. In 1944–45, he himself, as a young man, served in the Nazi Army, before becoming a prisoner of Soviet Russia. He witnessed horrors, perpetrated by all sides. 'Mourning', he concludes sombrely, 'is not divisible'. Understanding and empathy (meaning emotional grasp, *not* sympathy) are due to all, including those on the 'wrong' or losing side of history.

Koselleck's affirmation of shared humanity is vital, although all kinds of warfare—international and civil—still raise issues for moral and legal judgment (as noted below).

Communities and nations regularly create further poignant memorials 'back home', away from battlefields. Sites are locally tended and appreciated (And, sometimes, if comparatively rarely, left to fall into disrepair).

Moreover, commemorative war-mementoes circulate in multiple formats. They include books, films, games, and a variety of souvenirs. Ideally, such mementoes should *not* demonise real-life human opponents, who are fallible fellow mortals. *Nor* should they glorify violence as a means of resolving differences. And, certainly, too, mementoes of warfare should *not* encourage people to forget the harsh lessons and realities of organised killings.

Messages of grief and hard-gained experience are notably offered to the world at two key venues in Hiroshima, Japan. The Genbaku Dome [広島平和記念碑, *Hiroshima Heiwa Kinenhi*] is kept as a Peace Memorial, being the city's only building to survive the atomic bomb attack in August 1945. And, at the nearby Hiroshima Cenotaph (built in 1952), a memorial plaque pledges: 'Rest in peace! For we shall not make the same mistake again'. If past experience cannot control the future, it can certainly warn and advise…

Assessing Criminality in Warfare

Needless to say, the long history of wars and communal violence has not unfolded without vigorous countervailing efforts to control, or at least to minimise, these explosive forces. And to apply due punishment for transgressors.

Religious teachings have long offered moral frameworks to judge personal and communal behaviour. States, meanwhile, establish legal systems and enforcement officers, seeking to control criminality and to apply suitable punishments for detected offenders. Cultural attitudes also provide a counterpart of firm support for many forms of punishment, as well as a willingness to wink at minor transgressions. (The globally varied state of gun laws within 'advanced' societies today indicates that there is no common set of regulations, even though all societies officially ban inter-personal violence.)

Getting agreement is even trickier when it comes to regulating behaviour in wars between rival nations, with differing jurisdictions. But there are legitimate concerns about the sort of weaponry that can be used—and how captive soldiers should be treated—let alone how combatants should behave, especially when warfare is no longer confined to battlefields but can engulf entire societies.

Using rape as a weapon of war is one sign of how disastrously norms of civilised behaviour can collapse. Hostile soldiers transform sex into a symbol of contemptuous dominance (*not even love-hate; but hate-hate*).

Nations in the twentieth century, battered by World Wars, agreed to found organisations of international cooperation, which have begun, slowly, to construct agreed rules of engagement. The League of Nations (1920), extended as the United Nations (1945), began the process. There followed: the Geneva Conventions on the conduct of warfare (1949), the Comprehensive Test Ban Treaty on Nuclear Weapons (1996), and a judicial arena, in the form of the International Criminal Court (founded 1920; powers amplified 1998).

Monitoring and upholding conventions, amidst all-out combat, is an uphill task, as is, later, bringing alleged war criminals before a court. Nonetheless, the international society seeks not mob-lynchings of *baddies* but formal legal trials, based upon agreed global standards. Progress is painfully slow. But it remains vital that the international enforcement agencies are both endorsed and properly regulated. They must remain trusted by all. And hence, they must not be 'captured' by any one partisan interest.

Gradually, a set of globally-shared humanist values is becoming acknowledged. These endorse secular moral principles, which are broadly consonant with the teachings of the world's major religions. In sum, brutal violence and offensive force should not be used against other peoples and societies (especially if using banned weapons or other prohibited killing agents), as a routine matter of policy (There may be scope for exceptional actions in exceptional circumstances, but those remain exceptions).

Hence, all combatants, all army leaders, and all politicians, who direct them, can be held morally and legally responsible for atrocities in all theatres of warfare. They have perpetrated crimes *against humanity*.

Bringing the most heinous wartime culprits to measured legal justice, whenever possible, remains a crucial part of a post-conflict 'healing' process. As already noted, *forgive and forget* may work as a solution to minor tiffs. Yet, reconciliation after major conflicts requires that societies judge and punish, as well as forgive and heal.

Exercises in informed empathy, in order to understand the roots of people's behaviour, are entirely valid. Indeed, they are equally vital for historians; and for therapists, as well as for wider societies.

Nevertheless, that significant exercise still does not mean condoning atrocities. Not least because people who get away with breaking international laws once are likely to repeat the offence again and again.

Judgments, needless to say, must not be lightly made. Nor should verdicts be vengeful, made in hatred. Instead, impartial judgements are needed in the most dispassionate legal style; and punishments must be seen as fair. Such objectives are mightily difficult to achieve, no need to labour an all-too-obvious point. Yet they remain essential.

Above all, the world's 'great powers' tend to remain notably resistant to international vetting, making it very hard to bring 'great power' miscreants to justice. Nonetheless, international norms and judicial structures do now exist. A genuine global civic society is emerging (see Ch. 14). So conflicts now require not only post-conflict reconciliation but also redemptive justice.

Summary Next Step: Judging Conflicts at the Bar of History

Historical researchers into conflict strive to study, as coolly and as objectively as possible, all past manifestations of violence and hatred, not least in warfare and genocides. It is often grim work. And it certainly requires some stoicism. But researchers seek to understand, and their work also helps to dispel lurid exaggerations and persistent myths.

Dispassionate truth is owed to both the dead and the living. Retrospective acknowledgement is better than no justice at all. Japanese history provides another pertinent case. In the early 1940s, its Imperial Army coerced or lured into sexual slavery some two hundred thousand Asian women, many from Korea (and many very young). Their task was to 'service' the Japanese troops. For years, the fates of these so-called 'Comfort Women' were ignored. Yet, the efforts of determined survivors, aided by numerous Japanese and international historians, have shattered the silence.

Today, memorials to the 'Comfort Women' have been erected by American support groups, who now campaign to halt all sexual trafficking of women everywhere. There are also calls for direct redress to be made to the dwindling numbers of surviving victims. It's a controversial topic, particularly in Japan itself. Yet wartime sexual slavery is no longer a 'taboo' subject.

Calmly but purposively, people need to understand what humans can do to other humans, at the worst of times. Such assessments work for the long-term…but they add to collective human understanding. History is not just about 'nice' matters. Understanding the worst offers a chance (certainly not a guarantee) of minimising negative aspects of human aggression; of finding policies which enhance community cooperation; of developing mechanisms of non-violent conflict resolution; of curbing the worst excesses of fighting, should that ensue; and of redressing its worst effects afterwards.

Full understanding also gives a basis for considered judgment. Humans on their collective journey need reliable information. What is more important than to understand the capacities of their own species, not just for good but for the reverse? They should not rush to judgment, still less to vengeance. That reflex response only adds further momentum to cycles of violence.

Competition and rivalry have some dynamic effects. But they need to be kept within bounds and matched with policies to boost cooperation and solidarity. So should clashing interests escalate into organised warfare, as undoubtedly happens, then fellow humans should do their best to halt the fighting—to broker a fair and lasting peace settlement, to promote healing—but also to judge all perpetrators of war crimes impartially and fairly, at the bar of history, *in the full glare of Time…*

Human Behaviour in Biological Context

Bekoff, M. Pierce, J. (2009) *Wild Justice: The Moral Lives of Animals.*
Wrangham, R. W. (2019) *The Goodness Paradox: How Evolution Made Us Both More and Less Violent.*

Hatreds

Boyce, T. D., Chunnu, W. N. (eds) (2020) *Historicising Fear: Ignorance, Vilification and Othering.*

Eibl-Eibesfeldt, I. (1971) *Love and Hate: On the Natural History of Basic Behaviour Patterns*, transl. G. Strachan.

Violent Conflicts

Archer, I., Ferris, J. R., Herwig, H. H., Travers, T. H. E. (eds) (2003) *World History of Warfare.*

Nye, J. S., Welch, D. A. (2013) *Understanding Global Conflict and Cooperation: Introduction to Theory and History.*

Genocides

Bloxham, D., Moses, A. D. (eds) (2010) *Oxford Handbook of Genocide Studies.*

Hewitt, W. L. (ed) (2004) *Defining the Horrific: Readings on Holocaust and Genocide in the Twentieth Century.*

Memorials to Warfare

Sodaro, A. (2018) *Exhibiting Atrocity: Memorial Museums and the Politics of Past Violence.*

West, B. (ed) (2019) *War, Memory and Commemoration.*

Retrospective Justice

Archibugi, D., Pease, A. (2018) *Crime and Global Justice: The Dynamics of International Punishment.*

Pirie, F. (2021) *The Rule of Laws: A 4000-Year Quest to Order the World.*

Royer, C. (2020) *Evil as a Crime against Humanity: Confronting Mass Atrocities in a Plural World.*

Stephen, C. (2024) *The Future of War Crimes Justice.*

Chapter 14
Boosting Cooperation

Chapter 14 investigates the countervailing forces of human cooperation, noting social mechanisms that enhance solidarity, and celebrating recent steps towards a global civics.

Being Resilient

Time is the great healer... If the human story was all one of warlike conflict, then things would be very different. But people live in peace locally more frequently than they make war, and they show a marked capacity to cooperate It's often said that there are very few years in which there is not, somewhere around the globe, bloody warfare. And that proposition is probably correct.

Yet, equally, there's rarely, if ever, an era in history when all peoples are engaged in warfare simultaneously. Even in pan-global conflicts, there are regions which are not involved, while, even within belligerent countries, far from all fight or are caught by attacks upon civilians. Routines of ordinary life continue during wars, though not invariably, and certainly not for refugees fleeing the carnage.

Edgy and competitive as people can be, there are thus countervailing factors which constrain mass blood-lettings. It's probably true that malignant diseases have actually cut short or harmed more lives, historically, than has warfare. Major pandemics, especially those that target young adults in the prime child-producing years, can drastically reduce aggregate population numbers for many years. However, humans recover. And today's global population of almost eight *billion* people suggests a highly resilient species.

Before the extinction of the dinosaurs, about sixty-five million years ago, the few hominid precursors of today's humans lived furtive, hunted lives. Yet, the disappearance of the gigantic 'top predators' left a power vacuum. Many species competed. And it was *homo sapiens* which succeeded to global dominance. Humans are good at finding and generating resources, while avoiding being eaten by hungry predators. On land, lions, tigers, leopards, wolves, and bears constitute potential dangers, as do, in or close to water, sharks, crocodiles and alligators. Today, however, most of those big species are much reduced in numbers and terrain, while human dominance is pan-global.

One case indicates the changing balance of power among predators. In Nepal and northern India, a Bengal tigress, known as the Champawat Tiger (Uttarakhand), killed and ate four hundred and thirty-six people (possibly more), before her demise in 1907. She was estimated to be about ten or eleven years old; and she terrified villagers as she roamed in search of prey. Eventually, the legendary beast was shot dead by a British hunter, a plaque now marking the spot. Yet, despite her reign of terror, the tigress was on the losing side in history. Her forest habitat was dwindling, as were her non-human food supplies. Today, the Nepalese man-eaters are at risk of extinction, being protected only by valiant human conservationists.

Their collective organisation and ruthlessness serve humans well. Together, they build cities. Remodel the countryside. Domesticate cattle. They protect themselves from predators and, inadvertently, push other species into extinction or near-extinction. They explore the globe and near Space. They send fellow humans to walk on the moon. They create art, music, literature, science, medicine, and all branches of learning. They use languages. They invent tools and guns. They build power grids and transport networks. Operate smart phones.

They follow religions. Organise secular states and legal systems. They play sports. Enjoy communal festivities. Laugh at themselves.

All these activities depend upon some degree of sharing… To be sure, groups may organise to promote sectional interests, against those of others. And tensions can escalate into overt conflict (as already noted in Ch. 13). Yet, the core truth is that humans are a communal species, who live, love, learn, raise families, work, worship, play, travel, and fight, not alone but together.

Intermarrying and Sexual Partnering Amongst the Human Family

Geneticists confirm that all humans today belong to one biological species. As already noted, they share variants of the human genome or biological template. They have a common set of blood groups. When humans mate with any other humans, living in no matter which part of the world, their offspring are fertile (a classic species denominator). Visual variations among the diverse branches of the human family are thus, biologically speaking, but 'skin-deep'.

Historically and currently, men and women from different parts of the world often meet and mate, even if there are cultural and sometimes legal barriers. Indeed, impediments may provide an extra spur, generating the allure of the 'forbidden'. As a result, people today who investigate their deep ancestral roots are often surprised at the varied backgrounds which are revealed.

Barriers to intermarriage have at different times been imposed on many grounds, including ethnicity, religion, nationality, class, caste, and/or family hostilities (as in Shakespeare's *Romeo and Juliet*). People try to 'save' their specific group of humans from alleged socio-sexual 'contamination' by another.

By contrast, there is also a parallel literature celebrating love across boundaries. The ability to feel affection for fellow humans is widely shared (though not by all). 'The law of love knows no bounds of Space or Time', declares Mahatma Gandhi, thinking spiritually. Affection is not deterred by distance: 'And I will come again, my love/Though it were ten thousand miles', sang Robert Burns, poetically. Stern parents who try to keep young lovers apart face an uphill struggle. Proverbially, 'Love laughs at locksmiths'. Songbooks are full of the quest to find true affection, not just a 'permitted' partner. Hence, as Virgil wrote pithily in classical Rome: '*Amor Omnia Vicit*' [*Love Conquers All Things*].

That said, not all unions across social/legal barriers are outcomes of romance. Sometimes the story features power and exploitation. Men in authority may misuse their position to extract—whether by blandishments, threats or force—sexual favours from women of 'lower' and 'different' social groups. So there are many forms of sexual partnerships, not all being legally sanctioned.

Biologically, the effect of breeding between the varied branches of the human family works to increase genetic diversity. And hence collective resilience. Too much in-group reproduction (known as 'endogamy') risks recycling genetic flaws within a localised community. That reason probably underpins the near-universal human ban on incestuous unions, although definitions of precisely what constitutes incest vary from culture to culture.

When people from diverse backgrounds live and work in close proximity, the chances of intermarriage are much enhanced, whatever the cultural taboos. That happened, for example, in Northern Ireland. Even during the sectarian 'Troubles' of the 1970s and 1980s, a persistent minority embarked upon interfaith unions between Catholics and Protestants. And that happened, despite tough unofficial neighbourhood 'policing', which tried to keep the religious communities apart. Nonetheless, some couples rebelled. And, since 1974, the Mixed Marriage Association has helped to support Northern Irish interfaith partners.

Wherever humans create cultural barriers, other humans will find ways to cross them. The outcomes, however, are not always successful. Some 'mixed' marriages falter under the strain. And even those that flourish may find that they have, unwittingly, left their offspring with a troubled legacy. Their children may face hostility from both sides of the 'mix'; and may doubt their own identities.

Potential tensions were enhanced by the advent, from the eighteenth century onwards, of what was then termed 'scientific' racism. It gave an apparently expert authentication to feelings of 'difference'. Various separate 'races' were identified—often implicitly ranked from 'high' to 'low'.

In practice, however, this strand of thought proved to be an intellectual wrong-turning. As already noted in Ch. 7 (above), no consensus about the precise total of 'races' ever emerged. Estimates ranged from two to sixty-three. That discrepancy was well beyond a minor margin of error.

Racist attitudes do, however, show great cultural longevity, partly because those at the 'top' sometimes have a vested interest in upholding 'difference'. There are many subtle variants. In some countries, an unofficial 'pigmentocracy' may operate. 'Light' skins are praised, while 'dark' are not. Such attitudes may then prove harmful if dark-skinned humans internalise them and wrongly believe in their own 'inferiority'. There are potential physical dangers too, if people use medically risky skin-lighteners, such as the controversial hydroquinone.

Generating harmony within the huge human family remains a continuing social challenge. But the great range of human skin colours indicates *de facto* the historic extent of intermarriage and/or sexual partnering.

An attempt to finesse such classifications was undertaken in Apartheid South Africa in the twentieth century. Citizens were classified as 'White', 'Indian', 'Black' and 'Cape Coloured'—the fourth category being people of 'mixed' European/African parentage. Official ideology decreed that all these groups should remain apart, being *separate but equal*. It was a cruel sleight of hand as power and wealth were monopolised by 'Whites'.

However, the rising numbers of Cape Coloured people indicated that laws could not always corral biology. 'Whites' and 'natives' continued to inter-breed successfully, despite South Africa's Immorality Act of 1927 which banned them not just from marrying but also from having extra-marital sex.

To repeat, biology declares humans to constitute one huge family, sharing common blood groups and one human genome. True, the growing human family has many branches, some being of close cousinage, others more distant. True, too, that family bonds do not guarantee perfect harmony. But having a shared biological inheritance—and a shared residence on Planet Earth—gives an impetus, historically, for billions of people to strive to live peaceably together. And in that endeavour, they are aided not only by pooled knowledge (say, of names and dates) but also by shared human traits.

Generating Conventions of Daily Behaviour

Communal behaviour everywhere is eased by collective conventions of personal self-management. These are followed semi-automatically, thus saving effort and worry. Unofficial 'norms' are promoted partly by instinctive biological behaviour; partly by social custom; and, in some cases, by formal laws and religious teachings. Agreed conventions build upon tradition but are not static.

Societies everywhere expect a proper degree of bodily self-control from adults. Much effort in child-rearing is devoted to making the young aware of such requirements. For instance, all humans are early trained to control their bowel movements. Generally, too, people are taught to show a degree of consideration for others. They should not snatch food from other people's plates. Or bump, jostle and cause needless harm, either at home or when outside in crowds. Or shout or scream suddenly, except for special reasons. Or disturb sleeping people. Or indeed throw ordure or other rubbish over fellow humans.

Quite how much uninterrupted personal 'body space' individuals expect to have around themselves varies from culture to culture. Some cultivate considerable physical aloofness, while others encourage hugging and tactility. Yet, everywhere, respecting agreed conventions is socially learned behaviour, which usually does not rely upon legal enforcement (except in extreme cases).

Communities also have unwritten rules about how to meet and greet others. Should people prostrate themselves? Or bow deeply? Remove hats (men) or curtsey (women)? Shake hands? Bump fists or elbows? Rub noses? Kiss? Hug? Put a hand on heart? Or hold two hands forward with palms pressed together? Further refinements are also required in some religious cultures, with special conventions about greetings between men and women. The collective variety is most impressive. As is the fact that all societies have such unwritten conventions, showing that the norm expectation is a peaceful greeting.

Notably, too, the diplomatic handshake emerged long ago as a compromise salutation between ambassadors from two equally mighty kings. Neither one could show signs of submission to the other. So shaking hands at arm's length was an acceptable sign of mutual respect. Moreover, the growing extent of international meetings is today seeing the *de facto* spread of the egalitarian handshake as a common (though not universal) international mode of greeting That salutation brings people close together but not *too* close, hence not offending people from cultures where greetings do not entail bodily touching. It means that social conventions, while deep-rooted, are not immutable.

Other strong assumptions, including religious codes, influence what people consider acceptable to eat and drink. Some consume horsemeat, for example, without a second thought, while others recoil with horror. These patterns follow group allegiances, not government decrees. The same applies to conventions about dress and undress. What clothes are acceptable to wear, in which circumstances? And how much bare flesh to reveal and when?

Laws can and do intervene to check the quality of goods on sale and to prevent grossly anti-social behaviour. Yet, they regulate, rather than direct, community preferences. As already noted, the top-down attempt in the USA in

1919 to prohibit by law the sale and consumption of alcohol was a total failure. Attitudes can be changed, but not by an instant ruling from the state.

Meanwhile, references to intimate bodily functions are similarly subject to unwritten conventions. Outside the medical context, women rarely mention menstruation (except with trusted female friends). The experience is often culturally viewed as 'unclean' and polluting. As a result, it remains a semi-secret form of 'women's business'. Equally, men don't talk publicly about unwanted erections and/or nocturnal emissions of semen (if any). Even comedy shows, which enjoy challenging taboos, rarely mention these intimate matters.

Privacy is also sought for real-life sexual activities between consenting adults. True, public displays of mutual affection (hand-holding, kissing) are tolerated in some cultures (but not all). True, too, there are occasions when erotic exhibitions are shown semi-publicly, as in sex-shows. Yet, their overt imagery gains its 'buzz' by being in such marked contrast to the norm.

Doubtless, one ancestral reason for seclusion when mating was the need to avoid being caught 'off-guard' by enemies or by animal predators. Or onlookers might be distracting, perhaps laughing unfeelingly at heaving buttocks, flailing limbs, and moans of pleasure. At any rate, humans almost universally keep their mating activities private, not through shame but through erotic preference.

A similar caution also promotes a deep fastidiousness about excrement. Smelly droppings might alert dangerous animal predators, let alone leave clues for human enemies. So best to keep a distance. Humans, like most mammals, don't seek to wallow in their own excrement. Adults generally urinate and defecate in private. Even anti-social youths, who piss in town alleyways, usually do so furtively; while, in their homes, they adhere to social conventions.

What's more, humans generally talk very little (again, outside a medical context) about their bowel movements. Hence scatological or 'toilet' humour derives its shock value (especially for children) by breaking taboos of general silence about such private matters.

Keeping a fastidious distance from human excrement no doubt conferred, historically, good sanitary benefits. In fact, the ancestral practice of open-air defecation in fields or forests, away from homes, survives in some communities today. Yet, social attitudes and technologies of waste removal have long been changing. In densely populated societies, the old practice of open-air defecation is generating new health hazards, which medical officials are combatting (An unglamorous updating of 'gutter politics' but an essential one).

Conventions are thus not immutable. And they can always be flouted or ignored. On their own, unwritten rules do not hold mass societies together. Yet, they do indicate the deep cooperative reflexes which sustain humans in groups. Such instincts are as basic as the human capacity for competition. And both are traits that societies can either boost or discourage.

Human inventiveness is a great capacity that aids the struggle for survival. At the same time, however, daily life unfolds within a thick web of socially known rules and conventions. It is not necessary to reinvent everything from scratch. Versatility thrives when springing from a common launching pad.

Enjoying Concord and Cooperation

Plenty of experience confirms that cooperative team-working does not depend solely upon top-down power structures. *Ad hoc* groups run things together informally. Sometimes one dominant or well-organised individual will take the lead. At other times, however, people share tasks between themselves. (There are plenty of songs about group cooperation, often work songs, designed to coordinate physical labour: '*Yo-heave-ho!*' as sung by the Volga boatmen.)

Discontent, however, arises if participants in a cooperative group feel that some people are extracting benefits without doing any work. Many a well-intentioned commune has begun with goodwill but collapsed with acrimony. Nonetheless, not all do. So there are American communes today which began in the 'hippy' 1960s and still flourish. Key factors for success include good communal group management, a strong positive bond or ideology, economic viability, cheerful temperaments, and smart action to nip troubles in the bud.

The instinct of trust is, after all, deeply ingrained. From birth, human babies have no choice. Their complete dependency leaves a residual feeling of shared common bonds. As they grow older, people learn to become more cautious. Not every smiling person is actually a friend.

Nevertheless, an appeal to the 'kindness of strangers' does often work. People go out of their way to help. They jump into rivers and seas to save strangers in difficulty. They donate body organs for transplant to assist invalids they have never met. They share limited resources with others who are even worse off. They provide altruistic service to the community, without seeking financial recompense or personal praise. These are all examples of species solidarity, even if (no surprise) not all feel such commitment.

Added to instinctive feelings, there is the input of civic education, plus religious teachings. All condemn undue egotism and stress the need to think of others. No person is *the only pebble on the beach*. The gain is human companionship, in lieu of psychological isolation. Hence, the greater the unbroken trust that children experience in infancy, the greater the trust in others that they are likely to show in later life.

At times, it is true, self-defined groups can reserve solidarity only for those within their own circles. They may hate and fear 'others'. And they may direct special hostility at the government as well if it is seen as led by 'enemies'.

Universal goodwill is far from universal. Nonetheless, all but the most seriously troubled people usually manage to mingle with others daily, without fearing danger everywhere.

Coordinating the mutual dependence of human societies is the task of an immense array of organisations, both formal and informal. The history of government is very lengthy, from the traditional rule of tribal elders to the nation-states of today. But they all share basic tasks of setting rules (for example, regulating the disposal of human waste) and keeping order.

Dictatorial authorities officially concentrate the directive power in a single ruler or single institution at the 'top'. In pluralist states, by contrast, there are multiple sources of authority. Even in monolithic dictatorships, however, there are usually some unofficial channels whereby organisations (like churches and businesses) exercise power 'behind the scenes'. Systems often have a degree of flexibility. However, the lack of accountability in dictatorships can too generate public discontent, especially when economic hardships multiply. Moreover, when and if such grievances are felt by individuals in the agencies of repression (army, police, secret services), then dictatorships are especially liable to totter.

Pluralist governments, meanwhile, tend to delegate a lot of business. Some specific matters are sent 'outwards' to arms-length national organisations or to privatised services. Other tasks, meanwhile, are delegated 'downwards', to regional and local authorities, all the way to village councils. (These days, the powers of many localised bodies are eroding, although there are sometimes rather notional pledges to reverse the process.) Furthermore, pluralistic systems generally encourage many other non-governmental organisations. These include churches, businesses, national utilities, charities, universities, schools, and sporting associations—with their own structures and their own civic roles.

People living in pluralist societies are thus accustomed to dealing with multiple bodies in what is termed 'civil society'. They also expect to exercise a degree of choice, when electing the holders of political power. Yet, politicians' promises can be hard to deliver, especially in economic downturns. Accordingly, democratic societies may contain their own levels of disenchantment, especially if wealth and power appear to be monopolised by a small clique. Voters, however, generally don't wish to surrender their right to vote, even though not all exercise it regularly.

Taking a long view, liberal optimists predict that the spread of literacy and education, plus the interconnecting powers of trade, will foster a global rise of peace-loving, open and tolerant democratic states. It's certainly an excellent hope. Yet, such forces are working only slowly. (Not totally surprising, since the advent of near-universal literacy is, historically, very recent news.)

Dictatorships maintain intimidating powers of censorship and repression. Furthermore, democratic societies are not all equally open and tolerant. They may become vulnerable either to domination by one 'strong' leader or to internal coups.

While there is no universal 'march' towards global democracy, however, there have been some remarkable international innovations, which are changing the rules of inter-state engagements. Notably, the twentieth century witnessed the formation of the League of Nations (1920) and its successor, the United Nations (1945). These have brokered new conventions about the conduct of warfare, as already noted. And there are now international agreements to coordinate: global health, global policing, global trade and commercial tariffs, global shipping, global telecommunications, global banking, global environmental policies, and global cooperation in Space.

Of course, the resulting systems are far from perfect. But democracies and dictatorships accept these frameworks (even if they sometimes flout them on specific policies). And there are additional world-regional organisations and alliances, both political and military. The international stage is not a vacuum.

Furthermore, many non-governmental bodies now have their own international networks. These include churches, banks, businesses, professional societies, sporting associations, including the Olympics, educational networks, social clubs, charities, and campaigning bodies. These organisations, some large and well-funded, others small and 'niche', collectively provide an intermediate stage—beyond the control of nation-states—for global encounters.

Together, these non-governmental organisations are generating an entirely new form of global 'civil society'. They do not represent anything like a global public opinion. And their coverage is undoubtedly far from worldwide.

Nonetheless, this change is epic. It beckons towards a future of global negotiation, not confrontation. Even, one day, perhaps, a future of global governance?

Individuals belonging to international associations can be proud of being national citizens and, simultaneously, 'citizens of the world'. They are generating a new global civics, based upon shared global networks, friendships, and a common interest in the welfare of Planet Earth and its residents.

Seeking Reconciliation After Discord

Attempts at peace-making after warfare and civil conflict also have a long history. Can once warring parties agree to share a classic 'pipe of peace'? Or in a different context, can they 'shake hands' and draw a line under the past? And, even if leaders agree, will grass-roots participants follow suit? The role of redemptive justice has already been noted, at the end of the previous chapter.

Humanity is, in fact, evolving a repertoire of strategies for reconciliation. These provide options, rather than a single template. They can be applied not only to the aftermath of wars and civil war but also to reconciliation after historic injustices, such as the centuries-long trans-Atlantic trade in enslaved Africans, with which later generations today seek to come to terms.

Memorials and rituals of collective remembrance, even long after grim past events, are one mark of humanity's willingness to learn from history. Of course, tributes are best made with restrained dignity. Memorials that push messages too aggressively or mawkishly *in your face* can backfire. Hence, the need for reasoned public discussions about both past wrongs and later attempts at due acknowledgement.

Sharing memories across past dividing lines can also help to reunite. Truth and Reconciliation Commissions (or similar forums under other names) offer a public platform for 'truth-telling'. As in therapies for troubled individuals or unhappy couples, the aim is to bring problems into the open, allowing space for understanding, reflection and a measure of forgiveness. It is an admirable liberal hope that *truth will set people free.* All viewpoints, no matter how contentious, should be acknowledged at the bar of history—with empathy, albeit not necessarily with sympathy.

Accurate knowledge will help to prevent the recurrence of grim past conflicts, though, of course, it offers no guarantee. The work of historians, as already noted, is particularly helpful here. Their patient research often debunks the myths and exaggerations that cluster around emotive past conflicts.

Exercises in collective remembrance, however, need to be undertaken with sensitivity. Behaviours in warfare, when social norms are set aside, can be brutally repulsive and painful to recover. Emphasising solely past injustices can augment, among the victims, feelings of bitterness and anger. But equally, emphasising solely past culpabilities can prompt, among the aggressors, a subterranean guilt which may switch into an even more venomous disparagement of the victims, as a retrospective self-justification.

Truth-telling about bad times needs, therefore, to be set in a credible counter-framework of positive change. And one that is embraced on all sides.

Similarly, public apologies for historical injustices go far but not far enough. Expressions of contrition, made by later political and religious leaders, can provide salve for old wounds. Such statements underline the good intention not to replicate past horrors. But contrition works best when complemented by positive and publicly supported policies of ecumenical renewal.

Education in shared humanist values is also crucial. But, again, that task requires careful thought. Civic education should be participatory *and* inspiring. There's no point in lecturing dogmatically 'at' people. Nor does it help to dwell solely or even chiefly upon negative blaming. Individuals don't learn by being told that they are 'bad' and their views 'wrong'. Instead, all need to know not only how past wars and injustices have happened but also how to halt their recurrence, in the name of a global humanity.

All such exercises in learning from history require patience and repeated effort. Such a coming-to-terms with the past was undertaken with dignity in post-1945 Germany. It did not happen overnight. However, it was slowly fostered by both political and religious leaders. A few hard-right ideologues remain unrepentant. Overall, however, mainstream German culture has managed, not to 'forget' Nazism, but instead to 'remember-in-order-to-reject-decisively'.

Reconciliation additionally calls for hard-headed decisions about recognising economic injuries and making measured responses. Warfare causes damage, not only to lives but also to livelihoods. Moreover, conflicts often stem from rival economic interests, as well as rival ideas. Post-war settlements cannot please everyone. But they can make some recompense for wartime damages, help communities to rebuild, and address the most glaring injustices and inequalities that trigger discontent and resentment. These are long-term policies, calling for a new social compact of fairness to all parties.

Healing tensions between warring groups, who claim exclusive rights to the same territory, is a particularly hard task. Answers may well require a degree of managed sharing, probably with international arbitration to ensure honest dealing. It is important to uphold principles of 'fair play'. And it is equally vital the arbitrators are themselves trusted as being non-partisan and above the fray. Who knows? Perhaps future wars will be deflected by referring big disputes to international arbitration instead.

Collectively, and slowly, the world is developing *ad hoc* guidelines. There is now an international compact (not always honoured) on giving protection to refugees. And there are principled global affirmations. In 1998, the date of 23 August was adopted by the United Nations Educational, Scientific and Cultural Organisation (UNESCO) as an annual day of remembrance to recall both the trade in enslaved populations and its abolition.

Moreover, such acts of remembrance fortify continuing campaigns to halt clandestine people trafficking and neo-slavery of all kinds. These social horrors are proving hard to eradicate…but global opinion has been clearly stated.

Always there are lessons to learn. Symbolic actions are mightily assisted when supported by positive actions, to assist all historically injured parties. Efforts at reconciliation are strengthened when placed in the context of a shared humanist education. And good intentions need to be backed by effective global enforcement. *Well! Optimistic, yes! But it's now high Time to see whether humanity can cooperate globally, across the planet.*

Summary: Building a Global Civics

Building global civics is emphatically not the work of a day. It requires immense tolerance, flexibility, mutual understanding, education in the principles of mutuality, a readiness to heal justified grievances, and hope.

Formulating and sharing universal human values needs input from political and religious leaders, as well as from community workers, teachers, lawyers, medics, journalists, broadcasters, and all manner of social arbitrators, provided, of course, that these are not the ones actively fomenting discord. And in practice, all people, rich and poor, power-brokers and grass-roots, have to play their part. As part of fostering concord, it's important too that there should not be dangerous gulfs within communities, for example with a gilded few enjoying excessive wealth while the masses live in dire poverty.

Not that all human lives should be the same. That is impossible. But the bonds that unite communities should be greater than the issues that divide them.

Globally, what is needed now is global solidarity. Evidence from the past one hundred and fifty years indicates that humans have begun to build international associations based upon trust. As already noted, these changes are not happening solely at inter-governmental levels—important as those are in sustaining a framework of international law. But a myriad of global associations are also emerging spontaneously from below, giving practical experience in global cooperation.

Unquestionably, the human capacity for conflict cannot be discounted or forgotten. Yet, humans have a countervailing capacity for cooperation, which they can take reasoned steps to boost. They also have good evidence to show what factors bind communities together and what divides them.

Immediately, today all people everywhere are getting a mighty prod into collective action by the ramifications of climate change. Being one species, living on just one planetary home, has unavoidable consequences.

Constructive action is needed globally, not only to adopt the best eco-policies but also to strengthen global civics. That latter development has already begun spontaneously. And, in the cause of human survival, urgent actions are also needed to reduce gross inequalities and to boost global togetherness. *Now is the Time…*

Risk and Resilience

Hart, D., Sussman, R. W. (2018) *Man the Hunted: Primates, Predators and Human Evolution.*

Schoon, I. (2016) *Human Development in Context: The Study of Risk and Resilience.*

Intermarriage

Cavalli-Sforza, L. L., Cavalli-Sforza, F. (1995) *The Great Human Diasporas: The History of Diversity and Evolution.*

Farber, P. L. (2011) *Mixing Races: From Scientific Racism to Modern Evolutionary Ideas.*

Conventions of Daily Behaviour

Bethanne, P. (2011) *An Uncommon History of Common Courtesy: How Manners Shaped the World.*
Bremmer, J., Roodenburg, H. (eds), (1991) *A Cultural History of Gesture: From Antiquity to the Present Day.*

Amity and Reconciliation

Allen, S. H. (2022) *Interactive Peace-making: A People-Centred Approach.*
Araujo, A.L. (2017) *Reparations for Slavery and the Slave Trade: A Transnational and Comparative History.*
Boje, T. P. (2021) *Civility and Participatory Democracy: The Importance of Civil Society and Active Citizenship.*
Quigley, P., Hawdon, J. (eds) (2018) *Reconciliation after Civil Wars: Global Perspectives.*

Humanist Principles

Altinay, H. (2011) (ed) *Global Civics: Responsibilities and Rights in an Interdependent World,*
Tremblay, R. (2010) *The Code for Global Ethics: Ten Humanist Principles.*

Chapter 15
Putting the Pieces Together

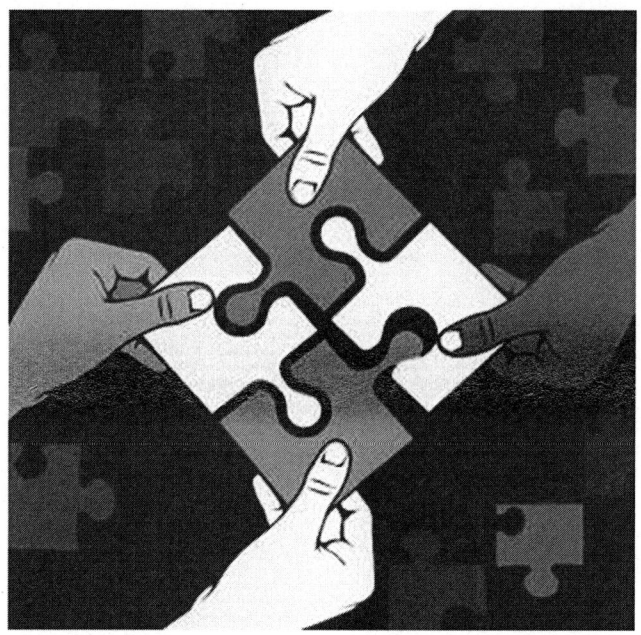

Chapter 15 acclaims the deep human interest in the past, whether enjoyed in the form of historical fiction or investigated via painstaking historical research. The result means that humans travel together from past to future, fortified by reliable knowledge.

Understanding the Knowledge Spectrum

Time to think… Time to share thoughts…and Time to act. The past constitutes a gigantic reservoir of cosmic experience. Tracking the human story—and its wider cosmic context—reveals not only deep continuities and reassuring truths but also plentiful upheavals and/or disasters. Yet, the past is no prison. It supplies ample evidence for learning. It supplies warnings. It suggests many options but not the option of halting the march of all-encompassing Time-Space.

Note, meanwhile, that knowledge covers a spectrum. Between the polarities of confirmed truths and outright errors, there is room for a great range of probabilities, possibilities and imaginative speculations. These permutations can provoke stimulating debates and creative rethinking, provided that fake news and fabrications are not mistaken for the 'real thing'.

Some framework truths are so basic that they count as 'truisms' (*obvious truths*). Thus reliable evidence from history and biology confirms that living creatures start young and grow older, not *vice versa*. Or here is a negative truth. Evidence from history and physics confirms that humans cannot jump physically from one planet to another (Future technologies may possibly facilitate interplanetary travel but not on the basis of human motor power alone).

Many other aspects of the human story remain, however, within the range of probabilities and possibilities. On a number of issues, there is not just one 'right answer'. There may instead be competing sets of good interpretations, requiring further research and debate to check and choose between them.

Yet, at the same time, there are seriously 'wrong' versions of the past. These are either based on false arguments or false evidence, or both. And given that there are liars who may have an interest in peddling falsities (as shown in Ch. 11), evidence on all important points should always be rechecked and retested.

Understanding the past (both human and cosmic) is so important that it's worth restating once more. Having a warped view of past experience leads people to make erroneous judgments. And, at worst, it can lead them to journey unknowingly into serious danger.

Enjoying Historical Fiction as Fiction

What then is the role of openly fictional accounts of the past? Do these constitute a problem? The answer is emphatically: *Not at all*. Historical fictions, in all their myriad variety, may look backwards or onward through Time. By so doing, they trigger fresh thoughts, stir imaginations, and explore mentally the myriad of options in historical pathways taken and not taken. These fertile inventions provide wonderfully creative grist to the mental mill, provided that the boundary between 'fact' and fiction is clearly understood.

Because the past is such a gigantic reservoir of experience and rival options, it is not surprising that its material is regularly raided. Historical scenarios and personalities are re-imagined in countless novels, poems, plays, pageants, films, toys and games. The range is immense. Hence they don't all fall into simple categories ('realist'; 'escapist'; 'romantic'; 'sci-fi'). Instead, historical fiction are endlessly protean. And the best are wonderfully inventive.

So it's not surprising that historical fictions find ready markets. Even those individuals who claim to have no interest in 'olden times', can find themselves enjoying (say) a digital replay of a past battle when the attacker is required to match the historical outcome (or do better) and the defender to avert defeat (and, ideally, to counterattack successfully). Great fun.

Moreover, successful creators of historical fiction have usually researched their materials carefully. They don't seek total verisimilitude. There's no market in referencing the sickening reek of real blood in a battle scene. Or in showing leading characters on screen with historically accurate bad teeth (though blackened fangs do well for villains). Instead, creators of historical fiction work hard to achieve enough authenticity to keep their audiences convinced and interested, while leaving ample scope for invention and imagination.

Fiction writers thus have untrammelled licence to play with the past. It's their privilege. By contrast, historians don't have the same freedom.

That point was well made by the English playwright and screenwriter, Alan Bennett. His career began with a brief stint as an academic historian at Oxford University. He then used his professional expertise to write his acclaimed play (later filmed), entitled *The Madness of King George* (1991). However, Bennett later confessed that he'd felt residual guilt at putting invented words into the mouths of real people from the past. The result is often funny. So the deluded George III announces that he is '*here—here—but not all there*'. At that point, Bennett cleverly manages to raise a laugh while simultaneously helping audiences to sympathise with the monarch's authentic predicament.

Nevertheless, things become problematic if and when fictions are seriously taken as fact. To minimise that possibility, authors often take precautions. Some historical novelists reference their sources. And others provide cast lists, differentiating the *bona fide* historical personages from the invented ones.

A further source of deception can arise, these days, from the great technical skills of film-makers. They splice authentic news-reel footage from earlier eras so seamlessly into later films that casual viewers can easily be misled. One example is the absorbing film about Britain's King George VI and his speech therapist, *The King's Speech* (dir. Tom Hooper, 2010). A later exchange in print between a stern reviewer and the director helpfully elucidated which material was interpolated and where. It was good to have this information on the record.

Indeed, some historical films do provide fact-checking websites, so that interested viewers can check for themselves. And, where such production information is not supplied, vigilant reviewers may furnish it instead.

Spot-checks of that sort are not intended to curb the creative imagination. Nor could they. The past cannot be policed or declared 'off-limits'. But there are enough 'factoids' in circulation already (see Ch. 11), without inadvertently adding more. So having fact-checking advice available for consumers of historical fiction of all sorts is beneficial.

Significantly, too, such precautions are now 'on trend'. Today's world of super-fast information exchange by mass media is speeding the spread of 'fake news' and disinformation. As a result, the twenty-first century is witnessing a notable rise in public fact-checkers. They are helping everyone to keep a grip on ordinary life, without denying a role for human inventiveness. (Interested in exploring the overlaps between historical research and crime detection? Try reading the majestic murder mystery by Umberto Eco: *Il nome della rosa* (1980); in English translation by W. Weaver as *The Name of the Rose* (1983). Or compare with another arresting historical puzzle, in a very different style: Josephine Tey, *The Daughter of Time* (1951).)

Testing Factual Evidence

Historians seek to present reasoned arguments, which are backed by reliable evidence. They do not just list fact after fact. They explore all relevant source materials from the past, whether in the form of art, artefacts, buildings, documents, songs, statistics, or anything else... And their overriding commitment is to use the evidence fairly and accurately. All information should be carefully checked and tested. Evidence should never be manipulated to mean something that it doesn't. Nor faked.

Furthermore, in the event of finding significant evidence that contradicts a researcher's pet theory or favoured interpretation, good practice demands that such evidence be declared and emphatically not concealed.

It is also essential for historical researchers to explain how they use their evidence. For example, if they classify data to provide an aggregate overview, the basis of the classification should be explained (briefly but clearly). Everything should be on the record. Hence, others can go back to the originals and cross-check. And then, if they wish, they can provide an alternative interpretation. The result of checking and cross-checking means that research can often be slow and painstaking. But retrieving the past is also enthralling.

Incidentally, readers of historical studies cannot go back to check all the original source materials. So their best alternative is to check the credentials of historians and their publishers.

One case history shows how debates may persist, even after in-depth research. It features the death of the exiled French Emperor Napoleon Bonaparte on the Atlantic island of St Helena. Did he die on 5 May 1821? *Yes; there is plenty of first-hand testimony.* Did he die of stomach cancer? *That seems probable, according to contemporary evidence and later medical reviews.*

But, wait a minute: do surviving locks of Napoleon's hair contain traces of arsenic? *Yes.* Does that prove that he was poisoned? *Not necessarily fatally. Arsenic traces survive in many nineteenth-century household furnishings and in samples of European hair from that era.* Did a human assassin enter Napoleon's residence? *Probably not, though that charge was made in 1822, not long after his death.* Did the British government, which was not sorry when its most dangerous prisoner died aged fifty-two, order his assassination? *Probably not, since it already kept the ex-emperor under close control. Nonetheless, Napoleon's will, written on his deathbed, did state that he himself viewed his impending death as suspiciously premature.*

Alternatively, how about a completely different set of questions? Was Napoleon's death faked, allowing him to escape to South America where he died of ripe old age? *No, there is no evidence to support that later myth.* Was his entire captivity faked, by sending a body double to St Helena and allowing the defeated general to live incognito in Verona, where a spectacle-maker looked notably like him? *No, that is another myth and not a very plausible one.*

Or what about another, even more dramatic, possibility: was the very existence of Napoleon Bonaparte faked by the British government? Did it invent him as a bogey-man to frighten Britons into supporting the costly war against France? *No.* But that sly argument was actually made in 1819, in an intellectual *jeu d'esprit,* entitled *Historic Doubts Relative to Napoleon.*

This intriguing polemic was written by Archbishop Richard Whateley. His aim was to challenge the religious sceptics of his day. They argued against the historical existence of Jesus Christ, by questioning the scrappy historical evidence. In response, Whateley sought to show his fellow Christians that too much doubt could undermine everything, including things (like the existence of Napoleon) which everyone across Europe 'knew' unhesitatingly to be true. Hence Whateley urged his flock to cease doubting and to have faith.

Tit-for-tat propositions of that nature are intellectually diverting. However, they do not actually resolve the basic questions of evidence. After all, there are many legendary historical figures—some of whom did exist in earlier times, and some of whom did not. All myths are well worth studying as myths. They should not, however, be taken literally without careful cross-checking.

Meanwhile, Whateley's polemic can be given yet another twist. Rather than scoffing at doubts about Napoleon or Christ, his deeper message can be read as stressing the need to check everything. And that can be applied in his case too. After all, who was Whateley? Did *he* really exist? Or was he perhaps a double agent in the secret pay of Napoleon, raising doubts about the ex-emperor's existence so that the real defeated Corsican could escape quietly in disguise, and live out his life in South America?

Well! *In fact, not so.* There is ample evidence to confirm that Whateley was a flamboyant and argumentative philosopher-theologian, who was also a reforming Anglican Archbishop of Dublin.

Nonetheless, the general point remains a good one. Liars, deceivers and exaggerators operate at all times and in many guises. There are also plain errors, which get copied and repeated inadvertently. *Check everything, including the basics!* (Noted already; but always worth repeating). Elaborate superstructures of knowledge, which are built upon sand, remain just that, built on sand.

Exposing Biases

There's no doubt that individuals from all walks of life have their own personal viewpoints and preferences. Generally, however, it's not hard to spot the difference between what happened in history and what might have happened in one's ideal scenario.

People manage to make such distinctions in their daily lives. And researchers do so consciously. For example, a present-day supporter of republican government could explain why Napoleon decided in 1804 to crown himself emperor, without needing to berate the Corsican for betraying true republican values. Historians are not invited to give a personal thumbs-up or thumbs-down for every twist and turn in past events. That said, however, it would be perfectly fair and accurate to report that such criticisms of Napoleon were voiced at the time, by numerous of his former political allies.

Certainly, a proportion of professional historians do have specific ideological commitments, which may affect their interpretations. They may be Marxists. Or have (say) strong nationalist, political or religious beliefs. Or have strong opinions on questions of gender roles and ethnic identities.

However, historical researchers are trained to reflect upon their personal attitudes and to acknowledge any strong commitments in their writings—usually within the preface to a book or essay. In that way, they play fair with their readers, just as they are committed to playing fair with the evidence.

Matters become seriously difficult only if partisan researchers take their partisan views as a licence to ignore obvious evidence and/or to fake their sources (a point already made in Ch. 11). Things become even trickier, too, if financial inducements are offered, to get people to warp the research outcomes.

By the way, it's worth repeating that many ideologies today—whether secular or religious—are very variegated. So Marxist theory has diversified in the one hundred and fifty-plus years since Marx and Engels first wrote. Historians who follow their inspiration will look first for underlying economic issues in any social confrontation. Yet, Marxists do not all agree on (say) the career of Napoleon Bonaparte.

Similarly, most other schools of thought are also diverse. There are rival versions of conservatism (say) and feminism. And the same point applies to the world's major religions. Ideological diversification is actually gaining force, within the context of growing global travel and cultural mixing.

All the interest and intellectual excitement of studying the past is actually lost, if researchers have begun with a pre-set conclusion. They have missed the point entirely. It is helpful to start with some broad ideas, theories, conjectures and hypotheses. But then it's essential to test those against the evidence and to debate the outcomes with fellow researchers. As Arthur Conan Doyle's great fictional detective. Sherlock Homes once observed: *'It is a capital mistake to theorise before you have all the evidence'*.

No overly rigid theory, then. But, equally, input from a thinking researcher is an essential part of the process of understanding. No one could or should approach the past with a completely blank mind. In practice, many researchers borrow ideas from a pick-and-mix of approaches. And they often find, too, that they are refining and adapting their own views as their work proceeds.

Personal attitudes may also have an impact. So it's helpful for researchers to self-assess their own temperaments. Some people are naturally more traditionalist. Some are more liberal. Some more radical. Others have firm views on ecology. Others on gender issues; or ethnic identities. Some are pessimists, who fear that *the end is nigh.* Others are bright-eyed optimists, who always hope for the best. (*This author confesses to that tendency, which she tries to keep under control*).

Critics, meanwhile, are always on hand to argue. They will bring their own minds to bear on things. Researchers constantly present their work at conferences and seminars. The ensuing debates are often intense. Once historical studies are published, too, reviewers add their views and a proportion of them don't hold back.

Readers also respond, favourably or unfavourably, as do audiences at lectures and viewers of documentaries. They do not have blank minds either. They argue too. *But! What? When? Why? Really?*

Evidence is mighty. Yet, to coin a phrase, *it cannot speak for itself.* It is the researchers who put the evidence together to understand the past and, simultaneously, to unfold Time's mysteries. Yet, none work alone. It is the community of all who study, debate, criticise, and recheck who help to iron out biases and seek the truth.

Seeking Impartiality

To assist the clarity of thought, there are some working rules of engagement that are worth summarising. The first is to ensure that all key research methods, concepts and terminologies are carefully defined. That's needed to avoid ambiguity. Otherwise, it's very annoying to get caught in a long wrangling discussion, which ends abruptly when the participants realise that they are talking at cross-purposes: *Oh, if that's what you mean by X, why didn't you say so earlier?*

Another rule advises that researchers, when making a case about the past, should always clarify their aims. If they wish to invent an alternative past, they can present their work as fiction (*Once upon a time, there was a planet…*). Or, if they want to advocate one particular version, they can write polemics, propaganda, and all forms of mission statements, through to campaign songs (*Vote, vote, vote to save Planet Earth!*).

When presenting serious research, however, the high ideal is the unadorned quest for truth. Of course, people do not always succeed. But they constantly strive. Philosophically, therefore, total doubt in all things is rejected (See the earlier discussion of historians' responses to postmodernist doubt in Ch. 4).

If, however, researchers cannot find the full truth, often because of patchiness in the surviving evidence, then it's perfectly fine—indeed necessary—to offer instead assessments in terms of probabilities and possibilities.

As they strive to provide impartial verdicts, historians are in some ways acting like trial judges. They too have personal feelings and beliefs. Yet, they are expected to suppress them when acting in their judicial roles.

Football coaches provide another—slightly less majestic—analogy. Their players do not want purely partisan good cheer (*Wonderful!*) or even total negativism (*Rubbish!*). Instead, they seek frank and fair assessments of their strengths *and* weaknesses (As well as practical advice on how to improve).

Equally, all those people who hope to learn serious things about the past want to learn from a judicious assessment. They don't need to know whether the researcher individually loves or hates (say) Napoleon or any other historical figure. Instead, the serious-minded public seeks the best evidence-based truth that the historical researchers can muster. It's fine if their accounts contain elements of doubts and difficulty. That's part of the story. And that public interest exists because seeking to understand their collective journey is what humans do.

Summary End Station: Travelling Together from Past to Future, Fortified by Reliable Knowledge

Knowledge (yes, it's worth restating again) does not come from the future. It comes from the reasoned study of ideas and evidence, from both past and present—the outcome constituting a shared legacy for everyone. That proposition applies in all fields of learning, from astrophysics to zoology.

Pessimistically, the novelist George Orwell once proposed that knowledge of olden times constitutes a form of power that can be used for totalitarian purposes. '*Who controls the past controls the future*', he wrote, adding chillingly: '*Who controls the present controls the past*'.

Fortunately, things are not so easy. In even the most absolute states, counter-information and rival ideas continue to offer challenges, even if only subversively at the 'edges'. And if it's difficult to reduce the present to total uniformity, it's even trickier to corral all global knowledge to support one totalising view. In the 1930s, for example, Josef Stalin tried to force Soviet scientists to endorse, on ideological grounds, Trofim Lysenko's theories of biological transformationism. Rival genetic studies were dismissed as merely the product of 'bourgeois capitalism' or, even more aggressively, as 'fascist science'.

Within Russia, Stalin did manage brutally to enforce compliance, at least outwardly. Yet global research into plant biology could not be so easily halted. Lysenkoism was eventually refuted, both empirically and theoretically. And scientists continued to build upon past research to advance the subject.

Orwell's dictum, nevertheless, offers a timely reminder of the critical significance of sound knowledge from the past. It's something that all people on Planet Earth share. And make. And need to understand (warts and all).

How then to tell the difference between 'fake news' on the one hand and reliable history and reputable science on the other? There's no magic bullet. But alert global citizens can all learn from the past, without being stuck-in-the-mud and refusing to change. They can test and debate, without rancour or rudeness. And they can all cultivate a reasoned scepticism, while avoiding the traps of weary cynicism and undue nihilism.

Red herrings and black lies are often well concealed. That's the cunning of humans. Yet, who are best placed to spot frauds, scams and deceptions? Why, other humans, of course, especially if they are willing to learn from experience.

Specifically, too, humans in the here and now need to learn urgently from both past science and history. Such studies warn of crisis and provide advice on crisis management. The science is clear. Many warnings have highlighted the adverse impact of climate change. And today, there is ample corroboration from abnormal fires, droughts, heatwaves, rainstorms, floods, rising seas, habitat loss, and biodiversity collapse. There are also serious longer-term risks of global economic disruption or even collapse, large-scale population displacements, and possibly, mass starvation.

Can people understand and take action swiftly enough? Brainpower and willpower, plus accurate knowledge and a readiness to improvise, are strong human qualities. The collective journey has proceeded thus far, despite setbacks (including serious current conflicts). Humans have generated a huge corpus of reliable knowledge. They need now to use it to find workable and globally fair solutions that can be implemented quickly and effectively.

It's also vital to boost collective cooperation worldwide. One positive measure would be to reduce the damaging gulf between those humans (and world regions) with immense wealth and those who live in dire poverty.

Today's crisis is global and active global solidarity is needed in response. Not just tree-planting! Not just enhancing biodiversity! Not just cutting the emission of harmful greenhouse gases! Not just shifting to green energy! But boosting cooperation throughout the human family, by reducing deep-rooted divisions and greatly strengthening mutual aid. *Is it Time? Yes, it really is Time.*

The Quest for Historical Truth Revisited

Banner, J. M. (2021) *The Ever-Changing Past: Why All History is Revisionist History.*

Carr, H., Lipscomb, S. (eds) (2021) *What is History, Now? How the Past and Present Speak to Each Other.*

History and Fiction

Greiner, R. (2021) *Cinematic Histospheres: On the Theory and Practice of Historical Films.*

Lukacs, G. (1969) *The Historical Novel.*

Southgate, B. (2009) *History Meets Fiction.*

Testing Evidence

Harrison Smith, S. (2004) *The Fact Checker's Bible: A Guide to Getting It Right.*

Poovey, M. (1998) *A History of the Modern Fact: Problems of Knowledge in the Sciences of Wealth and Society.*

Williams, R. C. (2015) *The Forensic Historian: Using Science to Re-Examine the Past.*

Checking Research Methods

Crymble, A. (2021) *Technology and the Historian: Transformations in the Digital Age.*

Schiuma, G., Carlucci, D. (2018) *Big Data in the Arts and Humanities: Theory and Practice.*

History and Civics

Guldi, J., Armitage, D. (2014) *The History Manifesto.*

Hess, D. E. (2009) *Controversy in the Classroom: The Democratic Power of Discussion.*

Matto, E. C. (eds) (et al.) (2021) *Teaching Civic Engagement Globally.*

Time Summary
Next Steps Together...in Time

Time present and Time past
Are both perhaps present in Time future
And Time future contained in Time past...

[opening lines from T. S. Eliot, *Burnt Norton* (1936), being the first of his *Four Quartets* (co-published, 1943)]

Step One: Being in Time

Time is in everyone and everything—and all are in Time, which provides the dynamic power within the cosmic Time-Space continuum.
That means that

*everyone and everything are 'fixed' in one Time-Space
which unfolds from past to future—
and people thus cannot escape
by abruptly leaving their current point in Time-Space
in order to travel to another era
or to an entirely different sector of the cosmos.*

*Unfolding Time-Space,
moreover, brings birth, life and death to all,
and makes no exception
for those individuals
who deny the reality of Time and claim it to be merely an 'illusion'.*

Step Two: Appreciating Time's Three Dimensions

*Time, like Space with which it is integrally yoked,
has three interlocking dimensions—
which incorporate deep continuity (ballast),
slow change (momentum)
and explosive discontinuity (turbulence).
Any changes made today to calm global climate turbulence
may hope to mitigate its worst effects,
but cannot erase those three fundamental dimensions.
Instead, humans can seek to abate the impact of turbulence by utilising
framework continuities
(the laws of science)
and by enhancing the cumulative might of gradualism
(by very many incremental micro-adaptations).*

Step Three: Living Together on Planet Earth

*Time is closely studied and measured by the thinking humans,
whose collective journey is undertaken within its ambit.
Between them, they build considerable knowledge
both about the great cosmos and, locally, about life on Planet Earth.
They study human life particularly closely,*

*being aware of the long history of hatred and conflicts
yet simultaneously recognising the human capacity for cooperation.
In Planet Earth's current state of climate crisis,
humans need to devise and implement policies
to keep Planet Earth habitable
for all its living creatures.
Specifically, too, humans need
a collective optimism of the will,
a pragmatic intelligence to find the best solutions,
and global solidarity to implement all necessary changes
communally and fairly.
In other words, policy solutions must
not serve just a few sectional interests
but must help inter-connected humanity as a whole.*

*To that end, economic policies are needed
to boost collective solidarity, by reducing the dangerous gulf
between those humans (and global regions) with great wealth
and those who live in dire poverty.
The human journey has already been long and eventful.
It is now facing a new crisis on a planetary scale.
All humans are collectively involved.
There are no exceptions.
No bolt-holes for escape to another era or another planet.*

*So the next steps need to be taken wisely and globally…
all together in Time.*

*** End ***

Global Climate Change

Bendell, J., Read, R. (eds) (2021) *Deep Adaptation: Navigating the Realities of Climate Chaos.*

Gale, J. (2020) *The Sustainable(ish) Living Guide: Everything You Need to Know to Make Small Changes that Make a Big Difference.*

McGuire, B. (2022) *Hothouse Earth: An Inhabitant's Guide.*

Future Prospects

Dunn, R. R. (2022) *A Natural History of the Future: What the Laws of Biology Tell Us About the Destiny of the Human Species.*

Hayhoe, J. (2021) *Saving Us: A Climate Scientist's Case for Hope and Healing in a Divided World.*

Monbiot, G. (2022) *Regenesis: Feeding the World Without Devouring the Planet.*

Weighing the Case for Optimism or Pessimism

Pinker, S. (2018) *Enlightenment Now: The Case for Reason, Science, Humanism and Progress.*

Scruton, R. (2010) *The Uses of Pessimism and the Danger of False Hope.*

Global Citizenship and Challenges

Langran, I., Birk, T. (eds) (2016) *Globalisation and Global Citizenship: Interdisciplinary Approaches.*

Stiglitz, J. E. (2012) *The Price of Inequality: How Today's Divided Society Endangers Our Future.*

Zielonka, J. (2023) *The Lost Future: And How to Reclaim It.*

Index

ABBA
- *Slipping through My Fingers* (1981) 122

Adams, Douglas
- *Hitch-Hiker's Guide to the Galaxy (1979)* 86

Althusser, Louis 68
Anderson, P.W. 63
Anti-semitism 198
Archilochus, Greek poet 62
Archimedes, Greek scientist 130
Argentina
- Equipo Argentino de Antropologia Forense 203

Aristotle, Greek philosopher 69
Augustine, St. of Hippo 94
Austen, Jane
- *Emma* (1815) 35, 36

Australia
- Indigenous people's 'walkabouts' as memory-markers 55
- Northcote, inner-urban suburb Melbourne, Victoria 100
- Prairie dogs 196
- Uluru/ Ayer's Rock 185

BadBadNotGood, Canadian band 121
Bakhtin, Mikhail 109
Barbour, Julian 162
Baudrillard, Jean 37
Beckett, Sanuel
- *Endgame* (1959) 142

Beethoven, Ludwig van 151
Bennett, Alan
- *Madness of King George III* (1991) 227

Berlin, Isaiah 62, 63
Blake, William 94, 142
Bonaparte, Napoleon 229, 231
Bowie, David/ inventive family names 183
Braudel, Fernand 115
Buddhism 156
Burke, Edmund 112, 116
Burns, Robert 30, 212

Carroll, Lewis
- *Alice through the Looking-Glass* (1872) 85

*Casablanc*a (1942 film dir. M. Curtiz) 107

Catullus, Roman poet 197
Caves
    Child burial in Panga ya Saidi
        Cave, Kenya 191
    Mammoth Cave, Kentucky,
        USA 128
    Postojna Cave, Slovenia 128
Chaucer, Geoffrey 130
Chernobyl / Chornobyl, Ukraine
    Alienation Zone 192
    Monument to those who 'Saved
        the World' 192
Chesterton, G.K
    King's Cross Station (1900). 136
Christianity
    Anglican Prayer Book 126
    Biblical quotations 119, 127
    Christ, debates over existence of
        .... 229, 230
    Christian anti-semitism 198
    Christian tolerance 229
    Global celebrations of the 2nd
        Christian millennium 189
    See also
        Augustine, St 94
Civil warfare
    see warfare 200
Climate change .. 83, 133, 143, 223, 234
Comte, Auguste 66, 67, 68, 72
Confucius/ Kong Qiu, Chinese
    sage 45
Cook, Sam 127
Covid-19, global pandemic 144
Cowley, Abraham 112
Cromwell, Oliver 125

Cummings, Ray 86

Darwin, Charles 62, 127
Davenant, Charles 116
Davies, Paul 154
Derrida, Jacques 157, 158
Dickens, Charles 172, 188
Donne, John 156
Dostoevsky, Fyodor 172
Doyle, Conan 176, 231
Dworkin, Andrea 175
Dylan, Bob
    It's A Hard Rain's Gonna Fall
        (1962) 126

Eco, Umberto
    Il nome della rosa (1980),
        transl. as *The Name of the*
        Rose 228
Edison, Thomas 96
Einstein, Albert 59, 86, 99, 100, 101, 102, 139, 154, 156, 158
Eisenman 158
Eliot, T.S 62, 109, 122, 237
Engels, Friedrich . 67, 82, 139, 146, 231
Ermarth, Elizabeth Deeds 73

Fabius Maximus, Quintus 124
    Fabianism 124
Factoids or pseudo-facts .. 174, 176, 178, 228
Festivals
    Islamic 187
    Mud Festival, Boryeong, S.
        Korea 187

Phoenix Festival, Tullamore, Co. Offaly, Ireland 187
Ford, Henry 27, 28, 30, 32, 41
Foucault, Michel 82
Franklin, Benjamin 86, 88, 115
Funerary Monuments
    Egypt, Pyramids and Sphinx 191
    India, Taj Mahal 190

Gage, Matilda 175
Galileo de' Galilei 147
Gandhi, Mahatma 212
Garbo, Greta 184
Germany
    Berlin Europa-Center water-clock 95
    Coming to terms with Nazism 221
    Deutsche Kammerphilharmonie Bremen 151
Gibbon, Edward 45, 65
Gray, Thomas 131

Haggard, Rider
    She (1886) 84
Halley's Comet/ IP/Halley 41
Hamasaki, Ayumi 66
Hannibal, Carthaginian general 124
Harvey, Arnold D., alias Harvey, Stephanie 172
Hawking, Stephen 86, 106
Hegel, Georg Wilhelm 139
Henry, Patrick 45
Herrick, Robert 113
Hesiod, of Ephesus 113
Historical fictions 82, 83

Imaginative value 226
Not to be taken as fact 227
Hitler Diaries/ Hitler Tagebücher 171
Holmes, Sherlock 176
Holocaust Denial 71, 173, 180
Housman, A.E 77
Hume, David 116
Huntington, Samuel P 65

Ice Age 82
Internationalism
    Conventions relating to warfare 206
    Handshaking as an international greeting style 219
    League of Nations 206, 219
    UNESCO annual day of remembrance for the slave trade and campaigns to abolish slavery 222
    United Nations 206, 219
Irving, David 172, 173
Islam
    fasting 187
    festivals 187
    holy places 199

Jagger, Mick 16, 39
Japan
    'Comfort Women' in WW2, memorials 207
    Hiroshima Peace Memorial and Cenotaph 205
    Shinto household gods 199
Jerusalem, holy sites 191

Johnson, Dr. Samuel 96
Julian, Roman Emperor
    Julian Days 76

Karr, Alphonse 109
King's Speech, The (2010 film, dir.
    T. Hooper) 227
Koestler, Arthur 141
Koselleck, Reinhart 205
Kuhn, Thomas 139
Kumar, Abbay
    Earth Anthem (2008) 133

Lampedusa, Giuseppe di
    The Leopard (1958) 112
Laughter/ jokes 16, 30, 37, 117,
    152, 163, 164, 183, 198
Lawrence, D.H 64, 73, 82, 102,
    117, 126, 142, 159
Lecky, William 65
Lenin, Vladimir 140
Lewis, C.S 22
Linnaeus, Carl 79
Longfellow, Henry 125
Lorenz, Konrad 117
Lysenko, Trofim 234

Machiavelli, Niccolò 177
Mailer, Norman 174
Mansfield, Katherine 64
Mao Zedong, Chairman 139, 145
Marquez, Gabriel Garcia 142
Marvell, Andrew 95
Marx, Karl 67, 82, 112, 139, 231
McColl, Ewan 97
Milton, John 113, 148

Minkowski, Hermann 99
Mitchell, Joni 77
Mola, Carmen 184
Monroe, Marilyn 174, 184
Museum of Crime
    Madame Tussauds Waxwork
        Museum, London 203
Museums
    Greenfield Village Museum,
        Dearborn, Michigan, USA 28
    Museum of American
        Innovation , Dearbor,
        Michigan, USA 28
Music, and Time .. 49, 51, 152, 154,
    158, 162

Nabokov, Vladimir 150
Naiman. Eric 172
Neanderthal people 80, 82
Neruda, Pablo 184
Newton, Isaac 59, 100, 103, 139,
    144, 147, 158
Northern Ireland
    'Mixed' Marriages in Northern
        Ireland 213
    Peace-making in Northern
        Ireland after civil war 204

Ockham, William of 69
Orewell, George
    Nineteen-Eighty-Four (1949)
        .... 198, 233, 234

Paul, St., formerly Saul 35
Penis Park/Haesindang Park, nr.
    Samcheok, S. Korea 189

Planck, Max 103, 113
Plato, Greek philosopher 158
Private Eye 171
Prohibition, US alcohol restraint
    (1919-33) 116
Proust, Marcel 48, 49

Quaggy, River, S.E. London 110
Quantic, a.k.a. Holland, Will 16

Randall, Dudley 141
Red, radical colour 140
    The Red Flag (1889) 140
Rollins Band
    Liar (1994) 171

Sagan, Carl 78
Sand-spits
    Arabat Spit, Sea of Azov,
        Crimea 129
    Long Point, Lake Erie, Ontario,
        Canada 128
Sardinia 80
Shakespeare, William .. 33, 48, 130,
    139, 142, 145, 193, 199, 212
Shelley, P.B 193
Smith, Zadie
    White Teeth (2000) 130
Songs 66, 68, 88, 97
    Songs about Time 40, 42, 49,
        58, 66, 68, 98, 125, 138
South Africa
    'Racial' classifications under
        Apartheid 214
Space 99
Space-Time 99

Spain
    Confronting legacy of civil war
        .... 203, 204
Spencer, Herbert 125, 127, 128
Spengler, Oswald 65
Stalin, Josef 68, 234
Standing Stones 55, 81
    Carnac, Brittany, France 189
    Stonehenge, Wiltshire, England
        189
Statues
    Buddha, cave statues destroyed,
        Afghanistan 190
    Buddha, in Fodushan, Henan,
        China 190
    Statue of Unity, in Kevadiya,
        Gujarat, India 190
Streets, renaming of controversial
    cases
    Budapest 186
    London 185
    Norwich 185

Taliban, Afghanistan 190
Tegmark, Max 157
Terence, Roman playwright 118
Tey, Josephine
    The Daughter of Time (1951)
        228
Thompson, E.P 68
Thoreau, Henry David 35
Tiger, the Champawat, Nepal ... 211
Time-Space 99
Tolstoy, Leo 63
Toynbee, Arnold 65
Trade in enslaved Africans 220

Trevor-Roper, Hugh 171
Twain, Mark 184

United States of America
    Communes 217
    Restrictions upon alcohol, see under Prohibition 153
    Tectonic plates / San Andreas Fault , California 160

Vaughan, Henry 102
Vico, Giambattista 64, 118
Virgil, Roman poet 212

Wallace, Alfred Russel 127
Warfare
    Civil wars 145
    Confronting legacy of civil wars 209

Wells, H.G
    Time Machine (1895) 84
Whateley, Archdeacon Richard 229, 230
Whymper, Edward 134
Wilde, Oscar
    An Ideal Husband (1899) 148
Williams, R.L. performing as R.LUM.R 235
Wilson, Dooley 107
Winkle, Rip Van (1819) 84
Winteler, Jost 154

Xenakis, Iannis 152

Yawn Song 122
Yeats, W.B. 139, 144